The Scandal of Evangelism

The Scandal of Evangelism

A Biblical Study of the Ethics of Evangelism

⁂

ELMER JOHN THIESSEN

CASCADE Books · Eugene, Oregon

THE SCANDAL OF EVANGELISM
A Biblical Study of the Ethics of Evangelism

Copyright © 2018 Elmer John Thiessen. All rights reserved. Except for brief quotations in critical publications or reviews, no part of this book may be reproduced in any manner without prior written permission from the publisher. Write: Permissions, Wipf and Stock Publishers, 199 W. 8th Ave., Suite 3, Eugene, OR 97401.

Cascade Books
An Imprint of Wipf and Stock Publishers
199 W. 8th Ave., Suite 3
Eugene, OR 97401

www.wipfandstock.com

PAPERBACK ISBN: 978-1-5326-1788-1
HARDCOVER ISBN: 978-1-4982-4294-3
EBOOK ISBN: 978-1-4982-4293-6

Cataloguing-in-Publication data:

Names: Thiessen, Elmer John, 1942–, author.

Title: The scandal of evangelism: a biblical study of the ethics of evangelism / Elmer John Thiessen.

Description: Eugene, OR: Cascade Books, 2018 | Includes bibliographical references and index.

Identifiers: ISBN 978-1-5326-1788-1 (paperback) | ISBN 978-1-4982-4294-3 (hardcover) | ISBN 978-1-4982-4293-6 (ebook)

Subjects: LCSH: Evangelism | Evangelistic work—Biblical teaching | Ethics | Missions | Evangelistic work—Philosophy

Classification: BV3793 T49 2018 (print) | BV3793 (ebook)

Manufactured in the U.S.A.   APRIL 20, 2018

Unless otherwise stated Scripture quotations are taken from the HOLY BIBLE, NEW INTERNATIONAL VERSION. Copyright © 1973, 1978, 1984 by Biblica. Used by permission of Hodder & Stoughton Publishers, a member of the Hachette Livre UK Group. All rights reserved. 'NIV' is a registered trademark of Biblica UK, trademark number 1448790

Contents

Acknowledgments | *vii*

Chapter 1　Introduction | 1
Chapter 2　An Approach to Biblical Ethics and the Ethics of Evangelism | 20

Part I: Ethics of Evangelism in the New Testament

Chapter 3　The Gospels and Jesus | 39
Chapter 4　Acts and the Apostles | 57
Chapter 5　Paul's Epistles | 75
Chapter 6　General Epistles and Revelation | 94
Chapter 7　Summary of Biblical Analysis: Guidelines for Ethical Evangelism | 110

Part II: Applied Topics

Chapter 8　Evangelism of Children | 137
Chapter 9　Evangelism in Professional Life: The Academy | 155
Chapter 10　Evangelism and Humanitarian Aid | 172
Chapter 11　Ethics of Proselytism | 196
Chapter 12　Conclusion | 216

Bibliography | 233
Subject Index | 245
Author Index | 255
Scripture Index | 259

Acknowledgments

MANY PEOPLE HAVE HELPED in the birthing of this book. Several chapters have their origins in papers presented at conferences or articles written for journals, resulting in valuable feedback from participants at these conferences or from editors and referee reports of draft articles. Specifics regarding these conferences or earlier articles will be given in the appropriate chapters of this book. The text has also been enhanced by frank and valuable feedback from a number of readers. Of course, acknowledging them does not necessarily imply that they agree with the content of this book or that they are responsible in any way for its shortcomings, which lie entirely with me.

For their assistance, I want to publicly express my heartfelt gratitude to Philip Barnes, who read an earlier version of the entire manuscript, and to Robert Kruse, who read an earlier version of most of the chapters. Thanks also go to individuals who gave me feedback on one or two chapters: Ron Mathies, Jennifer Cheek, Daniel Hillion, Rachel Uthmann, Tim Grass, and David Armstrong.

I am also very grateful to the team at Wipf and Stock Publishers who have shepherded this work to publication. Here I want to thank especially Robin Parry, who expressed an immediate interest in the book and who has guided it to its present form.

Finally, I want to thank my wife, Maggie, who has read through several drafts of the manuscript. More important though has been her encouragement and support through the many hours, days, months, and years where I was rather preoccupied with this writing project. The stability and sense of well-being she has provided over the years, and her tolerance for my long hours in front of my computer, have as always, contributed immeasurably to seeing this book through to its completion. I dedicate this work to her, on this our 50th wedding anniversary.

Elmer John Thiessen
August 10, 2017
ejthiessen@sympatico.ca

Chapter 1

Introduction

The topic of evangelism made national headlines in Canada in the spring of 2012.[1] It all started with a Grade 12 student in Nova Scotia wearing a T-shirt boldly emblazoned with the words, "Life is wasted without Jesus." William Swinimer continued to wear his yellow T-shirt even after the vice-principal at his school asked him not to do so. The vice-principal's request was prompted by some students who had complained that they found the message offensive. William's refusal to obey led to a series of in-school suspensions, and finally a five-day at-home suspension. The normally shy 19-year-old refused to comply even if it might mean permanent suspension and the loss of his chance of graduating. "I believe this is worth standing up for," he said. "It's not just standing up for religious rights, it's standing up for my rights as a Canadian citizen; for freedom of speech and freedom of religion."

The regional school board initially supported the actions of the school administration. The school board issued a statement clarifying that "students may choose to wear clothing that embraces their beliefs. However, it is expected that students will not wear clothing with messages that may offend others' beliefs, race, religion, culture, or lifestyle."

The vice-principal of the school even went so far as to suggest that the message on the T-shirt spewed "hate talk." Some of the students at the school agreed with these assessments, while others suggested that the T-shirt message was simply expressing William's personal beliefs. William himself is quoted as saying, "I don't do it to be disrespectful or to put down anyone else's beliefs."

---

1. An expanded version of this story first appeared in firstthings.com on June 8, 2012, and is here used with permission. See my original article, Thiessen, "Offensiveness of Evangelism." For the details of the story, I drew on several accounts found in two Canadian national newspapers: *Globe and Mail* and *National Post*, May 4–5, 2012.

In the end the school administration and the board, after consulting with a human rights activist, backed away from their controversial decision. However, they tried to save face by scheduling some follow-up "open dialogue" on how students can express their beliefs "in a complex multicultural school environment." Sadly, William's father did not let his son participate in this dialogue.

WHILE THERE MIGHT BE some dispute as to the central issue raised in this story, I am choosing to interpret it as a story about evangelism. Thus interpreted, the story provides a good illustration of how many people in contemporary Western societies view evangelism as scandalous. Evangelism is thought to be rude, disrespectful of the beliefs of others, and even comparable to hate speech. Here I will only respond briefly to some of the objections to evangelism raised in the above story and the nationwide debate ignited by this incident.

"Life is wasted without Jesus." What is so offensive about this statement? I agree that there is at least an implicit criticism of others' beliefs in this message. But so what? Those making objections to William's apparel are also making a criticism. Should this too be viewed as offensive? Making judgments or criticisms of the beliefs of other people is surely not inherently wrong. Nor should criticisms be seen as inherently disrespectful. I would even suggest that making a criticism of someone's belief is a way to honor that person. I am taking you and your beliefs seriously enough to critique them. The further claim that the message on William's shirt involved hate speech is so absurd that it doesn't merit comment.

Journalist Emma Teitel brought to the fore some other reasons for considering William's T-shirt message offensive. He is not being "discreet," but "rude." Religious beliefs are "far too precious to flaunt," and should be kept private, according to Teitel.[2] What is rather strange here is that we don't demand this of other similar sorts of value declarations. We seem to have no problem with the flaunting of commercial messages in the form of advertising. Why single out religion as something that needs to be kept private? In truth, I suspect Teitel simply disagrees with religious beliefs and is annoyed by their being expressed in public. Perhaps her opinions too should be kept private because I and others find them disagreeable.

But there is more to Teitel's tirade against the T-shirt episode. "There is a great difference between cherishing a belief and wielding it like a weapon,"

---

2. Teitel, "Tiring Tempest in a T-shirt," 12.

Teitel argues.[3] The old skeptical sawhorse of coercion is now being leveled against evangelism. But to talk about a message on a T-shirt as a kind of weaponry borders on the absurd, of course, unless one is drawing on the insights of French postmodernist Michel Foucault who interprets all truth claims as "fruits of a poisoned tree of power relations."[4] But if so, then this also applies to Teitel and her company of critics. The weapon analogy is ultimately self-refuting.

Another online critic was a little less dramatic: "The problem . . . with religious people is that they get so righteous and full of themselves that they think they have a duty to impose their beliefs on others."[5] But William was merely wearing a T-shirt with a message on it. In what sense is this an imposition? Is a highway billboard advertising toothpaste also an imposition on those driving by? We must be careful not to stretch the notion of imposition to the point where it becomes meaningless.

Given the feverish and absurd nature of the criticisms of William Swinimer, it is not surprising that the school eventually backed away from its controversial decision. Still, the reader might be wondering whether this comparatively minor, local incident merits the attention I have given it. It does, because it is not an isolated incident. The arguments used against William Swinimer are representative of the kinds of arguments frequently raised against all forms of Christian evangelism.

RESPONDING TO OBJECTIONS TO EVANGELISM

Much more could be said by way of responding to the objections to evangelism raised by those who found the message on William Swinimer's T-shirt offensive. But that is not the central purpose of this chapter or of this book. My purpose in describing the Swinimer case and responding briefly to the objections raised is to provide a backdrop for a description of the objectives of this book. Before doing so, let me draw attention to an earlier book of mine where I provide a detailed response to a variety of objections to evangelism, including the ones raised in the above example. My earlier work is entitled *The Ethics of Evangelism: A Philosophical Defense of Proselytizing*

---

3. Ibid., 12.

4. This phrase is used by James Smith to summarize Foucault's thinking. Smith, *Who's Afraid of Postmodernism?*, 87.

5. This statement was made by Snollygoster, in one of 690 comments on an article written by Sarah Boesveld, "Suspended Nova Scotia Student," May 3, 2012. Unfortunately, the comments on this article are no longer available on the *National Post* website.

and Persuasion, and was published in 2011.⁶ Ethics is a branch of philosophy that has to do with the evaluation of human actions, activities, motivations, or character. Ethics has to do with making judgments of approval or disapproval, right or wrong, good or bad, and virtue or vice. The ethics of evangelism is therefore concerned with evaluating the methods, goals, and motivations behind evangelism. Critics maintain that evangelism is often or even inherently unethical. The focus of my earlier work was to respond to these critics.

The Ethics of Evangelism was written with two readerships in mind—skeptics opposed to evangelism, and religious adherents who are committed to evangelism. In that book, as in my previous books, I was concerned with bridging the language barriers that often make communication between religious adherents and skeptics difficult. I had two basic objectives in mind when I wrote my 2011 book: to defend evangelism against a variety of objections; and to develop criteria to distinguish between ethical and unethical forms of evangelism. I thought my two objectives would run parallel to the two very different audiences I was writing for. My defense of evangelism was meant for a skeptical readership—atheists, agnostics, and those opposed to any religion. The chapters devoted to developing criteria to distinguish between ethical and unethical forms of evangelism were meant for religious adherents committed to evangelism, including Christians. What I have discovered since the book came out is that my sharp separation of objectives and readerships was rather naïve. I am finding there are many Christians, including evangelical Christians, who have quite a few suspicions about evangelism per se. Indeed, some of them are nearly as skeptical about evangelism as are atheists and agnostics.⁷ This has come as a surprise to me, and it raises the question as to why this is the case. I will return to this question in the concluding chapter of this book.

---

6. Thiessen, *Ethics of Evangelism*.

7. For example, Katie Sawatzky objects to evangelism in a column in my own denominational paper: "I become frustrated when I read or hear anything about spreading the gospel in the hope of converting others." She objects to the harvesting image for evangelism that Jesus uses (John 4:34–38), because "the time for 'harvesting' is over. It's now time for listening, and for helping with open hands and closed mouths." She goes on to express concerns about what her four-year-old son might be learning in Sunday school. "I don't want him to grow up thinking he needs to tell other people about Christ. I want him to see Christ in the people that he meets in his daily life, no matter what race, religion or economic status, and welcome them . . . I want him to recognize the religion and culture that people already have, and not assume that his trumps theirs . . . The colonial history of Christian evangelism is a severe reminder of how damaging it can be to preach Jesus as Saviour to people who seem 'ready' for it." Sawatzky, "Ready to Listen," 9.

OBJECTIVES

The objectives of this book are different from my 2011 book. In order to better understand them, it will be helpful to underscore an important feature of my first book. I was forced to take a unique approach to ethics in my earlier book because I was not writing only for Christians. As already mentioned, I wrote that book for both skeptics and religious believers. Even with regard to religious believers, I had in mind adherents to any religion committed to the propagation of its particular faith. Writing about the ethics of evangelism for multiple readerships brings to the fore an important question: What ethical framework can one use to deal with the subject? Given that I was writing for both the religiously committed and those who are skeptical of religion, I had to base my argument on a broader ethical foundation that would hopefully be accepted by both readerships. I was well aware of the fact that not all readers would find this approach acceptable.[8] Indeed, the question of ethical foundations is the subject of endless debate in philosophy. There are also philosophers and theologians who would question the very possibility of finding an ethical framework that can be shared by Christians and those who reject Christianity. I disagree with this assessment, though I will not argue for my position here.[9]

However, I do acknowledge the limitations of basing a treatment of the ethics of evangelism on an ethical framework that is shared by believers and unbelievers. Neither group will be entirely happy with my treatment of the subject. There is therefore a need for another approach in treating the ethics of evangelism for Christians. Indeed, in the concluding chapter of *The Ethics of Evangelism*, I argue that resources for encouraging ethical evangelism must be found within each of the religions that engage in evangelism.[10] Thus Christians need to find the resources for encouraging ethical evangelism within the Christian tradition itself. It is within this context that I state, "I intend to write a sequel to the present monograph in which I will deal with

---

8. For example, Edgar French, in a review of my 2011 book states: "Thiessen runs into a significant challenge, however, in his aim to make his appeal through a liberal/secular ethical framework. His conception of ethics is abstracted from the life and practice of the community of faith. There is a point at which the notion of the good life is not intuitively accessible. Christian ethics depends heavily on revelation, i.e. the incarnation, and is only formative within the setting of community life." French, Review of *Ethics of Evangelism*, 111.

9. I provide a brief defense of the possibility of a common ethical framework for Christians, people of other faiths, and those who claim to have no religious faith, in Thiessen, *Ethics of Evangelism*, 46–50.

10. Ibid., 219–23.

the ethics of evangelism from an explicitly Christian perspective."[11] This book is an attempt to keep my promise!

So what are my objectives in this book? The first and basic aim of the present work is to provide a biblical and theological grounding for an explicitly Christian ethics of evangelism. Secondly, I want to apply a biblical ethics of evangelism to some specific contexts that pose some unique challenges for doing evangelism ethically. For example, what are the ethical constraints in doing evangelism within the context of relief, development, and advocacy work? Or, within professions, e.g., the secular classroom? What about child evangelism? I also want to explore the tensions inherent in proselytizing, understood as sheep-stealing, e.g., evangelicals evangelizing in Orthodox or Catholic countries.

Is there a need for a book like this? Surprisingly, the existing literature on evangelism pays little attention to this important task of distinguishing between ethical and unethical approaches to evangelism.[12] There are countless articles and books written by Christians on how to do evangelism. But these same articles and books tend to skirt the ethical questions surrounding the practice of evangelism. One gets the impression that evangelism is so important for some Christians that there is no need to bother with the problem of doing evangelism in an ethical manner. Thankfully, there have been several attempts in the last decade or so to develop criteria to distinguish between ethical and unethical evangelism, the most recent one being the joint work of the World Evangelical Alliance, the World Council of Churches, and the Vatican's Pontifical Council on Inter-religious Dialogue, "Christian Witness in a Multi-Religious World: Recommendations for Conduct," released in 2011.[13] However, these attempts tend to be very brief, and they do little by way of showing how these criteria are grounded in the Scriptures. My aim is to provide a careful and systematic treatment of a biblical approach to the ethics of evangelism.

Perhaps a few words are in order about who is writing this book and why I am writing it. My interest in the ethics of evangelism arises in part from the fact that I am an evangelical Anabaptist Christian. Evangelicals are by self-definition very much committed to evangelism. I share this

---

11. Ibid., 219n7.

12. For a detailed analysis of existing literature on the ethics of evangelism, see Appendix II, in Thiessen, *Ethics of Evangelism*, 238–53. See also Schirrmacher and Johnson, "Why Evangelicals Need a Code of Ethics for Mission."

13. World Council of Churches et al., "Christian Witness in a Multi-Religious World." For a review of how this statement has been received, see Schirrmacher, "The Code," 82–89. For a list of further recent statements on the ethics of evangelism, see Thiessen, *Ethics of Evangelism*, 249–51.

commitment, though I would hasten to add I have some concerns about the evangelical understanding and practice of evangelism, concerns which will become apparent as I proceed. As an Anabaptist, I am also committed to peace and reconciliation, and so I am particularly sensitive to ways in which evangelism can become coercive and even violent. Words can be used as weapons, though I don't believe William Swiminer's T-shirt message is an example of evangelistic violence, as I have already argued. While my treatment of evangelism is probably best described in terms of being evangelical and Anabaptist in orientation, my thinking has also been shaped by other Christian traditions. I am particularly indebted to the Reformed tradition for my theological and philosophical outlook.

I am also a philosopher with a keen interest in theology. My specialty is philosophical theology, a happy blend between these two disciplines. As a philosopher, I will bring an analytical mindset to the Bible. I will be analyzing biblical texts carefully to see what they have to say about the ethics of evangelism. I will be looking for common threads in the books of the Bible regarding the ethics of evangelism. A philosophical background in ethics and applied ethics will also help me to examine the theoretical and practical implications of what the Bible says about the ethics of evangelism. Philosophers are also concerned with language and the clarification of concepts. Hopefully I will be able to add some clarity to concepts surrounding evangelism that are sometimes fuzzy at the edges. Philosophers also like to argue. I hope to provide a sustained argument for a biblical approach to the ethics of evangelism.

MEANING OF EVANGELISM

What do we mean when we use the word "evangelism?" Unfortunately, defining this word is not as easy as it might seem. David Bosch, a leading South African missiologist, in a survey of the ways in which evangelism is being understood and practiced today, makes mention of a "bewildering variety of interpretations of evangelism."[14] Given this plethora of definitions, it would seem there is a need to pay more attention to a philosophical and theological treatment of the problem of defining evangelism.[15] A full treatment of this question is beyond the scope of this chapter or of this book.

---

14. Bosch, "Evangelism," 8.

15. William Abraham identified this problem several decades ago and tried to address this need in his *Logic of Evangelism*. In a later summary of his work, Abraham says this: "We need an analysis of evangelism that will be at once historically grounded, theologically credible, and practically apt." Abraham, "Theology of Evangelism," 18. On the need for a theology of evangelism, see also Kandiah, "Lesslie Newbigin's Contribution to a Theology of Evangelism," 56.

Instead, I want to examine briefly a common definition of evangelism and place it into historical and theological context. I will then suggest a slightly modified version of this definition which will then be assumed in the rest of this book. In the concluding section of this chapter, I will briefly answer some objections to my definition of evangelism and also consider some concepts closely related to evangelism.

Most Christians, if asked to define evangelism, would construe it in terms of announcing or communicating or proclaiming the gospel to those outside the Christian faith.[16] I believe this understanding is the dominant meaning given to evangelism in the New Testament.[17] Michael Green, in his masterful study of evangelism in the early church, highlights three main word groups used in the New Testament that capture the core meaning of evangelism—*euaggelizesthai* (to "tell good news"), *marturein* (to "bear witness"), and *kērussein* (to "proclaim").[18] Jesus began his ministry by preaching the good news (Luke 4:18). We will look at the content of this good news shortly. Jesus himself gave his disciples and us the mandate for evangelism in what is often referred to as the Great Commission. In Luke 24:48, Jesus commissions the disciples to be his "witnesses of these things." The book of Acts gives us yet a different version of this commissioning. "But you will receive power when the Holy Spirit comes on you; and you will be my witnesses in Jerusalem, and in all Judea and Samaria, and to the ends of the earth" (Acts 1:8). The word "witness" used in Luke and Acts is primarily a legal term which was frequently used in Greek to denote witness to facts and events, or to truths vouched for.[19] This meaning of "witness" continues to this day within the legal context, where witnesses, and sometimes "expert witnesses," are called to give testimony in court cases.

---

16. Abraham, *Logic of Evangelism*, 41. Kandiah, "Lesslie Newbigin's Contribution to a Theology of Evangelism," 54. Newbigin defines evangelism in terms of the verbal proclamation of the gospel. Ibid., 54.

17. For a good summary statement of those who disagree with this assessment, see Johnson, "Proselytism and Witness in Earliest Christianity." I find Johnson's argument unconvincing, guilty of special pleading, faulty either-or thinking, and full of glaring inconsistencies. For example, after cataloguing New Testament mandates for evangelism and examples of evangelism (150–53), Johnson argues that "the New Testament is remarkably reticent concerning the place of such evangelization either as the mandate of the church as such or as an element in the life of the ordinary believer" (Ibid., 154). But then Johnson is forced to admit the counter evidence of 1 Pet 3:15 and the power of "witness as living true to God," which of course is seldom separated from witness as verbal proclamation in the New Testament (Ibid., 154).

18. Green, *Evangelism in the Early Church*, 76. See chapter 3 for Green's treatment of "The Evangel," (*to euaggelion*).

19. Ibid., 106.

The early disciples clearly acted in obedience to this mandate. Thus we find Peter, in Jerusalem on the day of Pentecost, proclaiming Jesus as Lord and Messiah to an audience representing many nations (Acts 2:14-41). Later Paul, after his own dramatic conversion, tirelessly traveled the then-known world pleading with Jews and Gentiles to find salvation in Jesus Christ. Near the end of his life he explains his motive and mission in his letter to the church at Rome: "I am obligated both to Greeks and non-Greeks, both to the wise and the foolish. That is why I am so eager to preach the gospel also to you who are at Rome. I am not ashamed of the gospel because it is the power of God for the salvation of everyone who believes: first for the Jew, then for the Gentile" (Rom 1:14-16).

There is much to be said for defining evangelism as preaching the gospel. It is clear and concise, and it reflects dominant New Testament usage. There are, however, some problems with construing evangelism simply in terms of proclamation of the good news.[20] For one, we need a more careful analysis of the good news being proclaimed. This definition of evangelism also fails to address the hoped-for results of proclamation. What about conversion, baptism, becoming a disciple of Jesus Christ, and belonging to the body of Christ? Now it may be that these results are assumed to be implicit in the definition,[21] but in order to avoid possible confusion, I want to address these additional questions before I provide a more formal and complete definition of evangelism.

To help us move towards a more complete definition of evangelism, we need to pay more attention to a slightly different version of the Great Commission as found in the Gospel of Matthew. After declaring that all authority in heaven and on earth has been given to him, Jesus says, "Therefore go and make disciples of all nations, baptizing them in the name of the Father and of the Son and of the Holy Spirit, and teaching them to obey everything I have commanded you."[22] Here we have an articulation of the hoped-for results of evangelism. Evangelism should result in people being baptized

---

20. For a careful analysis of these problems, as well as problems with the related concept of conversion, see Abraham, *Logic of Evangelism*, 49-61, 120-34.

21. Brueggemann also worries about reducing evangelism simply to proclamation, but his own three-stage taxonomy of evangelism simply makes explicit what is often assumed to be part of proclamation—the gospel verdict on the nature of reality, proclamation of the outcome of the verdict, and responding appropriately to the proclamation (allowing the good news to transform how one thinks and lives). See Brueggemann, *Biblical Perspectives on Evangelism*, chap. 1. My amplification of the meaning of evangelism runs roughly along these lines.

22. Matt 28:19. For a treatment of how the Matthew version of the Great Commission was emphasized by Erasmus and how it shaped the Anabaptist movement of the sixteenth century, see Friesen, *Erasmus, the Anabaptists, and the Great Commission*.

and becoming disciples who are obedient to Jesus Christ. This of course begs the question: When can we expect these results to occur? And should these results be included as part of the definition of evangelism? I want to answer these questions as part of my treatment of the issues that need to be addressed in providing a more complete definition of evangelism. I begin by focussing on the gospel being proclaimed in evangelism.

WHAT IS THE GOSPEL?

Michael Green highlights the uniqueness of the gospel, or the good news that burst on the scene in Palestine around the year AD 30.[23] The good news wasn't just about a carpenter-teacher who had been crucified under the Roman procurator, Pontius Pilate. It was the wonderful news that Jesus had been raised from the dead. "It was nothing less than the joyful announcement of the long-awaited messianic salvation, when God had come to the rescue of a world in need. Small surprise then, that the content of their message became known as *to euaggelion*, the good news."[24] Later, of course, this term was used to label the documents that recorded these momentous events, the written gospels.

Jesus, at the inauguration of his ministry in his home town of Nazareth, links himself to the Messiah of Old Testament expectations by quoting from Isaiah 61 which announces the "good news" of salvation (Luke 4:18–21). He dares to say, "Today this scripture is fulfilled in your hearing." In other words, he himself is the good news. Prior to this, we have John the Baptist "preaching a baptism of repentance" and announcing the coming of the kingdom, all of which is described in terms of proclaiming "the good news" to the people (Luke 3:1–18). Indeed, Mark introduces his gospel with the story of John the Baptist: "The beginning of the gospel about Jesus Christ, the Son of God" (Mark 1:1). Even prior to John the Baptist, we have an angel of the Lord announcing to the shepherds in the field, "I bring you good news of great joy that will be for all the people. Today in the town of David a Savior has been born to you; he is Christ the Lord" (Luke 2:11).

Near the end of Jesus' time on earth, after the resurrection, he commissions the disciples to be his "witnesses of these things" (Luke 24:48). What things? The context identifies the essentials of the gospel: Jesus is the Messiah and the fulfillment of Old Testament prophecies; Jesus suffered and rose from the dead on the third day; and there is a need to repent and put

---

23. Green, *Evangelism in the Early Church*, 76–77.
24. Ibid., 77.

one's faith in Jesus' name (Luke 24:44-47). These are the essentials of the good news, and evangelism involves the proclamation of this good news.

Yes, there were slight variations in the presentation of the gospel by the apostles after Jesus' ascension, but the core of the good news remained the same.[25] Paul liked to remind his readers of "the gospel," or "the gospel of God," or "the faith," or "the word of God," that he preached to the people.[26] Another favorite way in which to capture the essence of the gospel was to talk about the kingdom of God or the kingdom of heaven.[27] Thus we find Philip preaching "the good news of the kingdom of God" (Acts 8:12). Of course, here Philip is only following Jesus who began his ministry by "proclaiming the good news of God," saying, "The kingdom of God is near. Repent and believe the good news" (Mark 1:14-15). Indeed, Jesus' ministry continues to be described in terms of "preaching the good news of the kingdom" (Matt 4:23; 9:35). Paul therefore followed Jesus in preaching and even "arguing persuasively about the kingdom of God."[28]

The good news is here linked to the expansive notion of the reign of God over all creation. Paul also describes this bigger vision of the gospel in terms of the cosmic Christ, who came "to reconcile to himself *all things*, whether things on earth or things in heaven, by making peace through his blood, shed on the cross" (Col 1:19-20—emphasis mine). Yes, Paul goes on to talk about the reconciliation of individuals once alienated from God, but Christ's mission of reconciliation is not limited to the reconciliation of individuals to God. The good news of the kingdom involves the reconciliation of all things, including "powers and authorities" to Jesus Christ (Col 2:15). Evangelical Christians, I am afraid, have all too often limited the good news to personal salvation.[29] While this is certainly an essential part of the gospel, perhaps even the most important part, the good news is bigger than

---

25. Ibid., 80, 114-15. The technical term *kerygma* is often used by theologians to refer to what is supposed to have been a fairly fixed body of preaching material common to the early missionaries—"the pattern of sound teaching" (2 Tim 1:13). See C. H. Dodd, *Apostolic Preaching*, and Green's own review of the controversy surrounding the notion of *kerygma* (chap. 3).

26. 1 Cor 15:1; 2 Cor 11:7; Gal 1:8, 11, 23. References to preaching or receiving the "word" or the "word of God" occur no fewer than thirty-two times in Acts, e.g., 8:4,14. See Green, *Evangelism in the Early Church*, 210.

27. Herman Ridderbos, in his classic study of the kingdom of God, suggests this notion is the central theme of the whole New Testament revelation of God. See Ridderbos, *Coming of the Kingdom*. For a similar emphasis, see Abraham, *Logic of Evangelism*, chapter 2.

28. Acts 19:8; 20:25; 28:23, 31.

29. Brueggemann also expresses concerns about "conservative reductionism" in defining evangelism. See Brueggemann, *Biblical Perspectives on Evangelism*, 14, 44.

this. It is a wonderful message of personal and cosmic redemption. This is good news indeed! And we as Christians have nothing to be ashamed of in proclaiming this gospel.

CONVERSION

The concept of conversion is often introduced as one way to describe the goal of evangelism.[30] Two biblical stories have been particularly influential in shaping our understanding of conversion. Jesus, in his night-time conversation with Nicodemus, a high-ranking member of the Jewish ruling council, gave what has become for Protestant evangelicals the classic description of conversion as being born again. After some flattering comments from Nicodemus, Jesus seems to interrupt him with these words: "I tell you the truth, unless a man is born again, he cannot see the kingdom of God" (John 3:3). It is significant, I believe, that this description of conversion is linked to the kingdom of God. To be born again means being able to see and understand what God's reign is all about. Elsewhere Jesus talks about the need to change and become like little children in order to "enter the kingdom of heaven" (Matt 18:3). Then there is Paul's own dramatic conversion that transforms him, leads to his immediate baptism, and launches him on his missionary career (Acts 9:1–22). So significant is this conversion experience that Paul keeps recounting it at crucial points in his ministry (Acts 22 & 26).

These two accounts of conversion raise some important questions. What exactly does it mean to be born again? Does conversion have to be as dramatic as Paul's conversion? Should baptism follow immediately after conversion? Is conversion necessarily characterized as a one-time experience? I don't think the answers to these questions are as obvious as is often assumed by evangelical Christians. We must also be careful not to develop a paradigm of conversion only from these two accounts, both of which involve adult Jewish men.

Alan Kreider begins his masterful short study of conversion in the early centuries of the church by highlighting conversion as change.[31] In the ancient world, the words used for conversion—*epistrepho, metanoia, conversio*—all connote change. Kreider sums up the early church's understanding of

---

30. See the *International Bulletin of Missionary Research* 28.1 (January 2004), for several articles on conversion in the Old Testament and the New Testament, and for an attempt to adjudicate between conflicting understandings of conversion. For an interdisciplinary study of three orientations of conversion (socialization, liturgical, personal decision), see McKnight, *Turning to Jesus*.

31. Kreider, *Change of Conversion*, xiv.

conversion as involving a change of belief, behavior, and belonging.[32] The four gospels are full of conversion stories, and sometimes Jesus would demand people give up nearly everything in order to follow him. For those who chose to become a disciple of Jesus, following him meant an upheaval in their beliefs, a radical shift in their behavior, and also a change in their sense of belonging. Often a decisive turning to Jesus in repentance and faith was followed by baptism, as a physical sign and seal of conversion.[33] Part of the meaning of baptism includes identifying with the Christian community.[34] Baptized believers have shifted their sense of belonging. Jesus' conversation with Nicodemus described conversion as a new way of seeing, a worldview shift, which also included a change of heart brought about by the work of the Holy Spirit. Paul's conversion shattered his old assumptions and loyalties, and led to a radical change in his life.

Other conversion stories in Acts, like that of Cornelius and the Ethiopian eunuch, leave us wondering exactly what changed.[35] The New Testament gives us little indication what conversion might have meant for second-generation Christians. We need to be careful not to become too rigid in our understanding of what conversion means.[36] For example, we must not insist that conversion must necessarily follow the exact order in Kreider's analysis, moving from a change of belief to a change of behavior and then to a change of belonging. In today's fragmented society, it might very well be that belonging comes before believing.[37] Further, some conversions might just involve a long process of gradual change.[38] In addition, some Christians might not be

32. Ibid., xv, 1–2. In a later work, Kreider describes conversion in terms of a change of "habitus, that constitutes our profoundest sense of identity; that forms our deepest convictions, allegiances, and repulsions; and that shapes our response to ultimate questions." See Kreider, *Patient Ferment of the Early Church*, 40, 143–47.

33. See, for example, Acts 2:38; 8:12; 9:18; 10:47–48; 16:15; 18:8. Green, *Evangelism in the Early Church*, 214.

34. See Acts 2:41 and 1 Cor 12:15, where Paul links being baptized with becoming part of the body of Christ. Eric Tosi proposes the phrase "koinonic evangelism" as capturing an Orthodox understanding of evangelism where evangelism is seen as flowing out of the church and also involves helping new converts to become participants in the local Orthodox body of Christ. Tosi, "Koinonic Evangelism: The Community as the Evangelist."

35. Kreider, *Change of Conversion*, 2.

36. For a recent call to rethink the language of conversion evangelicals have inherited from revivalism, see Gordon Smith, *Transforming Conversion*. See also Chan, "Evangelical Understanding of Conversion."

37. See Richardson, *Evangelism Outside the Box*, chapter 10, which includes a delightful story of a Christian group at a university inviting non-Christians to their prayer meetings where they could experience real belonging.

38. A helpful contrast between the dramatic conversion experience of Paul and the

able to identify the precise moment they were converted. Like C. S. Lewis, it might be that some Christians can only in retrospect come to realize that they have been converted.[39] But what such retrospective reflection will reveal is that at some point in time there was a "turning" and life is now centered on Jesus Christ.[40] The person now acknowledges Jesus Christ as Savior and Lord, and is committed to following Jesus as a disciple, or an apprentice.

One final caution about conversion. Conversion is the work of the Holy Spirit. As Christians, we are called to be faithful in proclaiming the good news. Evangelism is a task given to Jesus' disciples. It is up to God to ensure that evangelism bears fruit. Paul highlights the limitations of human responsibility, after reminding us he and Apollos were merely servants: "I planted the seed, Apollos watered it, but God made it grow" (1 Cor 3:5–6). Yes, we as Christians have a responsibility to proclaim the gospel. But it is God who is responsible for the results of such proclamation.

DEFINITION OF EVANGELISM

The division of responsibilities between Paul and Apollos beg for a few more comments before I propose a formal and more complete definition of evangelism. It would seem that Paul saw his task primarily in terms of proclaiming the gospel. He recognized that there was more to do in terms of follow-up, and thus he acknowledges the work of Apollos in grounding the new believers and teaching them to become faithful followers of Jesus Christ. This distinction between proclamation and follow-up is important in defining evangelism. Here I return again to the Great Commission as given in the gospel of Matthew. The focus of this version of the Great Comission is on making disciples and teaching them to obey everything Jesus had commanded (Matt 28:19). But how do these ingredients relate to evangelism?

---

gradual conversion of the twelve apostles is found in Peace, *Conversion in the New Testament*. Kreider suggests in the second century the church in various times and places decided "to slow conversion down by insisting that their converts embody change that reflected the teaching and character of Jesus." Kreider, *Patient Ferment of the Early Church*, 176. The *Apostolic Tradition*, the famous manual of church order in the early centuries of the church, suggested that the process of becoming a baptized Christian, who is considered a full member of the church, could take 2–3 years (Ibid., 177).

39. Lewis, *Surprised by Joy*, 237.

40. On conversion described as "turning," see Acts 3:19, 26; 14:15; 15:19–20; 26:18. See also Green, *Evangelism in the Early Church*, 213. For a fascinating analysis of what conversion means, drawing on set theory in mathematics, see Hiebert, *Anthropological Reflections on Missiological Issues*, chapter 6. Hiebert prefers to see conversion as a turning around and becoming centered in Jesus Christ (126–27, 133–34).

I have already suggested baptism, being a disciple of Jesus, and growing in obedience to Jesus Christ are the hoped-for results of evangelism. Indeed, as has been argued by Dallas Willard, among others, being a disciple of Jesus is at the heart of what it means to be a Christian.[41] Here we need to be careful to distinguish between *being* a disciple of Jesus, how to *become* a disciple of Jesus, and how to *make* someone into a disciple of Jesus. According to Willard, evangelism is centrally concerned with helping people to *become* disciples of Jesus Christ. The task of *making* disciples is an important process that continues after a person has decided to become a follower of Jesus. The same can be said for the important task of teaching new believers to obey Jesus Christ. Here again, the task of teaching (disciple-making) continues after a person has become a Christian. This does not preclude the possibility of evangelists doing both preaching and teaching, or being engaged in both evangelism and the follow-up work of making disciples.[42] Paul clearly did both. But there is still a conceptual distinction that needs to be made between Paul's work as an evangelist and his work as a pastor-teacher.[43] Making this distinction does not entail that these two functions might not overlap at times *in practice*. But for clarity's sake, I believe it is still important to make *a conceptual distinction* between the task of evangelism and the task of teaching or making disciples.

In light of the above analysis, I am proposing the following as a definition of evangelism:

> Evangelism is the verbal proclamation of the gospel of Jesus Christ, having as its goal the conversion of another person or

---

41. Willard has highlighted the importance of discipleship in the third of a trilogy of books on the spiritual life (Willard, *Divine Conspiracy*, chap. 8). He makes the observation that evangelism today is "never" to his knowledge, "directed towards getting people to be disciples" (414n4). I disagree with this assessment and would recommend Willard take a look at Anabaptist theology which is largely in agreement with his position. See Friesen, *Erasmus, the Anabaptists, and the Great Commission*, especially 108. See also Bonk, "Gospel and Ethics."

42. Abraham uses this factual observation to object to D. H. Dodd's famous and widely adopted attempt to show that the early church made a distinction between preaching and teaching (Abraham, *Logic of Evangelism*, 50–56). Michael Green similarly argues that evangelism is sometimes called "teaching" in Acts 5:21, 25, 28 (Green, *Evangelism in the Early Church*, 224). But Abraham admits Dodd did not apply his distinction to evangelism (43), and he is forced to concede his own collapsing of the two functions admits of anomalies (106). Green fails to see evangelistic teaching is still different from teaching new believers how to be faithful followers of Jesus.

43. A good example of this distinction is found in Acts 14:21–22: "They preached the good news in that city (Derbe) and won a large number of disciples. Then they returned to Lystra, Iconium, and Antioch, strengthening the disciples and encouraging them to remain true to the faith."

group of persons, conversion being understood as involving a change of a person's belief, behavior, and sense of belonging.[44]

OBJECTIONS AND CONCEPTS RELATED TO EVANGELISM

It is important not to bring to this definition of evangelism preconceptions as to *how* or *when* verbal proclamation occurs in the process of helping someone to *become* a disciple of Jesus Christ. Indeed, a consideration of the ethics of evangelism might just have some important implications as to the *how* and *when* of proclamation. Nevertheless, what is important in understanding evangelism is that at some point some verbal proclamation of the good news must occur.

I am well aware that this view of evangelism will be considered too narrow by some of my readers. William Abraham, for example, is very critical of defining evangelism simply as proclamation.[45] Abraham describes his overall project in terms of bringing the variety of definitions of evangelism into "a unified and coherent whole."[46] He conceives of evangelism as "that set of intentional activities which is governed by the goal of initiating people into the Kingdom of God for the first time."[47] But he is forced to concede that proclamation and the call to repent and come to faith in Jesus Christ are two of the "central acts" in evangelism "that will very naturally crop up again and again."[48] In the end, I believe Abraham exaggerates the uniqueness of his approach to evangelism. My definition is in fact very close to that proposed by Abraham because I am including the hoped-for results of evangelism in my definition.[49]

---

44. This definition is similar to that given in my previous book (Thiessen, *Ethics of Evangelism*, 11). The one difference is my present definition is addressed specifically to a Christian readership and thus makes reference to the gospel of Jesus Christ and the changes involved in becoming a disciple of Jesus Christ. Brueggemann similarly describes evangelism in terms of inviting people into the biblical stories that define our lives, thereby authorizing them to give up and renounce other stories that have shaped their lives in false or distorting ways (Brueggemann, *Biblical Perspectives on Evangelism*, 10).

45. Abraham, *Logic of Evangelism*, chap. 3.

46. Ibid., 113.

47. Ibid., 95, 104.

48. Ibid., 104, cf. 114. In a later chapter in which he explores the implications of his proposal for the ministry of evangelism, he again admits that "proclaiming the good news of the kingdom is foundational in evangelism" (170).

49. For example, I include initial disciple-making in my definition of evangelism. This is in line with Abraham's own description of evangelism as "the initial formation of genuine disciples of the Lord Jesus Christ." Abraham, "Theology of Evangelism," 30.

David Bosch brings to the fore another problem with a narrow definition of evangelism, specifically objecting to the notion "that evangelism consists in verbal witness only. It consists in word *and* deed, proclamation *and* presence, explanation *and* example."[50] This attempt to broaden the definition of evangelism is in fact fairly common among Christians who like to emphasize evangelism by attraction, or incarnational evangelism, or indirect evangelism.[51] Now I quite agree that deeds are a very important part of the larger mission of the church. I would even concur that deeds have an important part to play with regard to evangelism. Deeds can serve as a demonstration of the gospel. But deeds by themselves cannot tell the story of Jesus Christ, his death and resurrection, and all that this means for us and for a broken world. Only words can tell this story.[52] And therefore I believe it is better to define evangelism in the narrow sense of verbal proclamation of the good news of Jesus Christ and his kingdom. Expressions such as "proclamation in deed" or "evangelism of presence" need to be understood as metaphorical, and will be put in quotation marks in the chapters that follow.[53]

Bosch also raises a more general version of the above objection. There has been and continues to be a lot of controversy surrounding the relation between evangelism and mission.[54] The trend today would seem to be to talk primarily of mission or of being missional.[55] The preference for the word missional has an interesting history related to a growing realization that we as Christians are participating in the mission of God, the *missio Dei*.[56] Others have argued it is not only unhealthy but very difficult to separate the notions of evangelism and mission. Thus, notions such as "integral

---

50. Bosch, "Evangelism," 11.

51. See, for example, Sider's definition: "Evangelism involves the announcement (through words and deeds) of the good news of justification, regeneration, the Lordship of Jesus Christ, and the fact of the new community wherein all relationships are being redeemed (Sider, "Evangelism, Salvation, and Social Justice," 200). See also chapter 10, footnote 35 for additional examples.

52. Sider's statement in the previous footnote illustrates the problem I am exposing. Deeds by themselves cannot include the "announcement" of the good news of justification, regeneration and the Lordship of Jesus Christ. Words are needed here. In fact Sider recognizes this problem in a later work where he clearly separates words and deeds, and argues that they complement each other (Sider, *Doing Evangelism Jesus' Way*, chap. 6).

53. Abraham, *Logic of Evangelism*, 44.

54. Bosch, "Evangelism."

55. Rick Richardson provides a helpful summary of the theological distinctives of "emerging missional movements" (Richardson, "Emerging Missional Movements").

56. Bosch, *Transforming Mission*, chap. 12. The mission of God is the Bible's "grand narrative," as Christopher Wright has argued throughout his book (Wright, *Mission of God*). See also Wright, *Mission of God's People*.

mission" or "holistic mission" have come into vogue more recently.[57] As should be evident from what I said earlier in this chapter, I have a very healthy regard for the larger mission of the church. But in the end I believe it is necessary to distinguish between mission and evangelism. I further align myself with those who regard mission as the wider, and evangelism as the narrower concept.[58]

Those who want to subsume evangelism under the broader concept of mission are invariably forced to admit there is still a conceptual distinction to be made.[59] I also worry about making everything the church does evangelism. It has been well said that if everything is evangelism, then nothing is.[60] Now I agree that everything the church does can contribute in some way to the task of evangelism, but *contributing* to the task of evangelism is different from *being* evangelism. I further believe my narrow definition of evangelism reflects the prominence that is given to proclamation in the New Testament. Given that this book is primarily a New Testament study of the ethics of evangelism, the focus will be primarily on the ethics of proclamation. I would remind those who are unhappy with my narrow definition of evangelism that an analysis of the ethics of proclamation can be extended to other activities of the church.

Much more could be said about the relation of mission and evangelism. I could provide additional justification for my treating evangelism and mission as different concepts, and for treating mission as broader than evangelism. A question could also be raised as to the relative importance of each in the life of the church. More could also be said about attempts to integrate evangelism and social action using concepts like "integral mission" or "holistic mission." These are issues that will be dealt with in more detail in later chapters, particularly in chapter 10, where I will deal with the topic of evangelism and humanitarian aid.

In this chapter I have argued we still need the word evangelism. Faithful Christian mission will require that we evangelize, proclaim or spread the good news, and initiate people into the kingdom of God. While

---

57. See, for example, the Micah Network, "Declaration on Integral Mission." This "Declaration of Integral Mission" is also found in Chester, *Justice, Mercy and Humility*, 17–23.

58. Bosch, *Transforming Mission*, 411–12. Kreider and Kreider, *Worship and Mission*, 54. This is also Newbigin's position (see Kandiah, "Lesslie Newbigin's Contribution to a Theology of Evangelism," 53–54).

59. For example, the very definition of "integral mission" in the "Micah Network Declaration on Integral Mission" makes a distinction between evangelism and social involvement. See also Bradbury, "Micah Mandate," 112.

60. Abraham draws attention to this point in his review of arguments for a narrow definition of evangelism (Abraham, *Logic of Evangelism*, 44).

acknowledging there are other important aspects of Christian mission, the main focus of this book is on evangelism. I want to stress it is not the concern of this book to find the best methods for effective evangelism. Rather my central concern has to do with the ethical evaluation of methods used in evangelism. Part I examines what the New Testament teaches about doing evangelism in a way that is ethical. Part II will apply the biblical principles of ethical evangelism to some specific contexts. Some of the chapters in Part II will move beyond evangelism and consider the ethics of some dimensions of the broader mission of the church. But first we need to lay some further groundwork by considering an approach to biblical ethics generally. The next chapter will also look briefly at how the Old Testament contributes to an ethics of evangelism.

Chapter 2

An Approach to Biblical Ethics and the Ethics of Evangelism

Poor Jonah. The word of the Lord came to him and said, "Go to the great city of Nineveh and preach against it, because its wickedness has come up before me" (Jonah 1:1). I really can't blame Jonah for being hesitant to obey God's commission to evangelize in the foreign city of Nineveh. Nineveh was the chief city of the most powerful empire of the then-known world. Nineveh was also a city known for its wickedness. After its destruction in 612 BC, Nineveh was remembered in Greek and Jewish history as a city steeped in immorality and violence (cf. Nah 3:1–7). This is why the book of Jonah doesn't spend much time describing the moral degradation of Nineveh. It was widely known to be a wicked city. And poor Jonah was given an evangelistic message that was rather blunt—go and tell the people how wicked they are. There didn't seem to be any mercy included in the evangelistic message that Jonah was commissioned to preach.

Most of us probably know the story well. Jonah ran away from the Lord. After a dramatic rescue from the belly of a great fish, the word of the Lord came to Jonah a second time, and this time Jonah obeyed God's commission. On his first day, Jonah walked down main street crying, "Forty more days, and Nineveh shall be destroyed" (3:4). It seems as though the people of Nineveh began to respond to Jonah's preaching after just one day. "The Ninevites believed God. They declared a fast, and all of them, from the greatest to the least, put on sackcloth" (3:5). And then the king issued a proclamation: "Let everyone call urgently on God. Let them give up their evil ways and their violence" (3:8).

The people of Nineveh responded to the king's edict, and "they turned from their evil ways" (3:10). Now I am sure there was some self-interest involved here, as the king and his people were trying to avert God's judgment. But, nonetheless, we have here a recognition by a pagan people that some things are just wrong, and that there is a better way—God's way.

There is something else that should be noted about the king's declaration. He went on to give a rationale for his decree. "Who knows? God may yet relent and with compassion turn from his fierce anger, so that we do not perish" (3:9). The story does not indicate that this was part of Jonah's message. Thus, it is rather amazing to find a pagan king, having at least the beginnings of an understanding of grace. God might change his mind and turn from his fierce anger. And, in fact, God did exactly that. This is good news, found already in the Old Testament.

Sadly, Jonah himself still had some lessons to learn. He started pouting. He got very angry with God and even started to rationalize his original attempt to flee from God's commission. The story ends with God very patiently teaching Jonah a lesson about the extent of his grace, even to a reluctant evangelist.

I WILL RETURN TO THIS story at the end of this chapter in order to draw some lessons about the ethics of evangelism. Here I just want to draw attention to a background question I raised in the first chapter: Is there any common ground between believers and unbelievers with regard to ethics? The story of Jonah is rather clear in giving a positive answer to this question. After all, Jonah was an Israelite, a member of God's chosen people, and yet he was asked to deliver God's message of judgment to a city outside of Israel. And as we have seen, the king and his people understood the message. They recognized they were guilty of doing evil. So here once again we have a biblical suggestion it is possible for believers and unbelievers to have a common understanding as to what is right and wrong. This was the assumption underlying my 2011 book on the ethics of evangelism, which was written for both believers and unbelievers.

We need not concern ourselves with this issue in the present book, however, because this book is addressed to Christians who accept the authority of the Bible. In this chapter and in Part I of this book, I begin an in-house conversation. Can the stories of the Bible help us understand how we should think in the area of ethics? If so, how can these ancient stories speak to us about ethics today? How do we as Christians use these stories to talk about the ethics of evangelism within the Christian community? What does the Bible have to say about the ethics of evangelism? How do we as a church ensure we practice evangelism in a way that is in line with biblical norms and in keeping with the example and teachings of Jesus and the apostles?

BIBLICAL ETHICS

This book proceeds on the assumption that the canonical Scriptures are the foundation for the life of Christians and the church. I am not going to defend this starting point. I simply affirm the classic confessional position of catholic and orthodox Christianity, particularly as sharpened in its Reformation traditions. I take the authority of Scripture seriously. Indeed, in preparing to write this book I skimmed through the entire Bible taking note of any passages that might have something to say about the ethics of evangelism either directly or indirectly. I am well aware this exercise is somewhat subjective, but I felt this was an important first step in preparing to write this book. Any passages of Scripture that were seen as particularly important were starred and these passages were then later followed up by more serious study using commentaries.

It is one thing to start with Scripture, but it is quite another to interpret Scripture correctly and then to use it to address ethical questions. Indeed, hermeneutical problems abound and there are many approaches that could be taken in developing a biblical approach to ethics. It is quite beyond the scope of this book to adjudicate between competing approaches to doing biblical ethics. I will therefore simply provide an outline of the approach that will be taken in this book. My approach will draw on Richard Hays's groundbreaking work, *The Moral Vision of the New Testament* (1996).[1] I will be focusing primarily on the New Testament, though as Hays notes, "It is impossible to read the New Testament rightly without hearing the voice of Israel's Scriptures *within* these early Christian documents."[2] I will therefore provide a brief treatment of Old Testament themes in relation to ethics and the ethics of evangelism later in this chapter. However, given that Christian evangelism is centered on the gospel message of Jesus, there is justification for focusing more on the ethics of the New Testament, which will be the main focus of the chapters of Part I of this book.

While my approach is inspired by Richard Hays, it would be foolish for me to pretend to be following exactly in his footsteps. I am after all a philosopher, not a New Testament scholar. I also have a few quibbles with some aspects of Hays's approach and these will be dealt with in my footnotes. I take some encouragement from the last part of Hays's book where he applies his analysis of New Testament ethics to a number of test cases.[3] What I am

---

1. For a useful summary of Hays's approach, see Hays, *Moral Vision of the New Testament*, 212–13, 309–10.

2. Ibid., 306.

3. Part Four of Hays's book is entitled "The Pragmatic Task: Living Under the Word—Test Cases" (Ibid., 313–461). Hays devotes a chapter to each of the following

AN APPROACH TO BIBLICAL ETHICS AND THE ETHICS OF EVANGELISM 23

doing in the following chapters is applying Hays's approach to an area he does not cover—the ethics of evangelism.

So how will I approach a biblical and New Testament study of the ethics? First, we need to do a careful exegesis of the individual texts of the Old and New Testaments that relate in some way to the topic in question. Here it should be noted there are several ways in which Scriptural texts can relate to the ethics of evangelism. For example, some texts might deal directly with the ethics of evangelism. Others might involve a treatment of theological or ethical principles which might then be applied to the ethics of evangelism. We need to take care to understand all these texts in their historical and literary context. We then need to move on to a more synthetic approach, trying to find some coherence and common themes about ethics and the ethics of evangelism in the Old and New Testaments.[4] At times there will be a blurring of these two tasks, as I don't think they can or should be entirely separated.[5]

A common failure in thinking about a biblical approach to ethics is to think of ethics primarily in terms of rules. The Ten Commandments clearly fall under this description, and it is not too difficult to apply the prohibition against telling lies to evangelism (Lev 19:11). We ought to be truthful in proclaiming the gospel. But rules are not the only way in which the Bible speaks to ethical issues. If we limit ourselves to searching only for rules about ethical evangelism, we will not find very many.[6] Besides, this approach is too simplistic and narrow. We need to broaden our notion about modes of ethical discourse in the Bible. Following Hays, I suggest there are five different ways in which Old and New Testament texts can help us in making ethical judgments.[7]

---

topics—violence in defense of justice, divorce/remarriage, homosexuality, anti-Judaism/ethnic conflict, and abortion.

4. Hays tries to find coherence in the moral vision of the New Testament, by highlighting three focal images: community, cross, and new creation (Ibid., chap. 10). I found this emphasis rather arbitrary and not that helpful for my purposes.

5. I believe Hays goes too far in stressing the diversity of the New Testament texts, including the gospels. While I agree each writer of the gospels and the epistles had his own agenda and was writing for a unique context, I am convinced if all these writers would have been in the same room they would have been sharing their excitement about the many things they agreed on with regard to the life and teaching of Jesus. I believe there would also have been substantial agreement about ethics and the ethics of evangelism.

6. Some New Testament "rules" about doing evangelism ethically might include 2 Cor. 4:1–6 and 1 Pet 3:15–16.

7. Hays, *Moral Vision of the New Testament*, 209. I am rewording and reordering Hays's four approaches, although the changes here are minor. I am also adding an additional mode of ethical discourse, as a way of resolving an ambiguity in Hays where he sometimes refers to narrative texts (plural) while at other times he focuses on the story of the New Testament as a whole (Ibid., 295). Hence the addition of (d).

MODES OF ETHICAL DISCOURSE IN SCRIPTURE

(a) **Specific rules or commandments** that either require or prohibit certain actions and types of behavior or character.

(b) **Broader principles or frameworks** that govern particular decisions about actions.

(c) **Stories** of persons who model exemplary conduct and character. There can of course also be stories of persons who model bad behavior and character. The story of Jesus holds primacy in our understanding of ethics.

(d) **Narrative of the Bible as a whole** within which we locate our individual stories and the story of the church. The narrative of the Bible gives us a broad and storied framework within which we understand ethics.

(e) **Biblical worldview** which is grounded in the narrative of the Bible as a whole. A biblical worldview shapes how we interpret the world and gives us a parallel broad framework from which we do ethics.

It should be evident that the above five modes of ethical discourse move from the specific to the more general. I would further suggest this gradation also moves from the less important to the more important.[8] All five approaches to appealing to biblical texts in order to do ethics are important, but some are more important than others. Further, texts must be granted authority in the mode in which they speak.[9] It would be a mistake to turn a narrative into a rule, for example. We must also be very careful not to use one mode of appeal to Scripture to override the witness of the New Testament in another mode. If there are tensions between differing modes of appeal, these should be acknowledged and any attempts at synthesis must do justice to the whole canon of Scripture. And, as already mentioned, we must guard against the danger of reading Old and New Testament ethical texts in one mode only.

There is another important problem that needs to be addressed here. Each of the books of the Bible is written within a particular historical, cultural, and social context. Even the language used will reflect the particularity of a certain culture. The worlds of the Old Testament and New Testament are very

---

8. Hays isn't entirely clear about which mode of ethical discourse is primary. Sometimes this status is given to the paradigmatic mode (or narrative texts—my "stories") (Ibid., 295), sometimes the narrative of the New Testament as a whole (Ibid., 295), and sometimes the mode of symbolic world construction (my "worldview") (Ibid., 303).

9. The suggestions in this paragraph draw on Hays's interpretative guidelines with regard to his four modes of ethical discourse in the New Testament (Ibid., 294).

distant and different from our own. So how do we overcome this distance as we seek to apply the five modes of ethical discourse to our own world? Here we must avoid two extremes. On the one hand, we must not make the distance between the biblical text and the world today so great that the Bible is unable to speak to our contemporary situation.[10] On the other hand, we must be careful not to ignore the gap between these two worlds and therefore adopt a simplistic equivalency approach in moving from the Bible to our contemporary situation.[11] What is needed to bridge this gap is some imaginative creativity, or even improvisation.[12] Hays describes the challenge in this way: "the use of the New Testament in normative ethics requires *an integrative act of the imagination*, a discernment about how our lives, despite their historical dissimilarity to the lives narrated in the New Testament, might fitly answer to that narration and participate in the truth that it tells."[13]

One caution is in order. Acknowledging that all of Scripture is embodied in a particular culture does not rule out the possibility there might be some ethical norms that are transcultural.[14] Indeed, as I will argue in the next section, understanding God as creator entails there being some universal norms that apply to all cultures and peoples. Another indicator of transcultural ethical norms is when certain ethical norms are reaffirmed in several books of the Bible, both Old Testament and New Testament. I consider the Ten Commandments to be one example of transcultural ethical norms which are affirmed throughout the Scriptures.

There is a final hermeneutical issue that needs to be dealt with in relation to developing a biblical ethic and applying it to evangelism. So far I have focused primarily on the authority of the New Testament or the Bible as a whole. What about other sources of authority? It would seem we cannot

---

10. This is the error of biblical scholars (and lay Christians) who are oriented to the spirit of the Enlightenment and who therefore insist on an uncommitted approach to Scripture which in turn produces a "distancing effect." See Bosch, "Toward a Hermeneutic for 'Biblical Studies and Mission.'"

11. This tends to be the error of those who like to take the Bible literally. For a short summary of these two extremes in biblical interpretation see Goheen, "Critical Examination of David Bosch's Missional Reading of Luke."

12. See Wells, *Improvisation*.

13. Hays, *Moral Vision of the New Testament*, 298. Hays also describes this bridging activity in terms of "metaphor-making" (Ibid., 6, 299). "[W]e will have to formulate imaginative *analogies* between the stories told in the texts and the story lived out by our community in a very different historical setting" (Ibid., 298).

14. I believe Hays goes too far when he cautions against an approach that tries to separate out "timeless truth" from "culturally conditioned" elements in the New Testament (Ibid., 299). It nearly seems as if he is here ruling out the possibility of transcultural ethical norms. I would suggest Hays's overall approach allows for a transcultural ethical vision in the New Testament, if not explicitly, then implicitly.

appeal only to Scripture because the interpretation of Scripture never occurs in a vacuum.[15] We therefore need to take into account other sources of authority such as church tradition, reason, and experience.[16] But we must not see these extra-biblical sources as independent, counterbalancing sources of authority. The authority of Scripture must always remain primary. Normative Christian ethics must begin and end with the interpretation and application of Scripture.

The above caution will be especially important when dealing with the ethics of evangelism. Sadly, the history of the Christian church is littered with coercive approaches to evangelism, and justifications of the same by appeals to Scripture. As will be argued later, such justifications are unwarranted, and so here an appeal to tradition or experience for developing the ethics of evangelism would be seriously misleading. Similarly, with regard to an appeal to reason. While reason has a role to play in interpreting Scripture, we need to remember the gospel of the cross will frequently confound reason (1 Cor 1:25). Hence, we will need to be careful with "rational" postmodern arguments suggesting any appeals to exclusive truth make evangelism immoral, to give just one example. While I agree appeals to tradition, experience, and reason are inescapable components of understanding biblical texts, the authority of Scripture must be primary.

N. T. Wright has given us a helpful analogy to understand what we are doing when we apply the Scriptures to our world today.[17] He compares the Bible to a drama with five acts (creation, sin, Israel, Christ, church).[18] To help us understand what it means for the church today to place itself under the authority of the Bible, Wright posits a Shakespearean play, most of whose fifth act has been lost.

> The first four acts provide, let us suppose, such a wealth of characterization, such a crescendo of excitement with the plot, that it is generally agreed that the play ought to be staged. Nevertheless, it is felt inappropriate actually to write a fifth act once and for all: it would freeze the play into one form, and commit

---

15. Hays, *Moral Vision of the New Testament*, 10, 209–11, 295–98.

16. These four sources of authority are often referred to as the Wesleyan Quadrilateral.

17. Wright, *New Testament and the People of God*, 139–43.

18. There is of course a sixth act to the biblical story—the coming of the new creation. I believe this final act also should come into play when seeking to find out what Scripture says about the ethics of evangelism. See Bartholomew and Goheen, *Drama of Scripture*, 13, 207–13.

Shakespeare as it were to being prospectively responsible for work not in fact his own.[19]

Instead, it is felt better "to give the key parts to highly trained, sensitive and experienced Shakespearean actors, who would immerse themselves in the first four acts, and in the language and culture of Shakespeare and his time, and who would then be told to work out a fifth act for themselves."[20] Is there a way in which to evaluate the performance of the fifth act in relation to the previous four acts? Yes, some things are simply required by the earlier acts and are not open to variation. Even in the creative improvisation involved in the fifth act, "there will be a rightness, a fittingness, about certain actions and speeches, about certain final moves in the drama."[21]

This is the challenge I am undertaking in this book. I want to immerse myself in the canon of Scripture, especially the New Testament, and then creatively apply the rules, principles, stories, drama, and worldview of Scripture to the ethics of evangelism. In the remainder of this chapter I want to illustrate how these five modes of appeal to Scripture work themselves out as we look briefly at the Old Testament and try to draw some lessons about the ethics of evangelism for our time.

THE BIG PICTURE

Wright's analogy has already helped us focus on the biblical narrative as a whole. The Bible begins with creation, then comes the tragic fall of Adam and Eve. Already in Genesis, we see God beginning to work out his plan of redemption. This redemption plan centers in Jesus Christ, though its culmination is still in the future. We as Christians live in a period between the times, and are called to proclaim the good news of God's kingdom and also to work toward ensuring God's will is done on earth as it is in heaven. I want to focus on some of the highpoints of the biblical drama, which in turn form the basis of the major themes of a biblical worldview. I also want to apply these highpoints and themes to the ethics of evangelism. Obviously we need to start with the Old Testament to get the big picture. I will focus mainly on those parts of the Old Testament story that are picked up in the New Testament.

The biblical drama begins with creation. The story of creation makes it abundantly clear the creation of man and woman represents the pinnacle of God's creation. "Let us make man in our image, in our likeness," God

19. Wright, *New Testament and the People of God*, 140.
20. Ibid.
21. Ibid., 141.

said, "and let them rule over the fish of the sea and the birds of the air, over livestock, over all the earth, and over all the creatures that move along the ground" (Gen 1:26). Man and woman are created in the image of God. What this means, according to Richard Middleton, is that men and women are to be bodily representatives of God here on earth.[22] That gives us quite an honorable status. Man and woman are also instructed to rule over the rest of creation. Again, quite an honor. Man and woman are also called to continue the creative process begun by God. They are called to fill the earth, care for it, and develop the potential latent in it, a challenge sometimes referred to as "the creation mandate."[23] Adam is even given the responsibility to name all the animals—an intellectual challenge, and a sign of authority (Gen 2:19–20). In all this, man and woman are given the freedom to obey or disobey the instructions given by God. Such freedom involves an awesome responsibility. Clearly, man and woman have dignity.

This understanding of man and woman's relation to creation is repeated again and again in Scripture. The Psalmist, after reviewing the complexity and glory of all creation, asks a haunting question: "What is man that you are mindful of him, the son of man that you care for him?" The answer: "You made him a little lower than the heavenly beings and crowned him with glory and honor. You made him ruler over the works of your hands; you put everything under his feet" (Ps 8:5–6). Jesus reflects this same understanding of the unique worth of human beings in his memorable warning against worry in the Sermon on the Mount: "Look at the birds of the air; they do not sow or reap or store away in barns, and yet your heavenly Father feeds them." And then comes a rhetorical question: "Are you not much more valuable than they" (Matt 6:26)?

This understanding of human nature is a key component of a Christian worldview. It also becomes foundational for a biblical approach to ethics. In everything we do, we ought to uphold the dignity of persons. We have here also a foundational principle for a biblical approach to the ethics of evangelism. Evangelism must always be done in such a way that it protects the dignity of the persons being evangelized. Any approach to evangelism that reduces persons being evangelized to the status of an object is wrong. It is similarly wrong to violate in any way the freedom of persons when evangelizing, because an essential aspect of upholding the dignity of persons involves respecting their freedom.

---

22. See Middleton, *Liberating Image*.

23. Gen 1:28, 2:15. See also Goheen and Bartholomew, *Living at the Crossroads*, 44–45.

LAW

There is another dimension of the story of creation that is relevant to ethics generally, as well as the ethics of evangelism. God did not only create the sun, moon, stars, plants, animals, and human beings. He also created the laws by which each of these elements of creation are to function. For example, the law of gravity governs the sun, moon, and stars. Thus we find the Psalms sometimes describing God as giving commands to the earth, spreading the snow like wool, and hurling down his hail like pebbles (Ps 147:15-18). These physical laws cannot be broken. The sun, moon, and all of inanimate creation cannot help but obey God's physical laws.

There is another kind of law created by God that applies to human beings. God gives commands, already in the creation story, but human beings are free to obey or disobey these commands. We are also given the results of obedience and disobedience. Obedience to God's laws leads to human flourishing, while disobedience leads to alienation, disorder, and chaos. Adam and Eve are instructed not to eat from the tree of the knowledge of good and evil, for when you eat of it you will surely die (Gen 2:17). Hence, the frequent theme of blessings and curses found in the Old Testament as well as in the New Testament.[24] God's creation laws apply to the whole range of human activities.[25] The question being posed by this book is this: Are there God-given norms that govern the proclamation of the gospel?

Later in this chapter I will deal specifically with the call of Israel as part of the biblical drama. Here I would like to jump into the middle of Israel's story and note the importance of God's creation law in the story of Israel. The exodus out of Egypt is of course a central part of this story. At Mount Sinai, God speaks these words: "I am the LORD your God, who brought you out of Egypt, out of the land of slavery" (Exod 20:2). Then come the Ten Commandments. Note especially that the commandments arise out of a story. As already mentioned, one of these commandments (truth-telling) has a direct bearing on the ethics of evangelism.[26] In Deuteronomy, where Moses gives his farewell address to the people of Israel before they enter the land of Canaan, he again reviews the story of Israel which then becomes the foundation for both general and specific instructions on how to live. Here again there is a review of the Ten Commandments (Deut 5:1-21). And here again there are

---

24. See Deut 11:26-32, 30:15-20; Job 4:8; Pss 1 & 2; Hos 8:7; Matt 7:13-14, 24-27; Gal 6:7-8.

25. Some examples include the family (Gen 2:24; Eph 5:22—6:4), agriculture (Isa 28:23-29), government (Judg 21:25; Rom 13:1-7), and master/worker relations (Eph 6:5-9).

26. Exod 20:16; cf. Lev 19:11.

blessings connected with obeying these commandments. "Hear, O Israel, and be careful to obey so that it may go well with you" (Deut 6:3).

Then come two more general principles that are part of this story of God giving Israel the law. The first is the Shema which is still recited daily by every devout Jew: "Hear O Israel: The LORD our God, the LORD is one. Love the LORD your God with all your heart and with all your soul and with all your strength" (Deut 6:5). Why this general commandment? It is because God has shown his love to the people of Israel that they are called to love God in return, and also to obey his commandments (Deut 6:1–3). Then a little later God is described as a God who loves the alien (Deut 10:18). Love of the alien also grows out of the very character of God. And then follows another commandment: "And you are to love those who are aliens, for you yourselves were aliens in Egypt."[27] Here again, a general commandment grows out of a retelling of Israel's story.

This commandment and the story undergirding it are again reflected in Jesus' teachings. In a conversation over some details of the Old Testament law, a Pharisee confronts Jesus with this question: "Teacher, which is the greatest commandment in the Law?" Jesus responds by quoting from Deuteronomy: "Love the Lord your God with all your heart and with all your soul and with all your mind. This is the first and greatest commandment" (Matt 22:34–38). But Jesus goes on to suggest a second commandment which he says is like the first, and which again is found in the Old Testament: "Love your neighbor as yourself. All the Law and the Prophets hang on these two commandments."[28] Earlier in the Gospel of Matthew, Jesus gives us another version of this commandment, in what has come to be known as the Golden Rule: "In everything, do to others what you would have them do to you," and again we are told that this "sums up the Law and the Prophets."[29]

Love of God and love of one's neighbor are surely fundamental to a biblical approach to ethics, but love is not just an undefined and sentimental feeling.[30] The law and the prophets give concrete expression to what love entails, Jesus reminds us. And Paul too reminds us that the commandments are summed up in the rule of love (Rom 13:8–10). Love cares for the neighbor. Love reaches out to the stranger. Love respects the other. Love speaks

---

27. Deut 10:19; cf. Isa 56:3.

28. Matt 22:39–40; Lev 19:18.

29. Matt 7:12. Luke gives us the Golden Rule in the context of an exhortation to love your enemies (6:31).

30. As Stanley Hauerwas has observed, "The ethics of love is often but a cover for what is fundamentally an assertion of ethical relativism." Hauerwas, *Vision and Virtue*, 124.

plainly and truthfully (Matt 5:37). Love tries to make peace and live in harmony with others.[31] We are even called to love our enemy.[32]

Here again we have an important general ethical principle that needs to be applied to evangelism. Evangelism should grow out of love for God and neighbor. Hence, too, Paul's succinct description of the motivation for evangelism: "For Christ's love compels us" (2 Cor 5:14). But evangelism must also be done in such a way that it conforms to the principles of love. It should not destroy the other person. It should cherish the other person as someone loved by God. It should respect the other person, even though there may be disagreement with the beliefs of the other person. It should also care for the whole person.

CALL AND MISSION OF ISRAEL

Another essential element in the plot of the biblical drama is the call of Israel. An examination of the mission of Israel will help us uncover additional ingredients of a biblical approach to the ethics of evangelism. When God first calls Abram, he says, "I will make you into a great nation and will bless you. I will make your name great and you will be a blessing . . . and all peoples on earth will be blessed through you" (Gen 12:1-3). After the exodus from Egypt, at the renewing of the covenant at Mount Sinai, God says, "Although the whole earth is mine, you will be for me a kingdom of priests and a holy nation" (Exod 19:5-6). Prophets like Isaiah kept reminding Israel of its calling: "But you, O Israel, . . . You are my servant" (Isa 41:8-9). "I will also make you a light for the Gentiles, that you may bring my salvation to the ends of the earth."[33]

But the mission of Israel includes more than just being a holy nation which models righteousness. It also includes proclamation. "You are my witnesses," declares the LORD, "and my servant whom I have chosen" (Isa 43:10). The context here is really that of a courtroom, where Israel is called on to combat competing understandings of reality, to discredit other witnesses, and to give testimony to Yahweh as the true God.[34] The language here begins to sound quite evangelistic!

Earlier in Isaiah some interesting imagery is used which further addresses the mission of Israel and the way in which this mission is fulfilled.

31. Matt 5:9; Rom 12:16, 18.
32. Matt 5:43-48; Rom 12:17-21.
33. Isa 49:6; cf. Isa 42:6; 60:3. On Israel's mission as a light to the nations, see Kaiser, *Mission in the Old Testament*.
34. Brueggemann, *Theology of the Old Testament*, 747-50.

"In the last days the mountain of the LORD'S temple will be established as chief among the mountains; it will be raised above the hills, and all nations will stream to it. Many peoples will come and say, 'Come, let us go up to the mountain of the LORD, to the house of the God of Jacob. He will teach us his ways so that we may walk in his paths.' The law will go out from Zion, the word of the LORD from Jerusalem."[35] The mountain of the LORD is a symbol of the coming kingdom of God, in which a purified and restored Jerusalem is destined to play a crucial role.[36] But Isaiah clearly intends that this vision will inspire contemporary Israelites to live now in light of this glorious prospect (Isa 2:5). What is interesting here is the mission of Israel is fulfilled by all nations streaming to the mountain of the LORD and asking to be taught the ways of God. What we have here is "evangelism by attraction." And it is only after people from other nations have come to the mountain with a desire to be taught the ways of God that teaching and proclamation begins.[37] Clearly this approach overcomes the problem of coercion often associated with evangelism. People who are attracted to the way of life of the Israelites and who come streaming to the mountain of the LORD asking to be taught are clearly giving their permission to be evangelized.

If we fast-forward to the New Testament, we find similar imagery used to describe the mission of the church.[38] Jesus tells his disciples they are the light of the world (Matt 5:14). The Apostle Peter uses the very same language found in Isaiah, describing Christians who are scattered over Asia Minor as chosen by God, a holy nation, a royal priesthood (1 Pet 1:2; 2:4, 9). Like Israel, the mission of the church is also to be light in the midst of darkness.[39] Peter challenges Christians to live such good lives among the pagans that "they may see your good deeds and glorify God on the day he visits us" (2:12). Like Isaiah, the emphasis here would seem to be on the

---

35. Isa 2:2–3. This same imagery occurs in Mic 4:1–5; cf. Ps 67:1–2; Isa 62:1–2,12; Zech 8:20–23.

36. Webb, *Message of Isaiah*, 46.

37. This imagery and the seeming emphasis on evangelism has led to considerable debate within Judaic scholarship regarding proselytizing, with some scholars maintaining that the Jewish tradition does not seek to convert individuals to the Jewish faith, while others maintain that proselytizing activities are part of the history of the Jewish faith. See Novak, "Proselytism in Judaism," and Thiessen, "Christians and Jews and Proselytizing," for a response to Novak.

38. See Goheen, *Light to the Nations*.

39. Paul in Acts 13:47 quotes from Isa 49:6 to justify his mission to the Gentiles. Kaiser, *Mission in the Old Testament*, 8. Kreider points out that the Isaiah 2 prophetic text that was referred to earlier was one that the early Christian writers cited more often than any other, and that it was know by all the believers of the first few centuries (*Patient Ferment of the Early Church*, 92).

AN APPROACH TO BIBLICAL ETHICS AND THE ETHICS OF EVANGELISM 33

"evangelism of presence." But Peter moves on to address overt evangelism as well. "Always be prepared to give an answer to everyone who asks you to give the reason for the hope that you have" (1 Pet 3:15). We will consider Peter's admonition in more detail in chapter 6. But Isaiah's notion of witness as giving testimony in court is taken up again and again in the New Testament as a way of describing evangelism.[40]

I return to a later section of Isaiah where the servant imagery is used once again, but now seems to refer to a special person, God's perfect servant, a Servant of the LORD (Isa 42:1-7).[41] The calling of this Servant includes being an ethical witness to the nations, being "a light for the Gentiles" (v. 6). He will also be inspired by the Spirit to "bring justice to the nations."[42] But the Servant does more than just bear silent witness. The instrument of the Servant's rule will be "the word of God" which is delivered by instruction (v. 4b).[43] We are also told God's Servant "will not shout or cry out," which again suggests overt proclamation is also being assumed here (v. 2). There are also some significant ethical overtones here. The Servant's manner will be gentle rather than overbearing (v. 3a).

What is of particular significance here is that Matthew's gospel draws on this passage in Isaiah to describe the ministry of Jesus (Matt 12:15-21). The context is also very interesting. Jesus is facing opposition to his ministry. In fact, after Jesus has publicly challenged the Pharisees by claiming to be Lord of the Sabbath and then healing a man with a shriveled hand, we are told that the Pharisees were plotting to kill him. After this Jesus withdraws, but the crowds keep following him, and Jesus keeps healing their sick, though he warns them not to tell who he is. Matthew then inserts a statement suggesting this was to fulfill what was spoken through the prophet Isaiah:

> Here is my servant whom I have chosen, the one I love, in whom I delight; I will put my Spirit on him, and he will proclaim justice to the nations. He will not quarrel or cry out; no one will hear his voice in the streets. A bruised reed he will not break, and a smoldering wick he will not snuff out, till he leads justice

---

40. Luke 4:18; John 1:7, 8; Acts 1:8; 23:11; 1 John 1:2.

41. Webb argues the Servant of the LORD in Isaiah 42 is too ideal a figure to represent Israel in a direct sense. There seems to be a shift to a specific person who is giving a message to Israel regarding its weaknesses and failures. Webb, *Message of Isaiah*, 170-71.

42. The key term in verses 1-4 is "justice" (*mišpāt*), which means more than what we normally associate with justice. It includes the order God has given to the entire universe by his creative acts (Isa 40:14).

43. The Servant's "law" is literally "his *tôrâ*" which means instruction or guidance. Webb, *Message of Isaiah*, 172.

to victory. In his name the nations will put their hope." (Matt 12:18–21; Isa 42:1–3)

What is the ethical significance of Isaiah's description of God's Servant, and Matthew's description of Jesus using this same language? Jesus is healing the sick, but he warns them not to tell others who he is. In fact, this is not the only time Jesus urges those he heals to keep silent.[44] Jesus doesn't want to exploit his healings in order to enhance his message. Yes, he is proclaiming justice to the nations, but this proclamation cannot be characterized in terms of noisy street demonstrations, complete with placards and megaphones. Instead, "no one will hear his voice in the streets" (Matt 12:19). Nor does Jesus spend a lot of time condemning the injustices of society. He simply quietly corrects them by healing those who are vulnerable, feeding the hungry, showing love to children, and treating women as equals. Jesus takes a positive approach. He is not there to break a reed that is already bruised. Instead, he focuses on bringing it to full health. Nor does Jesus snuff out a wick that is already smoldering. Instead he tries to fan it into a full flame.

Yes, there are times when Jesus does raise his voice and when he does condemn what he finds wrong in people and in society at large. We will need to address this tension in the next chapter. But for now, I want to focus on Matthew's description of Jesus' ministry in terms of nurturing back to health, and encouraging the light that is already present. Do we have here a model for Christian witness for our time? This is very different from the ineffective culture wars of the evangelical right of the past few decades. The witness of Christian presence might just be much more effective.[45] And more ethical too!

Just a few days before writing these lines, I enjoyed the 2015 production of *The Sound of Music* at Stratford, in Canada. The continuing popularity of this classic surely lies in its truthful testimony to the human condition and the powerful witness to goodness in Maria, a postulant at a convent, who has the courage to take up her calling and help a family in need. Yes, there is a point where Maria does bravely challenge the captain to fulfill his calling to be a loving father to his children. But in the main, Maria's witness is more subtle—fanning the flickering flames of light and goodness still present in this broken family, bringing love and wholeness to a family which had lost its mother, teaching the children to sing, and teaching the captain to be fully human once again. Yes, there is teaching, but there is also faithful modeling that precedes and accompanies this teaching. It is very hard to find anything ethically blameworthy in this approach to evangelism!

---

44. See also Matt 8:4; 9:30 and Mark 5:43.
45. See Hunter, *To Change the World*, Essay III.

JONAH

By way of conclusion, I return to the story of Jonah which was told at the beginning of this chapter. What can be learned about the ethics of evangelism from this story? First, a minor point of interpretation concerning Jonah shouting his message in the streets of Nineveh. Doesn't this contradict Isaiah's and Matthew's description of the Servant of the Lord who does not shout or cry out in the streets? As mentioned earlier in this chapter, one must face tensions in Scripture where these seem to occur. The first thing to note here is that describing Jonah as shouting his message in the streets of Nineveh is already an interpretation. The text in fact tells us that Jonah "proclaimed" his message, though some translations use the term, "cried out" (NRSV). It might very well be that Jonah was shouting when he was delivering his message on the streets of Nineveh, given that ancient city streets were rather noisy and one would have to do some shouting in order to be heard.

Even so, I am not so sure Jonah is here betraying the description of the Servant of the LORD as found in Matthew and Isaiah. The story of Jonah involves a solitary figure proclaiming God's judgment to a majority culture steeped in sin. Given his overall reluctance to proclaim his message, Jonah's approach is hardly one of a quarrelsome kind of shouting, and his proclamation of judgment might very well have been done in fear and trembling. This brings to the fore another possible answer to the seeming tension in Scripture being addressed here. Not all stories in the Bible are positive in nature. So, Jonah might be an example of a prophet who does not follow the guidelines of ethical evangelism. He was after all initially disobedient to God's commission.

There is another reason to believe that Jonah was not a model missionary. In the final chapter of this narrative, we discover the underlying reason for Jonah's reluctance to go to Nineveh in the first place. Should the Ninevites listen to his message and repent, Yahweh would surely withdraw the judgment that Jonah was predicting was only forty days away. "I knew that you are a gracious and compassionate God, slow to anger and abounding in love" (Jonah 4:2). God's mercy was the last thing that Jonah wanted for Nineveh. After all, Assyria had inflicted a lot of suffering on Israel, and so Jonah wanted punishment, not love and compassion.

The story of Jonah is perhaps best read as a warning to all Israel to avoid the trap Jonah fell into, "and to encourage their adoption of Yahweh's heart for the nations—yes, even one's brutal enemies."[46] Hence, Yahweh's question that concludes the narrative. "Should I not be concerned about

---

46. Kaiser, *Mission in the Old Testament*, 69. cf. Brueggemann, *Theology of the Old Testament*, 220.

that great city" (4:11)? Ethical evangelism reflects the love and mercy of God.

There is even more to be learned from this story. We have here an Old Testament account of evangelism in the public square—Jonah proclaiming judgment on the streets of Nineveh. Today's methods can of course be much more sophisticated. But there is nothing wrong with God's people proclaiming moral judgment in the public domain. In Western societies this might be treated as offensive, but this rests on an arbitrary liberal divide between public and private domains. Also, the claim that this is offensive is really just an aesthetic judgment, not a moral judgment.

The king, together with the residents of Nineveh, responded to Jonah's message. They were perfectly free to dismiss Jonah as an eccentric religious prophet. Instead, they listened, and their consciences were pricked. Jesus in his later discourses gives us an interpretation of what is happening here. He informs his disciples that when he leaves this earth to be with his father in heaven, he will send the Holy Spirit, one of whose functions is to convict the world of sin and righteousness and judgment (John 16:8–11). We have a part to play in disturbing consciences. And there is nothing wrong in doing so. People are still free to accept or reject our reminders of the existence of ethical norms. Let's just remember to combine evangelism as ethical exhortation with the good news of God's mercy and love.

In this chapter I have outlined my approach to deriving ethics from the biblical canon, particularly the New Testament. I have also touched on some Old Testament themes that relate to the ethics of evangelism. Many of these themes recur in the New Testament. The chapters of Part I focus on the ethics of evangelism in the New Testament.

PART I

Ethics of Evangelism
in the New Testament

Chapter 3

The Gospels and Jesus

Levi was a tax collector, and as such was held in suspicion by most Jews. Tax collectors worked for the hated oppressors, the Romans, and were proverbially wealthy because the system of tax collection lent itself to corruption. No doubt Levi will have at least heard about the teachings of Jesus in the Capernaum area, and he might even have seen Jesus heal someone. He was probably wondering about this man everyone was talking about. And then suddenly Jesus stands in front of his taxation booth and says, "Follow me." Amazingly, Levi obeys. One can only imagine what prompted Levi's decision to follow Jesus. Was it a recognition of a deep hollowness in his own life? Was it the love and integrity he saw in Jesus? Was it a hunger for truth and beauty and goodness? Whatever it was that prompted his decision, Levi gave up his old way of life, began the process of changing his beliefs, and began adopting a new identity by following Jesus. A while later he puts on a large banquet for his new master, inviting his former fellow tax collectors, together with other friends identified as "sinners." This prompts the ever-present spying Pharisees to ask Jesus' disciples a question. "Why do you (and your teacher) eat and drink with tax collectors and 'sinners'?" Jesus overhears the conversation and responds, "It is not the healthy who need a doctor, but the sick. I have not come to call the righteous, but sinners to repentance." (Luke 5:27–32)

WE BEGIN OUR STUDY of the New Testament with the four gospel accounts of the life and teachings of Jesus. Although we use the plural term "Gospels," we need to remember there is really only one gospel.[1] The

---

1. The use of the plural term "Gospels" to designate the first four books of the New Testament only occurred in the middle of the second century AD. The plural form would not have been understood in the apostolic age or in the next few generations because they thought only in terms of one true gospel. Indeed, Paul suggests anyone

word "gospel" comes from the Greek word *euangelion*, meaning "good news," and is related to the English word "evangelism." So the very term used to identify the four Gospels already gets us into the subject of evangelism. The Gospels tell the story of Jesus. The gospel writers are sometimes referred to as evangelists who crafted the stories of Jesus to bear witness to what they had seen and heard while they accompanied Jesus; they were in effect doing evangelism in writing the four Gospels.[2]

If we look at the Gospels as a written form of evangelism, then it is interesting to note the introduction to Luke already addresses the issue of the ethics of evangelism. The prologue is dedicated to Theophilus, which in its present context might be a fictional form of address to any interested reader.[3] Luke begins by referring to various other accounts of the life of Jesus handed down by those who were eyewitnesses of the events surrounding Jesus. Luke describes himself as having "carefully investigated everything from the beginning," and wanting "to write an orderly account" of the life and teachings of Jesus. Luke's description of his objectives suggests he is aiming for historical accuracy and a carefully organized narrative. Luke's goal is also to ensure the reader "may know the truth" of the subject of his narrative (NRSV). The Greek word translated "truth" is *asphaleia*, meaning firmness, certainty, or security; the English word "asphalt" is derived from this root. So, Luke's claim could be paraphrased as aiming to assure his readers of the *solidity* of the instruction they have received.[4]

Given the evangelistic nature of the Gospels, we see here a model of ethical evangelism. Like Luke, our evangelistic message should not be haphazard, but based on careful research. It should be creative and well organized. We also need to be truthful in what we say. Listeners and readers should be able to have confidence in what we say because we have done our homework.

If we look at all four Gospels, we discover each is written with a unique purpose and audience in mind, but all of them tell stories about Jesus. These stories don't always line up in terms of giving us a chronological account of the life of Jesus, because each evangelist is keeping his unique readership and purpose in mind. Although the gospel accounts, especially Matthew, include some ethical instruction, which we will need to apply to our subject of doing evangelism in an ethical manner, we must not forget the primary

---

who teaches "a gospel other than the one we preached to you" is condemned (Gal 1:8; cf. Rom 1:1–3).

2. John is very specific about his intention in recording the miraculous signs of Jesus: "[T]hese are written that you might believe that Jesus is the Christ, the Son of God, and that by believing you might have life in his name" (John 20:30–31).

3. Luke 1:1–4. Hays, *Moral Vision of the New Testament*, 135n4.

4. Ibid.

mode of discourse of the Gospels is stories. As we have seen in chapter 2, stories are one mode of ethical discourse in the New Testament. Ethical instruction by way of stories is more indirect and in some respects more complex. Stories teach us how to see the world and what to hope for. Stories also give us models of behavior, some good and some bad. Stories instruct by way of the imagination.[5]

The story of Levi's banquet highlighted above is one of many stories of Jesus we will be considering in this chapter. There are some lessons about ethical evangelism to be learned from this story, but these will be considered later in the chapter. My purpose here is merely to highlight the importance of stories in our study of the Gospels. I would remind the reader that the focus of this book and the study of the Gospels in this chapter is not on methods of doing evangelism. This is not a "how-to-do" manual." Rather, the focus is on ethics. What can we learn from the story (stories) of Jesus regarding the ethics of evangelism?

GOD AS EVANGELIST

The Gospel of John is perhaps clearest in describing God as an evangelist.[6] John, unlike Matthew and Luke, doesn't give us the details of Jesus' birth in Bethlehem. Instead, John begins by identifying Jesus as the preexistent *Logos* who was with God before creation, and through whom all things were in fact created. Jesus' coming is described as bringing light and salvation to a dark world. And then this memorable description of the Incarnation: "The Word became flesh and lived for a while among us. We have seen his glory, the glory of the one and only Son, who came from the Father, full of grace and truth" (John 1:14). Jesus is the revealer of God. When God wants to evangelize, he does so by sending his Son into this world so people can see grace and truth in a person.[7]

Already in the first chapter of the Gospel of John we are told that there was resistance to God's revelation—the darkness didn't understand the light, the world didn't recognize Jesus, and his own people, the descendants of Israel, didn't receive Jesus. But a few did, and they became children of God in a very special sense, not born in the way in which babies are typically born, but born of God.

---

5. Ibid., 73.

6. Note the title of a book by Wells, *God the Evangelist*.

7. Of course, God was already concerned about evangelism in the Old Testament, as we found in chapter 2, but, as is noted in the introduction to the Epistle of Hebrews, God has spoken to us in a very special way through his Son (Heb 1:1–3).

In this description of God as an evangelist we already get some hints as to the nature of ethical evangelism. God didn't just send a written message to the world. He sent his Son to embody the message. Ethical evangelism is always incarnational in nature. Proclamation must always go hand in hand with a demonstration of the gospel. Further, people are given the freedom to reject the light that came into the world. Jesus as Creator doesn't come barging into the world demanding allegiance from his created subjects. John reinforces this point by contrasting the power and glory of Jesus as creator with the power and freedom of human beings to reject the Word made flesh. Even though the world was made through him, the world did not recognize him or receive him. Matthew and Luke also highlight the vulnerability of God becoming flesh—Jesus was born as a helpless baby, in circumstances of poverty, and was welcomed by the marginalized in that society. God as evangelist didn't come with the pomp and ceremony that would be appropriate to someone who is really the King of the universe. Instead, he came in weakness. He came as a human being with all the vulnerabilities attached to being human. He came filled with grace and truth. This is what ethical evangelism looks like.

The first chapter of the Gospel of John includes a brief reference to John the Baptist who was sent by God to prepare the way for Jesus. This story is told in greater detail in each of the other three Gospels. John was an eccentric and chose to stay in a desolate desert for his work as an evangelist. The Gospel of Mark describes him as "baptizing in the desert region and preaching a baptism of repentance for the forgiveness of sins" (Mark 1:4). In the Gospel of Matthew we find him proclaiming, "Repent for the kingdom of heaven is near" (Matt 3:2). Despite his eccentricity and isolation, people from Jerusalem and the whole Judean countryside were coming to John to be baptized, confessing their sins. Luke goes on to describe the life-changing dimensions of John's kingdom message and baptism of repentance (Luke 3:10–14). Soldiers were told to be content with their pay. Tax collectors were told not to collect more taxes than required, and the crowd was told to practice charity. This is what it means to prepare the way for Jesus and to preach "the good news" to people (Luke 3:18).

What is further significant about John the Baptist is his self-effacement. In all four Gospels, John is described as being careful to draw attention away from himself. When people began to wonder whether John himself might be the Christ, John responded, "I baptize you with water. But one more powerful than I will come, the thongs of whose sandals I am not worthy to untie" (Luke 3:16). The Gospel of John picks up the image of Jesus as light and then describes John the Baptist in this way: "He himself was not the light; he came only as a witness to the light" (John 1:8). Ethical evangelism is humble and self-effacing.[8]

In the end, John the Baptist got himself locked up in prison for daring to confront even a king with his kingdom message. The Gospel of Mark ties the beginning of Jesus' public ministry to this incident. "After John was put in prison, Jesus went into Galilee, proclaiming the good news of God. 'The time has come,' he said. 'The kingdom of God is near. Repent and believe the good news'" (Mark 1:14–15).

Jesus' message is very much in line with the message of John the Baptist. It is a message about the kingdom of God. At the heart of this notion is the idea of God's reign. You can't have a kingdom without a king. Jesus, like John, outlines some of the implications of God's reign. In Luke's gospel, Jesus inaugurates his ministry by quoting from Isaiah. He has been appointed to preach good news to the poor, to proclaim release for the prisoners, freedom for the oppressed, and the Jubilee Year (Luke 4:18–19). Jesus is here announcing that the good news of the kingdom touches on poverty, economics, freedom, and justice. This is pretty all-encompassing. Later, when the disciples ask Jesus to teach them how to pray, Jesus includes this couplet in what has come to be known as the Lord's Prayer: "Your kingdom come, Your will be done on earth as it is in heaven" (Matt 6:10). God's kingdom has to do with God's will being done in every sphere of human endeavor.

Then there is a call to repent. Why is there a need to repent? Because the King's subjects do not always obey the King's rules. Therefore, repent, change your ways, turn around, live according to the way the Creator originally designed his creation, because judgment is coming and God is about to establish his rule. This is part of the good news, the gospel of Jesus Christ.

Sadly, in the history of the Christian church, the gospel has all too often been reduced to personal salvation. This is certainly part of the reason for the gospel being good news. But there is more to the good news of salvation than this. The good news is about Jesus, who climactically and decisively brought about God's fresh kingdom-order to God's people, and thence to the world.[9] The good news is about God's will being done in all of creation. The good news is about a way that leads to life and wholeness and *shalom* for individuals and for society at large. The good news is about us becoming co-creators with Jesus in establishing God's kingdom rule here on earth. Of course, this goal will only be completed when God creates a new heaven and a new earth. This too is part of the good news. All of this is

---

8. Paul also picks up the theme of self-effacement in 2 Cor 4:5.

9. For an inspiring treatment of how Jesus initiated God's kingdom, see Willard, *Divine Conspiracy*.

the message God wanted to have proclaimed and lived here on earth when he sent his Son. This is what it means to see God as evangelist, and ethical evangelism too will proclaim and live the complete gospel of Jesus Christ. To proclaim an incomplete gospel is unethical.[10] To live in violation of this complete gospel lacks integrity.

JESUS AS A MODEL OF ETHICAL EVANGELISM

Early in his three-year ministry, Jesus called his twelve disciples. The calling of Levi, which has already been told at the beginning of this chapter, stands out from the earlier calls of several fishermen, which will be considered in a later section.[11] After Levi had responded positively to Jesus' invitation to follow him, Levi put on a "great" banquet for his new master, with guests including "a large crowd" of his former fellow tax collectors and other "sinners." In response to the Pharisees' criticism that Jesus and his disciples were keeping bad company, Jesus says this is precisely why he has come—to call sinners to repentance. What can we learn about ethical evangelism from this story?

Jesus mixed easily with tax collectors and sinners. Levi's banquet was not an isolated incident.[12] Jesus loved people who were obviously sinners. What is significant is that swindling tax collectors, prostitutes, and other sinners were quite comfortable associating with Jesus. This is really quite amazing and prompts the question as to why these people felt comfortable in Jesus' presence. Somehow Jesus didn't let their sinful lifestyle get in the way of relating to them. Confronting them about their sin was not his first priority. Jesus obviously did not come across as self-righteous and judgmental, and yet tax collectors and sinners were well aware that Jesus did not approve of their sinful choices and lifestyles. As a result of their encounters with Jesus, Levi and Zacchaeus declared or demonstrated they were changing their sinful ways.

---

10. For a good analysis of two incomplete "gospels of sin management," see Willard, *Divine Conspiracy*, chapter 2. Willard critiques both the theology of the right for proclaiming only a gospel of forgiveness of an individual's sins, and the theology of the left for proclaiming only a gospel of removal of social or structural evil.

11. The story of the call of Levi is told in all three Synoptic Gospels. See Matt 9:9–13; Mark 2:13–17; Luke 5:27–32.

12. There is the familiar story of Jesus inviting himself to the home of height-challenged Zacchaeus, another tax collector (Luke 19:1–10). Here again we have Jesus describing his passion: "For the Son of Man came to seek and to save what was lost." Another well-known example is Jesus' lengthy conversation with a Samaritan woman who had had multiple husbands and who was now trying out a sixth (John 4:1–42).

Not only was Jesus comfortable dialoguing with sinners, he sought them out. And sinners reciprocated by looking for Jesus. Ethical evangelism grows out of a genuine love for sinners. It seeks them out. Sinners should be attracted to us because we are not at all self-righteous or preoccupied with judging them. Instead, our focus should be on loving sinners, and when appropriate, telling them about the transformative news of the kingdom.

Here we must be careful not to assume Jesus interacted with sinners in only one way. The story of Levi's banquet is also about the Pharisees and teachers of the law who were complaining about Jesus to his disciples. Jesus' interaction with these self-righteous critics illustrates another dimension of ethical evangelism. Jesus lovingly and yet quite pointedly speaks the truth. "I have not come to call the righteous but sinners to repentance" (Luke 5:32). In other words, Jesus is here identifying the Pharisees as having excluded themselves from his invitation because of their self-righteousness. "It is not the healthy who need a doctor, but the sick." I can't help you until you humble yourselves and admit you too are sinners.

The Gospels include many other stories of Jesus interacting with the Pharisees and teachers of the law. Often the exchanges were quite antagonistic as the Pharisees and teachers of the law were constantly challenging Jesus' teaching and actions. What is fascinating is that Jesus did not go out of his way to avoid his critics. He accepted invitations to their homes.[13] Despite their antagonism, Jesus did not miss opportunities to converse with them.[14] But Jesus was never afraid to confront them with the truth even though it might not be well-received. Indeed, the conflict between Jesus and the Pharisees came to a head towards the end of his life. This is seen particularly in Matthew where Jesus pronounces a series of woes on the scribes and Pharisees, and condemns them for creating barriers for those who would like to enter the kingdom of heaven.[15] In this same context, Jesus specifically addresses the issue of evangelism. The Pharisees and teachers of the law are condemned for going "over land and sea to win a single convert, and when he becomes one, you make him twice as much a son of hell as you are" (Matt 23:15). Obviously, such evangelism is unethical. Ethical evangelism should be life-giving. Jesus' exchange with the Pharisees also teaches us that ethical evangelism does allow for confrontational truth-telling, though here we

---

13. Matt 23. See Luke 14:1–14 for another example of Jesus eating in the house of a Pharisee, even though "he was being carefully watched."

14. Jesus even met with Nicodemus at night in order to accommodate the desire of this high-ranking Pharisee to meet with him in secret (John 3).

15. Luke's account of Jesus' pronouncing a series of woes on the Pharisees comes as a response to a Pharisee who had again invited him to his home but then criticizes Jesus for not first washing his hands before the meal (Luke 11:37–54).

need to be careful not to misinterpret Jesus' pronouncement of woes on the Pharisees. These need to be read in context, and we must not forget these words were accompanied with words of love and grace.[16]

TRUTH

We have already touched on the notion of truth in the preceding paragraphs. Indeed, the notion of truth comes up repeatedly in the gospel accounts of Jesus' life and teaching. John describes the Word becoming flesh as "full of grace and truth" (John 1:14). Again and again in his interactions with other people, Jesus prefaces his words with the phrase, "I tell you the truth."[17] When facing opposition, Jesus defends himself as "a man who has told you the truth that I heard from God" (John 8:40). Even his enemies are forced to concede Jesus taught "the way of God in accordance with the truth" (Matt 22:16). Jesus describes himself as "the Way, the Truth and the Life" (John 14:6). When comforting his disciples after telling them he is going to the Father, he promises them a Counselor, "the Spirit of truth," who will be with them forever (John 14:15–16). At his trial, in conversation with Pilate, Jesus goes so far as to suggest he came into the world "to testify to the truth" (John 18:37).

As followers of Jesus Christ, we too should be truthful in all we say. As citizens of the kingdom, our words should be trustworthy. "Simply let your 'Yes' be 'Yes,' and your 'No,' 'No,'" Jesus tells us in the Sermon on the Mount

---

16. To the modern ear, pronouncing woes and calling people hypocrites, snakes, and vipers seems rather offensive. But the language of woes is reminiscent of Isaiah 5:18–23 and other places in the Old Testament, where woes are understood as a funeral lament, a mix of music and literary convention for mourning the dead. See Green, *Message of Matthew*, 242. In calling the Pharisees "snakes" and "vipers," Jesus is taking up the language of John the Baptist when Pharisees and Sadducees were coming to him to be baptized. John is here referring to a desert phenomenon where fire would sometimes sweep over dried-up grasses and bushes. This would prompt snakes and scorpions and other living creatures who found shelter in these grasses and bushes to run for their lives before the fire. John compares the Pharisees and Sadducees to snakes and vipers because they were scurrying for cover ahead of the coming judgment. See Barclay, *Gospel of Matthew*, 38–39. Finally, we need to read to the end of Matthew 23, where the seeming bluntness of Jesus' language is counterbalanced with some of the warmest and most loving language ever used by Jesus. "O Jerusalem, Jerusalem . . . how often I have longed to gather your children together, as a hen gathers her chicks under her wings, but you were not willing" (Matt 23:37). Jesus loved the Pharisees, even while he confronted them with the truth about themselves.

17. Other translations use expressions such as "Truly I tell you," or "Verily, verily." See Matt 5:18, 26; 6:2, 5, 16; 8:10; 10:15, 23; Mark 3:28; 8:12; 9:1, 41; Luke 9:27; 12:44; 21:3; John 1:51; 3:3, 5, 11.

(Matt 5:37). This entails that we should also be truthful when engaged in evangelism. Jesus credits John the Baptist with testifying to the truth (John 5:33). Ethical evangelism is careful to speak the truth, even uncomfortable truth, as we have already seen. Being truthful in evangelism will also entail that we dare to present Jesus as "the Way, the Truth and the Life." This is not easy to do in a culture where truth has become relativized and where any claims to exclusive truth are seen as intolerant.[18] But as followers of Jesus, we will need to speak such uncomfortable truth, with love, with humility, and a willingness to suffer as Jesus did. More on this shortly.

JESUS INSTRUCTS EVANGELISTS

Perhaps the most direct way to understand what the Gospels say about the ethics of evangelism is to examine the instructions Jesus gave to his disciples when he called and commissioned them to the task of evangelism. Here a caution is in order. These instructions are situated in a cultural and historical context far removed from our own, so we will need to address some contextual issues in order to apply these texts to our day. These instructive texts have often been used by evangelicals to exhort Christians to evangelize. My purpose is different. I want to examine these texts to see if they have anything to say about doing evangelism in an ethical manner.

All four Gospels give an account of Jesus calling his first disciples, though the details are somewhat different.[19] What is significant for our purposes is that the first disciples who responded to Jesus' call were humble fishermen. Further, fishing is the first metaphor Jesus uses to describe evangelism. Jesus was walking along the shore of the Sea of Galilee, and when he saw Andrew and Peter casting a net into the lake, he said to them, "Come, follow me, and I will make you fishers of men."[20] Crowds were surrounding Jesus as he stood on the shore of the Sea of Galilee, and so Jesus borrowed a boat from Peter and asked him to row out from shore a little so he could address the crowd from a convenient distance. After he has finished teaching the people from the boat, Jesus instructs Peter to row out further and again start fishing. Peter protests, "Master, we've worked hard all night and haven't caught anything. But because you say so, I will let down the nets" (Luke 5:5). One can imagine how Peter must have felt when Jesus first told him to row

18. For a discussion of the issue of exclusive truth in relation to evangelism, see Thiessen, *Ethics of Evangelism*, 62–71.

19. I will not try to harmonize these varied accounts (Matt 4:18-22; Mark 1:14-20; Luke 5:1-11; John 1:35-51).

20. Mark 1:17; Matt 4:19.

out and start fishing: "Who are you to tell a fisherman how to fish?" And yet Peter obeys, and the result is he and his crew are overwhelmed by the large number of fish they catch in their nets. Peter falls down in worship, acknowledging his own sinfulness. Jesus responds, "Don't be afraid; from now on you will catch men."[21]

What are the ethical lessons to be learned from this story? Jesus invaded Peter's area of expertise in fishing and he wants to do the same with regard to evangelism. Like Peter, we are tempted to rely on our own expertise and to protest when Jesus tells us when and how to fish. We need to listen to Jesus. We also need to realize that the results of evangelism are not really dependent on our own expertise. Success in catching fish is really God's doing. Conversion is finally the work of God's Spirit,[22] and so we need to be less concerned about methods and strategies in doing evangelism. Success in evangelism should not be our goal, but should rather be seen as a by-product of faithfulness to Jesus' command to cast the net.

The first few months of Jesus' public ministry were spent together with his disciples, mentoring and modeling ministry for them (Mark 3:14). The Gospel of Matthew sums up Jesus' early ministry: "Jesus went through all the towns and villages, teaching in their synagogues, preaching the good news of the kingdom and healing every disease and sickness" (Matt 9:35). Jesus was attracting crowds, and Matthew tells us when Jesus saw the crowds, "he had compassion on them because they were harassed and helpless, like sheep without a shepherd."[23] He then told his disciples "the harvest is plentiful but the workers are few" (Matt 9:37). In seeming response to this assessment, Jesus formally commissioned the twelve disciples to help him in his ever-expanding ministry. This commissioning is found in the three Synoptic Gospels, though the accounts vary in length and detail.[24] Luke and

---

21. Luke 5:10. Compare another intervention of Jesus when the disciples were fishing, occurring during a third appearance of Jesus to the disciples after his death and resurrection (John 21:1–14).

22. Jesus describes the Holy Spirit as convicting the world of sin and righteousness and judgment (John 16:8).

23. Matt 9:36. Jesus seems to be reflecting Ezekiel 34 which depicts the sheep as neglected, maimed, and scattered because of the unfaithfulness of the leaders of Israel. Mark places Jesus' description of the crowds being like sheep without a shepherd into a different context, after Herod had John beheaded and before Jesus fed the five thousand (Mark 6:34).

24. See Matt 9:35—11:1; Mark 3:7–19; Luke 9:1–6. Matthew is clearly assembling and editing a composite of instructions Jesus gave to the disciples on various occasions in order to clarify the principles of Christian mission. See Evans, *Matthew*, 218. See also Luke 10:1–24 where Jesus commissions seventy-two (or seventy) disciples. There is considerable overlap in the instructions given, and so for my purposes there is no need to treat them separately except for one detail which I consider in the main text.

Matthew include detailed instructions to the disciples as to how to carry on Jesus' mission and so I will focus on these accounts. These instructions need to be read at two levels. Their primary purpose was to describe the mission of disciples at the time of Jesus. But these instructions were no doubt also cherished by Matthew and Luke in terms of what they might have to say about the continuing mission of the church in their own time, a time when efforts at evangelism were met with persecution.[25]

The first thing to note is the similarity between the mission of Jesus and the mission given to his disciples. They too are to preach, heal and drive out demons.[26] Their mission too is caring for whole persons. Their mission too includes kingdom-building. Jesus and the disciples did not only do evangelism in the narrow sense of saving souls, they also dealt with the effects of sin—disease, demon-possession, and death. Jesus also made it a point to deal with other effects of sin like marginalization and injustice when he talked to women and healed them.[27] It would seem the disciples were rather slow learners with regard to understanding that preaching the good news of the kingdom included reaching out to women. When they found Jesus talking to a Samaritan woman, John tells us they were "surprised," but didn't dare challenge Jesus and ask him why he was talking to a woman (John 4:27). Jesus clearly demonstrated that the good news of the kingdom included breaking down barriers that were simply unjust, and this too is part of the good news that must be preached and exemplified. A narrow approach to mission which focuses only on evangelism, is not only contrary to the example and teaching of Jesus, but is also unethical. It fails to care for the whole person.

A treatment of the mission given to the disciples would be incomplete without some reference to what has been called "the Great Commission."[28] I have already touched on this theme in chapter 1, but there I was dealing with it in relation to the mandate for evangelism. My focus here is on examining the ethical overtones of the Great Commission as found in the Gospel of Matthew: "Therefore go and make disciples of all nations, baptizing them in the name of the Father and of the Son and of the Holy Spirit, and

---

25. See Green, *Message of Matthew*, 128.

26. See Matt 10:1, 7–8; Mark 3:14–15; Luke 10:9; 9:1–2. In Jesus' prayer for the disciples, he once again highlights the parallels between his being sent into the world and the disciples being sent into the world (John 17:18; cf. John 20:21).

27. See Jesus' encounter with the Samaritan woman (John 4), his healing of Peter's mother-in-law (Matt 8:14–15; Mark 1:29–31), his raising of the daughter of a synagogue ruler (Mark 5:21–43), and his healing of a woman who had been subject to bleeding for twelve years (Luke 8:40–48).

28. There are several versions of the Great Commission. See Matt 28:19; Mark 16:15–16; Acts 1:8.

teaching them to obey everything I have commanded you" (Matt 28:19–20). What is significant here is there is no mention of conversion, though as was mentioned in chapter 1, being a disciple presupposes conversion. But the focus here is on what follows after one has decided to become a disciple. Making disciples takes time and involves hard work. It involves teaching them to obey everything Jesus commanded.[29] To lead individuals to conversion without following up on the hard work of making disciples is not only a betrayal of the Great Commission, it is also unethical. The new convert is given a glimpse of the glorious kingdom of God, but is then dropped and not helped to grow to maturity in Jesus Christ. This is a betrayal of love and a denial of the dignity of the person. It is unethical.

COERCION

When Jesus sent out the twelve disciples (as well as the seventy-two disciples), he gave them an array of practical suggestions for their mission, suggestions that might be summed up as: "travel lightly." These suggestions must of course be interpreted in historical context. In mid-eastern cultures, the hospitality of strangers was a given, and so it was quite possible to travel lightly. Cultural context is also important in trying to understand the instructions of blessing a home, and then retrieving the blessing if the home was not worthy, or of shaking the dust off one's feet if a home or a city would not welcome the disciples or listen to their words (Matt 10:12–15). What is of ethical significance here is that Jesus' instructions anticipate that not all people would welcome the disciples or listen to their message. And when that happened, the disciples were instructed to move on. The freedom of individuals, homes, or cities to reject an evangelistic message was to be respected. Jesus is also giving the disciples "a theology of failure."[30] The dramatic gesture of shaking the dust off their feet would help the disciples to leave behind them any lingering sense of failure and free them to go on to the next home or village.

Jesus' rejection of any kind of coercion in evangelism becomes even clearer in a later story where he and the disciples enter a Samaritan village where the people do not welcome them (Luke 9:51–55). James and John ask Jesus, "Lord do you want us to call fire down from heaven to destroy them?" Jesus turned and rebuked them and then they went on to another village.

---

29. For a defense of the Anabaptists as having captured this dimension of the Great Commission, see Friesen, *Erasmus, the Anabaptists, and the Great Commission*.

30. Bailey, *Good Shepherd*, 157.

Ethical evangelism does not coerce people into listening to the kingdom message. Nor does it coerce people into becoming followers of Jesus.

Here we need to deal with a possible objection to this principle of non-coercion in evangelism. In the history of the Christian church, Jesus' parable of the great banquet has sometimes been used to justify coercion in evangelism. In this parable, "a certain man was preparing a great banquet and invited many guests" (Luke 14:15-23). When those who had been invited made a variety of excuses for not attending, "the owner of the house became angry" and ordered his servant to go into the streets and "bring in the poor, the crippled, the blind and the lame." After finding that there was still room, the master gave the following instructions to his servant: "Go out into the highways and hedges, and compel them to come in that my house may be filled" (KJV).[31] This certainly sounds like coercion.

However, there is an ambiguity in the Greek word for "compel."[32] It can also mean invite. In the parallel account of this parable in Matthew, the order given by the king uses the word "invite" rather than "compel" (Matt 22:1-14). I therefore conclude that this parable should not be used as a counter-example to the principle of non-coercion in evangelism.[33]

REJECTION, RESISTANCE, AND HOSTILITY

When Jesus gave his instructions for mission to his disciples, he not only anticipated that people would reject the disciples' message, he goes on at length to instruct the disciples on how to respond to resistance and outright hostility. "I am sending you out like sheep among wolves," Jesus says (Matt 10:16-31). You will be handed over to local councils, flogged in synagogues, and arrested. You will face betrayal even in your families. All men will hate you, just as they hated me. If I was called Beelzebub, you can expect

---

31. This parable was used to justify force in the crusades by Pope Innocent III who came to the papal throne in AD 1198, and who was surely the most important figure in the crusading movement after Pope Urban II. See Riley-Smith, *The Crusades*, 77–78. This line of argument goes back to Augustine, who reconciled the use of force with the demands of love and who used this same parable to justify force against heretics.

32. According to Bauer, et al., *Greek-English Lexicon of the New Testament* (52), there are two possible meanings for *anankaso*. The harder meaning of *compel* or *force* is fairly clear in Acts 26:11; 28:19; Gal 2:3, 14; 6:12; and 2 Cor 12:11. There is, however, a weakened sense of the word (*strongly urge/invite, persuade*) in Matt 14:22; Mark 6:45; and Luke 14:23.

33. Augustine's interpretation of this parable was already disputed in the seventeenth century by Pierre Bayle, *Philosophical Commentary*.

name-calling that is even more derogatory. Indeed, you as my disciples might face the same ultimate fate I will be facing—death.

So, how are Jesus' disciples to respond to such hostility? Again, we need to listen to the ethical overtones in Jesus' instructions to his disciples. "Therefore be as shrewd as snakes and as innocent as doves."[34] The disciples, when they evangelize, are to be wise, open, honest, and even simple, when it comes to interaction with the enemies of the gospel. Ethical evangelism does not resort to deceit. It does not involve hidden agendas or rely on elaborate scheming. Jesus goes on to advise the disciples not to "worry about what to say or how to say it," when they are brought to trial because of their witness (Matt 10:19). God's Spirit will tell them what to say. Indeed, evangelism is finally God's doing, for it is "the Spirit of your Father speaking through you" (Matt 10:20).

Another ethical aspect of Jesus' instructions to his disciples is already evident in his analogy of sending them out like sheep among wolves. Sheep are defenseless when it comes to attacks by vicious animals. Jesus also predicts men *"will hand you over* to the local councils and flog you in their synagogues" (Matt 10:17—my emphasis). There is no indication the disciples will be fighting back in self-defense. Instead, they are reminded of Jesus, their master, who did not talk back or retaliate when he was on trial, but who entrusted himself to God.[35] Servants should be like their master (Matt 10:25). In all this, Jesus is reinforcing a teaching that runs throughout the gospels and the epistles—we should love our enemies.[36]

What does it mean to love our enemies when doing evangelism? Jesus' instructions are pretty straightforward when opposition to gospel-preaching becomes physical or political or even violent, but there are also implications for the language we use in evangelism. We need to recognize words can be used as weapons and to incite violence. Such evangelism is not in line with Jesus' instructions to his disciples. There is no room for demeaning or

---

34. Matt 10:16. The idea that serpents are shrewd or wise or prudent goes back to the very beginnings of the biblical story where serpents are described as more crafty than any other wild animal (Gen 3:1). The idea that doves are innocent is more difficult to trace, but its meaning is clear. See Evans, *Matthew*, 222. Jesus' saying may be reflected in Paul's admonition to the Roman Christians, "I want you to be wise about what is good, and innocent about what is evil" (Rom 16:19).

35. Peter sums up this response when he reminds Christians of their calling to suffer, following the example of Christ: "When they hurled their insults at him, he did not retaliate; when he suffered he made no threats. Instead, he entrusted himself to him who judges justly" (1 Pet 2:21–23).

36. See Matt 5:9–12, 43–48; Rom 12:14–21; 1 Pet 2:21–23.

hateful language as we counter beliefs with which we disagree. We need to practice tolerance.[37] Ethical evangelism is expressed in the language of love.

There is an additional detail in Luke's account of Jesus sending out seventy-two (or seventy) disciples that is worth noting and has some implications for ethical evangelism (Luke 10:1–24). After the seventy-two returned from their missionary journey, they enthusiastically reported to Jesus, "Lord, even the demons submit to us in your name." The disciples were enamored with their success, maybe even a bit conceited about the new powers they had. Jesus responds by reminding them it was he who gave them the authority over demons (v. 18). Theirs is a borrowed authority. And then Jesus shifts the focus of their rejoicing: "Do not rejoice that the spirits submit to you, but rejoice that your names are written in heaven" (v. 20). Jesus is reminding them and us that having our names written in heaven is due to grace, not personal effort, or success in evangelism. What Jesus is also suggesting here is that success is not the fundamental objective of ethical evangelism. Our preoccupation should instead be focused on our belonging to Jesus and being faithful to him.

METAPHORS AND PARABLES

We have already examined some metaphors Jesus uses in order to describe evangelism. For example, when Jesus calls his first disciples who were fishermen, he challenges them to become fishers of men. Jesus also uses the analogy of sheep without a shepherd to highlight the desperate need of the people who were harassed and helpless, and hence the further need for workers to be sent out to proclaim the good news of the kingdom of God. Indeed, Jesus makes frequent use of the shepherd/sheep analogy, no doubt drawing on a long history of such usage in the Old Testament, starting with the familiar description of God as our shepherd in Psalm 23.[38]

I would like to focus on the parable of the Lost Sheep, which occurs twice in the Gospels, though the context is quite different in each case.[39] The setting that prompted the telling of this parable in Luke is somewhat similar to that of Levi's banquet, considered earlier in this chapter. Tax collectors and sinners were gathering around Jesus to hear him, but some members of

---

37. I am using tolerance in the traditional sense of putting up with what you disagree with and respecting persons even though you disagree with them. See Thiessen, *Ethics of Evangelism*, 105–14, 198–200. I will have more to say about tolerance in chapter 7.

38. For an excellent recent treatment of a thousand-year history of the Good Shepherd imagery in the bible, see Bailey, *Good Shepherd*.

39. Luke 15:1–7; Matt 18:12–14.

an elite club of Pharisees and teachers of the law were muttering complaints about Jesus, who was so obviously breaking their laws of ritual purity. Jesus responds by telling them a carefully nuanced parable in which the Pharisees and teachers of the law are asked to imagine they are shepherds, a trade they despised. "Suppose one of you has a hundred sheep and loses one of them" (Luke 15:4). Jesus then draws on the natural and expected response of anyone who loses something of value—he or she will make a determined effort to find what was lost.[40] The shepherd in the parable leaves the ninety-nine sheep, and at some risk to himself tries to find the one lost sheep. Once found, he brings it home and invites his friends to rejoice with him.

Throughout the Gospels, Jesus is described as the Good Shepherd who is very concerned about bringing lost sheep back into the kingdom.[41] Indeed, in the parable of the Lost Sheep, Jesus is declaring himself to be the fulfillment of what the psalms and the prophets were writing about when they describe God as the Good Shepherd who would one day enter history and make up for the failures of bad shepherds.[42] In effect, Jesus is telling the Pharisees and scribes he is doing what they should have been doing all along. He is inviting them to join him in restoring the lost sheep of the house of Israel to God.[43] Jesus is also saying to us today that it is a good thing to bring individuals who have left the faith back into the kingdom. Ethical "reevangelism" cares about sheep who get lost.

This parable also illustrates an interesting blend between divine initiative and personal responsibility. Yes, a caring shepherd will go out of his way to find a lost sheep. But a lost sheep will typically know it is lost, will be listening for the shepherd, will respond to the shepherd's approach with its bleating, and will accept the shepherd's rescue effort rather than run still further away.[44] In the same way, sinners need to respond to the Good Shepherd's call, and to accept being rescued. Ethical evangelism retains a delicate balance between human initiative in finding lost sheep, and giving lost sheep the freedom to participate in being found.

---

40. The parable of the Lost Sheep is in fact followed by two more parables about losing something or someone valuable: the parable of the Lost Coin (Luke 15:8–10), and the parable of the Lost Son (Luke 15:11–32). Bailey suggests these three stories were in fact given by Jesus as a single parable, indicated by the fact that Luke writes, "he told them *this* parable" (Luke 15:3; Bailey, *Good Shepherd*, 120).

41. See Luke 15:3–7; Matt 18:12–14; John 10:1–18. See Bailey, *Good Shepherd*, chap. 5, 7, and 8.

42. Ibid., 129. On the theme of bad shepherds, see Jer 23:1–8 and Ezek 34.

43. Bailey, *Good Shepherd*, 125.

44. Ibid., 136–37.

In the Gospel of John, Jesus gives us an expanded exposition of the contrast between good and bad shepherds (John 10:1–18). It is here where we have Jesus boldly claiming, "I am the good shepherd." I want to draw attention to the statement that follows immediately after this famous "I am" statement. "The good shepherd lays down his life for the sheep." Again, we need to ask what this entails for the ethics of evangelism. Such application is justified because in this passage Jesus himself applies the good shepherd imagery to evangelism. "I have other sheep that are not of this sheep pen. I must bring them also" (John 10:16). And then Jesus again reminds us that finding these other lost sheep will entail the good shepherd laying down his life for these sheep.[45]

Good shepherds are willing to sacrifice themselves for the sheep. There is nothing here about a triumphalist proclamation of the gospel. Instead, ethical evangelism will be characterized by a willingness to suffer and even die. Evangelism inspired by the cross is not conquest-minded or militant.[46] Instead, ethical evangelism will be characterized by vulnerability and sometimes even martyrdom.

There is a final set of parables that deserves mention. Matthew 13 gives us a series of parables about the kingdom of heaven. The kingdom of heaven is like a farmer going out to sow his seed, but as every first-century farmer knew, not all the seed sown would produce good crops. The kingdom of heaven is like a mustard seed, a seed so tiny that when it falls on the ground it can hardly be seen, and yet when it grows, it can become a large bush which provides a home for birds. The kingdom of heaven is like yeast that is invisible and yet has the power to permeate the entire dough.

Then there is the parable of the wheat and the weeds (Matt 13:24–30, 36–43). Again there is a farmer sowing good seed, but there is also an enemy sowing bad seed. The result is a field of both wheat and weeds. The farmer's servants suggest a campaign of weed-pulling, but the farmer objects. Jesus gives us an interpretation of this parable. The good seed stands for the sons of the kingdom, and the weeds are the sons of the evil one. Jesus wants the sons of the kingdom to co-exist with the sons of the evil one. Indeed, at times it might seem the weeds are crowding out the wheat. Never mind. Be patient. The final weed-pulling must be left to God at the end of time. Only then will "the righteous shine like the sun in the kingdom of their Father" (Matt 13:43). In the meantime, keep working and witnessing for the kingdom, even though your work and witness might not be all that visible in a world that contains a mix of the good and the bad.

---

45. John 10:17–18. Bailey, *Good Shepherd*, 227–38.
46. Thangaraj, "Evangelism Sans Proselytism," 344.

What might these parables say about the ethics of evangelism? Evangelism might very well be hidden, crowded out by the weeds, or be like yeast in dough. Not to worry. The "evangelism of presence" is still powerful, and it is obviously ethical. Ethical evangelism is like the farmer sowing seeds, but unable to ensure a good crop. When Jesus interprets the parable of the Sower to his disciples (not the crowd to whom the parable was first given), he seems to be telling the disciples they need to spread the seed purposely, yet indiscriminately, not worrying about soil types or receptivity. Forget strategizing and targeting of people groups. Just keep sowing. There is also an encouragement to accept powerlessness.[47] Kingdom-building is like the mustard seed, starting so small that it is probably the object of scorn and given little chance for success. And yet against all odds, the kingdom of God will grow and spread throughout the world, resulting in increasing justice and peace for all. Similarly, the proclamation of the good news of the kingdom can and should be done with humility and in weakness, but we should never underestimate its power to transform, though again that power lies not in ourselves, but in God the King.[48]

---

47. Mark highlights this in his telling of what might be another parable that focuses on the seed. After the farmer has scattered the seed it sprouts and grows, "though he does not know how. All by itself the soil produces grain" (Mark 4:26–29).

48. This point is highlighted again in Jesus' conversation with Nicodemus (John 3:1–15). Conversion is finally a work of the Spirit, and the Spirit like the wind blows wherever it pleases, and you cannot tell where it comes from or where it is going.

Chapter 4

Acts and the Apostles

Stephen was a good man. That is why the disciples chose him as one of seven men to take on the work of caring for widows in the rapidly growing church in Jerusalem. We are also told Stephen was "a man full of faith and of the Holy Spirit" (Acts 6:5). But clearly diaconal work was too limited a field of service for Stephen, who was at the same time involved in proclaiming the gospel and doing "great wonders and miraculous signs among the people" (6:8). Fierce opposition to Stephen's ministry of evangelism and miracle-working came rather quickly, and seems to have been centered in a particular synagogue composed of foreign Jews who were now residing in Jerusalem.

At first, these men simply argued with Stephen. Stephen responded with counterarguments, and his opponents were unable to stand up against the inspired wisdom with which he spoke. Next, his opponents started a smear campaign against him, persuading others to do the dirty work for them, accusing Stephen of speaking words of blasphemy against Moses and God. After further agitating the people, the elders, and the teachers of the law, they seized Stephen and brought him before the Sanhedrin. The charges were repeated here by "false witnesses," and here Stephen seems to have simply listened calmly. Indeed, the members of the Sanhedrin couldn't help but notice that Stephen's "face was like the face of an angel" (6:15).

Only after the high priest invited Stephen to respond to these charges did Stephen begin to speak. Indeed, his long speech is not only a careful and measured response to the charges, but also an "apologia" for the gospel. He reviews the history of Israel, highlighting four major epochs of Israel's history, dominated by four major characters.[1] His overall strategy is to point out that he is not at all against Moses or God, and that Jesus is the fulfillment of Old Testament prophecy.

---

1. Abraham and the patriarchal age, Joseph and the Egyptian exile, Moses and the exodus, and David and the monarchy. Stott, *Message of Acts*, 129–39.

In the end, Stephen points out that the current resistance to his message on the part of his accusers is very much in keeping with their forefathers. Then come words that were bound to antagonize. "You stiff-necked people, with uncircumcised hearts and ears! You are just like your fathers: You always resist the Holy Spirit! Was there ever a prophet your fathers did not persecute?" (7:51–52) It would seem Stephen had come to the conclusion some shock-therapy was needed, or maybe he realized his case was already lost. After reminding them that the prophets had predicted the coming of Jesus, Stephen closes in—"you have betrayed and murdered him" (7:52). In effect, Stephen is saying, "You, not I, are guilty of violating the law and the prophets."

As might be expected, the people hearing Stephen's concluding remarks "were furious and gnashed their teeth at him" (7:54). Stephen recognized the end was near, and looking up to heaven, he declared to all present, "I see heaven open and the Son of Man standing at the right hand of God" (7:56). This was too much for his opponents, so they dragged Stephen out of the city and began to stone him. While they were stoning him, Stephen prayed, "Lord Jesus, receive my spirit. Then he fell on his knees and cried out, 'Lord, do not hold this sin against them.' When he had said this, he fell asleep" (7:60).

THE GOSPEL OF LUKE and the Acts of the Apostles are really a two-part series in which Luke tells the story of Jesus and then the story of the work of the apostles which led to the emergence of the church. The opening of the second volume makes clear the relation between these two parts in the series. "In my former book, Theophilus, I wrote about all that Jesus *began* to do and to teach until the day he was taken up to heaven, *after* giving instructions through the Holy Spirit to the apostles he had chosen" (Acts 1:1—my emphasis). The Greek word order is even clearer in highlighting the fact that Luke's gospel only narrates the beginning of what Jesus set out to accomplish, and that the apostles whom he had chosen were instructed to carry Jesus' work forward under the guidance of the Holy Spirit.[2] I have dealt with Luke's gospel in the previous chapter, as part of my treatment of all four gospels. In this chapter, I want to examine the book of Acts to see what we can learn about the ethics of evangelism from the apostles and the early church.

The book of Acts is a story, and as such presents some unique challenges in terms of learning about the ethics of evangelism. As mentioned in the introduction to the previous chapter, stories shape our ethical values indirectly. Stories instruct by way of the imagination. Stories give us different

---

2. Hays, *Moral Vision of the New Testament*, 112.

examples of behavior and character, some positive and some negative. The last point is important because we cannot assume the apostles, unlike Jesus, were always acting in an ethical manner. We need to remember, for example, that at one point Jesus chastised Peter, even suggesting his words were prompted by Satan (Matt 16:21–23). The apostles were all too human, and hence their approach to evangelism might not always be ethical. The same can be said of the early church.

This raises some important questions. Is it even worthwhile to study the book of Acts in order to learn about the ethics of evangelism? If so, how do we distinguish between what is good and what is bad in the behavior of the apostles? Sometimes, of course, we are told quite specifically that certain behavior was not exemplary.[3] At other times, discernment on our part will be necessary.[4] The key here is to keep referring back to the life and example and teachings of Jesus.[5] So our analysis of the ethics of evangelism in the Gospels in the previous chapter must be seen as primary. Of course, as was noted in chapter 2, we must also strive for coherence with the rest of Scripture.

I have chosen to begin this chapter with the story of Stephen because his story surely gives us a positive example of ethical evangelism. His character and behavior are a reflection of Jesus Christ. We are specifically told he was a wise person, full of faith and the Holy Spirit. I will return to the story of Stephen at the end of this chapter to highlight how Stephen's final words are reminiscent of Jesus' own words on the cross, and thus exemplify an ethical response to opposition to evangelism.

THE KINGDOM OF GOD AND THE HOLY SPIRIT

In the Prologue to the book of Acts, Luke reviews some of the final events in the life of Jesus, events that were also recorded in his earlier gospel. The book of Acts, like some of the Gospels, begins by referring to the kingdom of God. Luke tells us that after Jesus' death and resurrection, he appeared to the apostles, "over a period of forty days and spoke about the kingdom of God" (Acts 1:3). The Greek is better translated, "Jesus kept on speaking

---

3. For example, the behavior of Ananias and Sapphira is clearly condemned and punished (Acts 5:1–11). Paul and Barnabas clearly condemned the people of Lystra for offering sacrifices to evangelists and healers (Acts 14:8–20).

4. On the need for ethical discernment, see Rom 12:2; Phil 1:9–10; Heb 5:14.

5. Here it is helpful to note that Paul, in his letters to the church at Corinth, at one point, in giving instructions about marriage, is careful to make a distinction between his own advice and the teachings of Jesus himself. "To the married I give this command (not I, but the Lord)" . . . "To the married I give this command (I, not the Lord)" (1 Cor 7:10, 12).

about the kingdom of God," because the verb used here is the present participle, *legōn*. As we have already seen in the previous chapter, the kingdom of God was the central theme of Jesus' message throughout his public ministry, and according to Luke he continued emphasizing it during the forty days between his resurrection and ascension. The Acts Prologue continues with a description of another encounter with the apostles after the resurrection, where Jesus reminded them about the Holy Spirit he had promised them earlier.[6] Jesus commands the apostles to wait in Jerusalem until they receive the gift of the Holy Spirit (Acts 1:4–5). Because the prophets had often associated the kingdom of God with the pouring out of God's Spirit,[7] the disciples asked Jesus, "Lord, are you at this time going to restore the kingdom to Israel?" Jesus responded, "It is not for you to know the times or dates the Father has set by his own authority. But you will receive power when the Holy Spirit comes on you; and you will be my witnesses in Jerusalem, and in all Judea and Samaria, and to the ends of the earth" (Acts 1:7–8).

Jesus' response to the disciples' question is most significant, and here again we see some themes already found in the Gospels. In his response to the disciples' question in Acts, Jesus again tries to correct their mistaken notions of the kingdom's nature, extent, and arrival.[8] The disciples' question assumes the kingdom will be territorial in nature. They are confusing the kingdom of God with the kingdom of Israel, and hoping for political liberation and the reestablishing of the monarchy. In responding, Jesus seems to change the subject when he talks about the coming gift of the Holy Spirit, but Jesus is very much on topic. The kingdom of God involves a different kind of power—the power of the Holy Spirit. The kingdom of God is not political in nature, as typically understood, nor is it brought about by political means. "It is spread by witnesses, not by soldiers, through a gospel of peace, not a declaration of war, and by the work of the Spirit, not by force of arms, political intrigue or revolutionary violence."[9] Yes, the kingdom of God has radical political and social implications (for example, its citizens will refuse to give Caesar supreme loyalty), but the kingdom of God is not built by political ingenuity. Instead, it is built by prayer, obedience to God, and dependence on the Holy Spirit.

There is another assumption implicit in the question the disciples ask Jesus. They assume the kingdom of God will involve Israel alone. Their

---

6. See, for example, John 15:18—16:16.

7. See, for example, Isa 32:15–18; 43:3; Ezek 11:18–20; 36:24–32; 39:29; Joel 2:28–32, which is quoted in Peter's Pentecost sermon (Acts 2:17–21).

8. Stott, *Message of Acts*, 41–45.

9. Ibid., 42.

aspirations are narrow and nationalistic. In his reply, Jesus broadens their horizons. The Holy Spirit will empower them to be his witnesses, starting in Jerusalem, continuing in the immediate environs of Judea, and then extending to the ends of the earth. God's overall mission was never intended to be limited to the people of Israel. As we saw in chapter 2, God's intent was always that Israel would be a blessing to all nations. Now with the promise of the power of the Holy Spirit, the apostles are asked to go and make disciples of all nations.[10] Indeed, at the end of time, when God's kingdom is consummated, there will be a multitude of people that no one can count, "from every nation, tribe, people and language," all standing before the throne of the Lamb (Rev 7:9).

A third misconception in the apostles' question has to do with the timing of the kingdom of God. They are thinking of an immediate inauguration of the kingdom of God here and now. Jesus responds to the timing question in two ways. First, he tells them that they need to be content with not knowing the answer to their question. Next, he tells them to be patient. I want you to focus instead on being my witnesses.[11]

The Prologue to the book of Acts concludes with the apostles seeing Jesus disappear into the clouds. While they stand looking intently up into the sky, two men dressed in white interrupt the apostles' heaven-gazing: "This same Jesus, who has been taken from you into heaven, will come back in the same way you have seen him go into heaven" (Acts 1:11). Here we see a restatement of the answer already given to the apostles' question about the timing of the kingdom. Yes, the kingdom of God has come, but only in part. The consummation of the kingdom is still future, when Jesus will return to Earth. The apostles and the church are reminded they are living in the already-not-yet time period of the kingdom. And during this time between the first and second coming of Jesus, the apostles and the church are commissioned to bear witness to Jesus Christ in the power of the Spirit.

There are several lessons to be learned about the ethics of evangelism and mission from this introduction to the book of Acts. First, ethical evangelism is dependent on the work of the Holy Spirit. Jesus was very clear in his instructions. The apostles were to wait for the gift of the Holy Spirit

---

10. Stott points to an interesting contrast between the witness of God's people in the Old Testament and in the book of Acts. In the Old Testament, the vision of the latter days is of a "pilgrimage of the nations" to Mount Zion (Isa 2:2–3). But in Acts, the apostles are told to go to the nations. Quoting another writer, Stott points out that a "centripetal missionary consciousness" is replaced by a "centrifugal missionary activity," and the turning point is the resurrection after which Jesus receives universal authority and then commissions his apostles to go and make disciples of all nations (Stott, *Message of Acts*, 43).

11. On the meaning of "witnesses," see chapter 1, page 8.

before they took up the challenge of being witnesses in Jerusalem, Judea, and to the ends of the earth. Yes, there is a place for human initiative in evangelism. But human initiative must always be coupled with reliance on the power of the Holy Spirit. We can't do it alone.

We also need to be very cautious about relying on human ingenuity in evangelism. Jesus was very clear in challenging assumptions that the kingdom of God would be built on political power and intrigue. Sadly, the apostles' misconceptions about the kingdom of God are still very much present in the contemporary church. We need to be reminded of Jesus' instructions to the apostles. The kingdom of God is not built by Christians aligning themselves with political power.[12] This also applies to evangelism. Ethical evangelism is careful not to become preoccupied with human strategies. It will be especially sensitive to the abuses of power. Instead, ethical evangelism will be bathed in prayer, and will recognize that, ultimately, effectiveness is due to the power of the Holy Spirit.

Ethical evangelism is also outward-looking and universal in vision. It does not limit itself to one tribe, one target area, or one nation. It is not preoccupied with building one's own church or one's own denomination. It seeks to make disciples wherever they may be found, and whatever their eventual choice in terms of church affiliation.

CONTINUITY OF MISSION

We have already seen that the author of the Gospel of Luke and the book of Acts is careful to highlight the continuity between the two-part series he wrote. In both books, the apostles are assigned the task of bearing witness to the kingdom of God, especially in terms of how Jesus came to decisively announce the inauguration of the kingdom of God. John the Baptist and Jesus were calling people to repentance and to a change of life that would be in accordance with the ideals of God's rule. In like manner, Peter, at the conclusion of his powerful Pentecost sermon, called people to "Repent and be baptized, every one of you, in the name of Jesus Christ so that your sins may be forgiven" (Acts 2:38). As a result of this appeal, about three thousand people were baptized and added to the number of believers in Jerusalem. But evangelism didn't end here. A community of believers was formed and "they devoted themselves to the apostles' teaching and to the fellowship, to the breaking of bread and to prayer" (Acts 2:42). Here again, the pattern is similar to that of Jesus who called and instructed a nucleus of new covenant

---

12. This is the central thrust of a fine book by James Davison Hunter, *To Change the World*.

people that God was calling to himself.[13] The goal of evangelism is not just conversion, but the making of disciples or apprentices of Jesus within the context of a fellowship of believers. "God's saving action intends the formation of a *people*, not merely the salvation of individuals."[14] And God's people are called to follow the way Jesus had marked out. Hence Luke's characteristic description of Christians as people of "the Way."[15]

There is another notable similarity between the mission of Jesus and the mission of the apostles in Acts. The mission was broader than evangelism. It also included signs and wonders and healings. In his Pentecost sermon, Peter highlighted the fact that Jesus performed "miracles, wonders and signs" (Acts 2:22). Soon after Pentecost, Peter and John healed a man who had been crippled from birth (Acts 3). This healing led to their arrest and appearance before the Sanhedrin. After their release, Peter and John returned to the fellowship of believers and reported all that the chief priests and elders had said to them. A fervent prayer meeting followed in which these early believers were not only praying for boldness in proclaiming the gospel, but also that God would perform miraculous signs and wonders that would confirm the gospel message and at the same time extend the kingdom of God (Acts 4:29–30).

Indeed, many of the miracles in the book of Acts parallel the miracles of Jesus in the Gospel of Luke.[16] There are also parallel summary statements about signs and wonders, healings, and driving out evil spirits.[17] There is also a parallel between the ministry of Jesus and the apostles in the Gospels, and the ministry of Paul and Barnabas later in Acts. During their first missionary journey they spent considerable time in Iconium, "speaking boldly for the Lord, who confirmed the message of his grace by enabling them to do miraculous signs and wonders" (Acts 14:3). Clearly the mission of the apostles after Pentecost included more than just evangelism. Like Jesus, they too were healing and driving out evil spirits.

Another parallel concerns the notion of the kingdom of God which, as we have already seen, was the burden of Jesus' message throughout his public ministry and even during the forty days between his resurrection

13. Hays, *Moral Vision of the New Testament*, 122.
14. Ibid.
15. Acts 9:2; 18:25; 19:9, 23; 22:4; 24:14, 22.
16. For example, Peter's healing of a paralytic, Aeneas (Acts 9:32–35) is similar to Jesus' healing of the paralytic (Luke 5:17–26). Peter's raising of Dorcas from death (Acts 9:36–43) mirrors Jesus' raising of the daughter of Jairus (Luke 8:40–42, 49–56). See Stott, *Message of Acts*, 183.
17. For example, compare the summary statements early in the book of Acts (5:12) and early in Luke's gospel (7:22).

and ascension. The apostles continued to preach the kingdom of God.[18] The early church also exemplified what the kingdom of God should look like. For example, we have repeated descriptions of the church giving to anyone who was in need (Acts 2:45; 4:34-35). The apostles further dared to challenge political authority, upset economic interests, and overcome systemic racism, whenever these obstructed or compromised the mission of the church to make disciples.[19]

A complete gospel for whole persons and for all of society—anything less than this is unethical. To present an incomplete gospel is to proclaim a half-truth and thus violates the spirit of the biblical principle of truth-telling. Ethical evangelism calls people to repentance from sin, but it is not only concerned about saving souls from sin. It needs to be combined with care for whole persons. Ethical evangelism also includes proclamation of the broader vision of building the kingdom of God. It will also be combined with a broader mission of actualizing God's rule in all of society. Sadly, these ethical requirements aren't always satisfied in evangelical discussions about evangelism.[20]

EVANGELISTIC SERMONS AND SPEECHES

A notable feature of the book of Acts is a number of lengthy evangelistic sermons or speeches.[21] I will limit my treatment to just three of these discourses. The first is Peter's Pentecost sermon, addressed to "God-fearing Jews from every nation under heaven," who had just witnessed the outpouring of the Holy Spirit which had led the disciples to declare the wonders of God in a variety of tongues.[22] The second sermon is given by Paul in a

---

18. For example, Philip in Samaria did miraculous signs and "preached the good news of the kingdom of God and the name of Jesus Christ" (Acts 8:4, 6, 12). In Ephesus, Paul spent three months "arguing persuasively about the kingdom of God" (Acts 19:8; cf. 20:25). In Rome, Paul's message again concerns the kingdom of God (Acts 28:23, 31).

19. See Acts 4:19-20; 10:1—11:30; 19:1-41.

20. Michael Green at the 1974 Lausanne Conference on World Evangelization asked rhetorically, "How much have you heard here about the Kingdom of God?" His answer: "Not much. It is not our language. But it was Jesus' prime concern." Cited in Willard, *Divine Conspiracy*, 59.

21. Stott points out there are no fewer than nineteen significant Christian sermons/speeches in the book of Acts, eight by Peter, one each by Stephen and James, and nine by Paul. All of these speeches are probably condensed versions of what was actually said. For a defense of their authenticity and accuracy, see Stott, *Message of Acts*, 69-72.

22. Acts 2-3. A second evangelistic sermon, again by Peter, followed the healing of a man crippled from birth (Acts 3). There are strong parallels to Peter's Pentecost sermon. The next evangelistic sermon given by Peter represents a major shift in the story of the

synagogue in Pisidian Antioch (Acts 13). Although there were some God-fearing Gentiles present, the audience is primarily Jewish.

John Stott points out that Paul's sermon in Pisidian Antioch is practically identical in structure to Peter's sermon on the day of Pentecost. In both we find a review of "the gospel events (the cross and the resurrection), the gospel witnesses (Old Testament prophets and New Testament apostles), the gospel promises (the new life of salvation in Christ, through the Spirit), and the gospel conditions (repentance and faith)."[23] While not all of these ingredients are found in the other sermons and speeches in Acts, what is clear from all of them is the early witnesses were very systematic in their presentation of the good news. There was also some essential content, a "pattern of sound teaching," that they were concerned to convey.[24] They were not just making emotional appeals, nor were they calling for quick decisions; instead, they were trying to help people understand some key elements of the broader biblical story and the story of Jesus.[25] Ethical evangelism is careful to present the essential elements of a biblical worldview and the good news about Jesus Christ.

The third evangelistic speech I want to consider was given by Paul to a pagan audience in Athens.[26] In Paul's day, Athens still had an unrivaled reputation as the empire's cultural and intellectual metropolis. When he arrived in Athens on his second missionary journey, Paul took a two-pronged approach, reasoning in the synagogue with Jews and the God-fearing Greeks, as well as in the marketplace with anyone who would stop to listen. Soon he found himself arguing with a group of Epicurean and Stoic philosophers. Some started to ridicule him, calling him a "babbler," Athenian slang which could also be translated seed-picker, plagiarist, parrot, or intellectual

---

book of Acts—the mission of the church is extended to the Gentiles (Acts 10). But first Peter has to have his eyes opened, his worldview changed, and his vision broadened so he can respond positively to an invitation from Cornelius, a God-fearing Gentile centurion. This sermon is quite different from the other two because of the different Gentile context, and it resulted in the Holy Spirit coming on all who heard the message, confirming Peter's extension of evangelism to Gentiles (Acts 10:44).

23. Stott, *Message of Acts*, 226.

24. 1 Tim 1:13. See chap. 1, pp. 10–12.

25. We see this again in Philip's Spirit-inspired encounter with the Ethiopian eunuch on a chariot who was reading from Isaiah. Philip starts with a question, "Do you understand what you are reading?" (Acts 8:26–40). Then follows what was probably a lengthy conversation in which Philip uses this passage to tell the eunuch "the good news about Jesus." It is only after this careful exposition of Scripture and witness to Jesus that Philip baptizes the Ethiopian eunuch at his request.

26. Acts 17:16–34. For another much shorter evangelistic message, to a pagan crowd in Lystra, on Paul's first missionary journey, see Acts 14:8–20. Here we find Paul taking a similar approach to the one under discussion.

magpie.[27] All this hubbub led to Paul being brought to a meeting of the Areopagus, which in Paul's day functioned as a council whose members were guardians of the city's religion, morals, and education.

What is significant is how Paul adapts his evangelistic message to a very different audience who did not have the background knowledge that could be assumed when speaking to Jews. Here Paul does not bother to prove Jesus is the Messiah, as he did when speaking to a mainly Jewish audience in the synagogues. Instead, he starts by finding some common ground, noting the people of Athens are very religious and are in fact searching for God. He then highlights some basic themes that would help the uninitiated understand the broad scope of a Christian worldview. He also describes God as sovereign Lord and final judge. And then there is a brief hint of Jesus as the revelation of God, and the resurrection of Jesus as proof of this, a point that Paul had already argued earlier in the marketplace.

What is of ethical significance here is that Paul adapts his message to his audience. Paul also tries to find areas where he agrees with his audience. He even quotes some of their poets (Acts 17:28). This is more than just good strategy. This is an expression of love and care for those with whom one is communicating.[28] Further, while Paul does engage in argument and counterargument, his defense of the gospel message is respectful of the beliefs of those he is talking to. He is tolerant. These are all characteristics of ethical communication and evangelism.

APOLOGETICS

Throughout the book of Acts we find the apostles and other witnesses providing a careful and reasoned defense of the gospel. When Paul and Silas arrived in Thessalonica on their second missionary journey, Paul went into the synagogue, "as his custom was," and "reasoned with them from the Scriptures, explaining and proving that the Christ had to suffer and rise from the dead" (Acts 17:1–4). The result—some Jews, God-fearing Greeks, and a number of prominent women were "persuaded and joined Paul and Silas." After some Jews organized a riot against Paul and Silas, they moved on to Berea, where they again went to the synagogue to evangelize. The Bereans, we are told, received the message "with great eagerness," but interestingly, they also "examined the Scriptures every day to see if what Paul said was true" (Acts 17:10–12). Here evangelism led to an honest and

27. Stott, *Message of Acts*, 282.
28. This point is also reinforced at Pentecost where God himself ensures the good news is communicated in many languages so all can understand.

careful investigation on the part of those being evangelized. And it would seem Paul had no objections to such exploration. Ethical evangelism does not object to honest investigation and hard questioning. Indeed, it takes the time to respond to honest queries. Sometimes conversions take time!

If there is one thing that characterizes evangelism in the sermons and speeches found in the book of Acts, it is the element of reasoning and persuasion.[29] Again and again we find Paul arguing in the synagogues trying to prove to the Jewish listeners that Christ's suffering and death was in keeping with their Scriptures. We have already seen that in Athens, Paul is arguing with Epicurean and Stoic philosophers in the marketplace. Then of course we find Paul defending himself in various trials, where again he gives reasoned defenses of the faith.[30] It would seem there is a closer link between evangelism and apologetics than is sometimes assumed by opponents of apologetics.

In today's postmodern culture there seems to be little patience with argument and persuasion. Often these are associated with coercion and even paternalistic militarism. Clearly these associations are not found in the book of Acts. Two features of persuasion in Acts should be noted here. First, it is striking that almost all of the examples of persuasive speeches in Acts are in response to questions being asked by those outside the church.[31] Secondly, there are frequent statements about the results of such persuasion, including statements to the effect that some believed and some didn't believe. Already

---

29. Green draws attention to the nuances of words used to describe apostolic evangelistic preaching (Green, *Evangelism in the Early Church*, 224): *diamarturesthai* (Acts 2:40; 8:25; 10:42; 18:5; 23:11) "to testify strenuously," *katagellein* (Acts 4:2; 13:5, 38; 15:36) "to proclaim forcefully," *dialegesthya* (17:2, 17; 18:4, 19; 19:8, 9; 24:25) "to argue," and *diakatelenchein* (Acts 18:28) "to confute powerfully." Another example of persuasion is found in Apollos who is described as a learned man, with a thorough knowledge of the Scriptures (Acts 18:24–28). He had been instructed in the way of the Lord "and he spoke with great fervor and taught about Jesus accurately." On arriving in Achaia, "he vigorously refuted the Jews in public debate, proving from the Scriptures that Jesus was the Christ."

30. For example, after Paul requests a trial before Caesar, Festus asks King Agrippa to help him prepare a brief for Caesar, and so Paul is given a final chance to defend himself (Acts 25 & 26). In the end, Paul responds to Festus' accusation that he is out of his mind. "I am not insane, most excellent Festus. What I am saying is true and reasonable." Paul then appeals to King Agrippa's familiarity with the history of Israel and the Christian Way, and he asks him if he believes the prophets. King Agrippa responds by saying, "Do you think that in such a short time you can persuade me to be a Christian?" It would seem that King Agrippa cannot help but interpret Paul's defense as having evangelistic overtones which involved "persuasion" and arguments that were meant to be "reasonable."

31. Lesslie Newbigin highlights this point in *Gospel in a Pluralist Society*, 116–17. See Peter's sermon at Pentecost (Acts 2:12), Peter and John before the Sanhedrin (4:7), Stephen before the Sanhedrin (7:1), Philip with the Ethiopian (8:31), Peter's meeting with the household of Cornelius (10:33), and Paul in the synagogue at Antioch of Pisidia (13:15).

at Pentecost, after God-fearing Jews from many nations heard the apostles declaring the wonders of God in their own tongue, some of the people were making fun of the apostles (Acts 2:13). Others listened carefully to Peter's subsequent evangelistic sermon and accepted his message and were baptized (2:41). During their visit to Iconium, on their first missionary journey, Paul and Barnabas are described as speaking "so effectively that a great number of Jews and Gentiles believed" (14:1–7). At the same time, there were "Jews who refused to believe," and who opposed the ministry of Paul and Barnabas. Much later, we find Paul speaking to a Gentile audience on Mars Hill, and again the response is mixed. Some sneered when Paul talked about the resurrection of the dead, while others wanted to hear more from Paul, and still others became followers of Paul and believed (17:32–34). This pattern is repeated again and again in Acts.[32]

Ethical evangelism expects mixed responses to the proclamation of the good news. It should further be noted that persuasion in itself does not force the listener to agree with what is being said. Typically, persuasion leaves people perfectly free to either believe or not to believe. Indeed, by trying to persuade you, I am honoring you by allowing you to consider my argument and make up your own mind on the subject at hand.[33] Ethical evangelism does not rule out persuasion and argument, but it is always careful to allow a free response either to agree or to disagree with what is being said.

SOME COUNTEREXAMPLES

Here it might be objected that the conclusions I have drawn from the evangelistic sermons and speeches in the book of Acts go too far in highlighting a careful presentation of the gospel message, including argument and persuasion, as essential to ethical evangelism. Surely there are exceptions to this rule. There is for example, the jailor of the prison in Philippi (Acts 16:16–40). After Paul and Silas could have escaped because an earthquake had loosened everyone's chains and opened the prison door, the jailor had to be stopped from killing himself. Trembling before Paul and Silas, he asked, "Men, what must I do to be saved?" Paul and Silas replied, "Believe in the Lord Jesus, and you will be saved—you and your household." This

---

32. For additional examples of mixed responses to hearing the good news, see Acts 17:4–5, 12–13; 18:8, 12; 19:9, 19; and 28:24. Of course, this is in keeping with the responses to Jesus, even after the resurrection, where we read that the disciples "worshiped him; but some doubted" (Matt 28:17).

33. James K. A. Smith describes persuasion as "a mode of convicted charity" (Smith, "Lost Art of Persuasion," 3). The entire issue of *Comment* (Spring, 2013), in which this editorial is found, is devoted to the subject of persuasion.

nearly sounds like a simplistic "four spiritual laws" approach to evangelism, and the jailor's conversion seems to be rather instantaneous and prompted by emotions arising from unusual circumstances.

But we need to read the text carefully. The story goes on to say that Paul and Silas "spoke the word of the Lord to him and to all the others in his house" (v. 32). So there was a careful presentation of the gospel message. It is only after the jailer had taken Paul and Silas to his home, washed their wounds, and set a meal before them, and listened to their presentation that we read, "the whole family was filled with joy, because they had come to believe in God" (v. 34).

Saul's conversion might be cited as another counterexample to my analysis of ethical evangelism as requiring a careful presentation and explanation of the content of the gospel message and even persuasion (Acts 9:1–18). Here we have a conversion prompted by a blinding heavenly light, and a voice which addressed him, "Saul, Saul, why do you persecute me?" Yes, Ananias is called by the Lord to visit Saul, but Ananias's speech is rather short: "Brother Saul, the Lord—Jesus, who appeared to you on the road as you were coming here—has sent me so that you may see again and be filled with the Holy Spirit." After this, we are told something like scales fell from Saul's eyes, and he could see again, and he got up and was baptized.

Surely, we have here an example of a sudden conversion that even seems to involve some coercion.[34] But I would suggest Saul's conversion was not as sudden as it appears to be. After all, he was blind for three whole days. What was going on in Saul's mind during those three days of blindness? I would guess he was experiencing considerable mental turmoil, a radical rethinking and change of attitude towards this Jesus who had confronted him on the Damascus road and told him bluntly, "I am Jesus whom you are persecuting." Further, in one of the other accounts of his conversion, Paul hints at some antecedent events that led up to his conversion.[35] Further, Saul already possessed a lot of the background knowledge and so his conversion is not as sudden is it might seem.

---

34. In one of his sermons, Augustine argued Christ used force to coerce Paul into conversion by blinding him (see Kreider, *Patient Ferment of the Early Church*, 288).

35. In his defense before King Agrippa, Paul describes the voice that confronted him on the Damascus road as saying in Aramaic, "Saul, Saul, why do you persecute me? It is hard for you to kick against the goads" (Acts 26:14). The latter phrase was commonly found in both Greek and Latin literature, to refer to a farmer using goads to break in a lively and recalcitrant young bullock. So the implication is that Jesus was pursuing Saul, prodding and pricking him, and it was difficult for Saul to resist. Stott provides a helpful analysis of three goads that eventually culminated in Saul's conversion (Stott, *Message of Acts*, 171–72).

It is also an error to assume Saul's experience was so overwhelming that he was not able to respond freely to his encounter with Jesus. Given Saul's background knowledge, he immediately recognized the voice speaking to him. Yes, the blinding light humbled him as he fell to the ground, but Jesus did speak to him and in fact confronted him with a probing question, "Saul, Saul, why do you persecute me?" Jesus was appealing to Saul's reason and conscience, and Saul clearly was not so overwhelmed by the vision and the voice that he was unable to respond. He answered Christ's question with questions of his own, "Who are you Lord?" and "What shall I do?" (Acts 22:8, 10) Jesus then told Saul to get up and go to a house in the city where he would get further instructions. And Saul did exactly that. Yes, Saul's conversion was a result of God's intervention and grace, "[b]ut sovereign grace is a gradual grace and a gentle grace."[36] And so too should ethical evangelism be gradual and gentle, at least for the most part.

All this is not to rule out the possibility of sudden conversions, or conversions that are prompted more by emotion than reason. Studies show there is a great variety of conversion experiences within the Christian family.[37] But when it comes to evangelism and efforts at bringing about conversions, these should for the most part involve patient and careful presentation of the gospel message. And such efforts might even include argument and persuasion.

REJECTION AND RESISTANCE

I have already drawn attention to the fact that in the book of Acts we repeatedly read of contrary responses to the evangelistic appeals of the apostles. Another example of this is found in Paul's evangelistic sermon in Pisidian Antioch. There were some people who were urging Paul to return the following Sabbath so they could hear more about Jesus. But when nearly the whole city came out to hear Paul the next Sabbath, some Jewish leaders "were filled with jealousy and talked abusively against what Paul was saying" (Acts 13:45).

The response of Paul and Barnabas is significant. First they make an announcement: "We had to speak the word of God to you first. Since you reject it and do not consider yourselves worthy of eternal life, we now turn to the Gentiles" (Acts 13:46). The response among the Gentiles was once again mixed. Some Jews stirred up resistance against Paul and Barnabas, and managed to recruit to their cause some God-fearing Gentile women of

---

36. Ibid., 173.

37. See McKnight, *Turning to Jesus*, and Kerr and Mulder, *Famous Conversions*.

high standing, and leading men of the city. This widespread resistance led to a second significant response from Paul and Barnabas. "[T]hey shook the dust from their feet in protest against them and went to Iconium" (Acts 13:51). Here Paul and Barnabas were following the instructions Jesus had given to his apostles.[38] Ethical evangelism eventually moves on when people say no.

The book of Acts also records more intense forms of rejection and resistance to evangelism. It is therefore instructive to see how the apostles responded to political efforts to silence them and also how they responded to outright persecution. Here I wish to consider two examples of escalating opposition. The first concerns a story already touched on: Peter and John healing a crippled beggar shortly after Pentecost (Acts 3). Peter again used the occasion to deliver a sermon, quite similar in structure to his Pentecost sermon. As a result of this evangelistic endeavor, the number of believers grew to five thousand men, probably not including women and children (Acts 4:4).

The priests and the captain of the temple guard, together with the Sadducees, were "greatly disturbed" by the content of Peter's message as well as the growth in the number of believers (Acts 4:2). Indeed, the Sadducees saw the apostles as both agitators and heretics.[39] Peter and John were brought before the Sanhedrin, the ruling body of seventy-one Jewish leaders presided over by the high priest, together with Caiaphas and other men associated with the high priest. No doubt memories of the trial of Jesus will have flooded the minds of Peter and John as they realized they were essentially before the same court that had condemned Jesus to death.

In response to the question as to what power has enabled them to heal the crippled beggar, Peter and John boldly declare it was in the name of Jesus this man had been healed. They then recount Jesus' death and resurrection and declare that salvation is only to be found in Jesus. Peter and John too can't help but use a trial for evangelistic purposes! The court was astounded at the courage of these men, and noted that they, like Jesus, were laymen with no formal theological training. They wanted to punish these men, but everyone in Jerusalem knew they had done an outstanding miracle and were praising God for what had happened. So, "to stop this thing from spreading any further among the people," they "commanded" Peter and John "not to speak or teach at all in the name of Jesus" (Acts 4:17–18).

---

38. Matt 10:14. For an explanation of this symbolism, see chapter 3, page 50.

39. The Sadducees were the ruling class of wealthy aristocrats who were politically aligned with the Romans. They also believed the Messianic age had begun in the Maccabean period and so they were not looking for a Messiah. They further denied the doctrine of the resurrection of the dead. See Stott, *Message of Acts*, 95.

Peter and John respond in three ways (Acts 4:19–31). First, they appeal to the God-honoring sentiments of the court and highlight the dilemma they themselves needed to face. Surely the court itself must acknowledge the first priority for anyone is to obey God rather than human beings. Next, they respond that they can't help but speak about what they have seen and heard. Anyone who has witnessed something exciting firsthand naturally wants to share the story with others. Again, the court couldn't gainsay this dimension of human nature. And third, Peter and John report their experiences to the body of believers, and "they raised their voices together in prayer to God." Here I want to draw attention to one aspect of their prayer: "Now Lord, consider their threats and enable your servants to speak your word with great boldness. Stretch out your hand to heal and perform miraculous signs and wonders through the name of your holy servant Jesus" (Acts 4:29–30). What is of note here is an appeal to the Sovereign Lord to consider or entertain the threats they have encountered. They are not praying these threats will fall under divine judgment, only that God would bear these threats in mind. They are not praying for a miracle of vengeance or destruction, such as fire from heaven, but for miracles of mercy.[40]

We also have something to learn from the response of Peter and John to pressures to stop them from engaging in evangelism and healing. They simply refused to obey. They appealed to a higher authority, the Sovereign Lord, in order to justify their disobedience.[41] And they, together with other believers, prayed for courage to continue ministry, even in the face of threats. This prayer meeting resulted in another moving of the Holy Spirit, which in turn led to the apostles testifying to the resurrection of the Lord Jesus "with great power" (Acts 4:31, 33). What you have here is the first Christian articulation of the principle of justified civil disobedience. Christians and the church will sometimes refuse to submit to social sanctions or legal prohibitions against proclaiming the gospel.

This becomes even clearer in a later incident where the Sanhedrin once again try to silence the apostles after many more people become believers in response to the apostles' preaching and healing ministries (Acts 5:12–41). Upon appearing before the Sanhedrin, the high priest addresses them: "We gave you strict orders not to teach in this name. Yet you have filled Jerusalem with your teaching and are determined to make us guilty of this man's blood." Peter and the other apostles boldly reply, "We must obey God rather than men!" Peter once again uses a court scene to review the

---

40. Ibid., 100. cf. Luke 9:51–55.

41. Generally, Christians are called to submit to human authorities (Rom 13:1–7; Titus 3:1; 1 Pet 2:13–17). But when an authority forbids something that God has commanded, then Christians are justified in disobeying that authority.

essential elements of the story of Jesus, and then reminds the court that he and the apostles and the Holy Spirit are witnesses to these things. This so infuriated the members of the Sanhedrin that they wanted to kill the apostles. Fortunately, Gamaliel, an esteemed Pharisee and teacher of the law, was able to calm the court. The apostles were flogged, once again ordered not to speak in the name of Jesus, and then released.

How did the apostles respond to this latest prohibition to evangelize? They left the Sanhedrin, "rejoicing because they had been counted worthy of suffering disgrace for the Name" (Acts 5:41). This too is part of ethical evangelism—a willingness to accept suffering when evangelism leads to persecution. The apostles were doing what Jesus, in the Sermon on the Mount, had instructed his followers to do when they faced insults and persecution, namely to rejoice and be glad (Matt 5:11-12). Indeed, it is an honor to be dishonored for the sake of Jesus Christ.

STEPHEN

Of course, this open defiance of the law did not go unnoticed. Nor did the continuing spread of the gospel. Indeed, shortly after the apostles' second appearance before the Sanhedrin, which we have just considered, we read this summary statement: "So the word of God spread. The number of disciples in Jerusalem increased rapidly, and a large number of priests became obedient to the faith" (Acts 6:7). Then follows the story of Stephen, which has already been told at the beginning of this chapter. Fierce opposition to Stephen's ministry of evangelism and miracles came rather quickly. Here again, there are lessons to be learned from Stephen's story. I would encourage the reader to look again at Stephen's careful responses to several levels of opposition.

In the end, Stephen is stoned, and we hear his final words: "Lord Jesus, receive my spirit ... Lord, do not hold this sin against them" (Acts 7:59-60). These concluding words are of course reminiscent of Jesus' own words on the cross (Luke 23:46, 34). We have here a final kind of response to rejection and resistance to evangelism—a willingness to become a martyr for the gospel. Indeed, the Greek word for witness is *martus*, from which we derive the word "martyr" in English.[42] Ultimately, ethical evangelism does not fight back in word or deed when it encounters opposition. It accepts failure. It

42. An interesting problem of translation arises in Paul's later speech in Jerusalem where he refers to Stephen. "And when the blood of your martyr Stephen was shed, I stood there giving my approval and guarding the clothes of those who were killing him" (Acts 22:20). There is some ambiguity as to whether this should be translated "martyr" or "witness." We see here the beginning of the semantic development from "witness" to "martyr" (cf. Rev 2:13).

adopts a posture of powerlessness. It expresses a willingness to forgive those who persecute. It surrenders its cause to God. Indeed, in the face of opposition and persecution, ethical evangelists entrust themselves to Christ, their heavenly advocate, standing at the right hand of God.

The story of Stephen ends with a note about a young man named Saul, who clearly endorsed the stoning of Stephen as he kept guard over the clothes of those who were expressing their murderous anger. But Stephen's death had a profound effect on Saul, as Paul acknowledged after his conversion (Acts 22:20). We find in Paul's witness to the gospel the very same responses to rejection and resistance as we have found in the story of Stephen. At times Paul counters objections to the gospel with arguments. At other times he simply endures ridicule. As we have already seen, Paul cannot help but use court scenes to present the gospel of Christ. In the end, it is likely Paul too suffered martyrdom, as did Peter.

Chapter 5

Paul's Epistles

You know, brothers, that our visit to you was not a failure. We had previously suffered and been insulted in Philippi, as you know, but with the help of our God we dared to tell you his gospel in spite of strong opposition. For the appeal we make does not spring from error or impure motives, nor are we trying to trick you. On the contrary, we speak as men approved by God to be entrusted with the gospel. We are not trying to please men but God, who tests our hearts. You know we never used flattery, nor did we put on a mask to cover up greed—God is our witness. We were not looking for praise from men, not from you or anyone else. (1 Thess 2:1–6)

PAUL'S LETTER TO THE church at Thessalonica, from which the above excerpt is taken, is probably the earliest writing in the New Testament canon. Most scholars agree that Paul's letters to the Thessalonian church were written in AD 51. These letters give us a glimpse into some of the issues facing a newly planted church just eighteen years after the death and resurrection of Jesus Christ. Paul, with a team consisting of Silas, Timothy, and Luke, first visited Thessalonica during his second missionary journey in AD 49 or 50.[1] As was his usual practice, Paul began by defending the gospel in the synagogue. After doing so on three successive Sabbaths, some Jewish listeners became believers. So did "a large number of God-fearing

---

1. Paul's visit to Thessalonica is described in Acts 17. Silas was Paul's chief missionary partner from the beginning (Acts 15:40). In Lystra, Paul invited Timothy to join them (Acts 16:1–3). It is assumed Luke was added to the team in Troas, because in Acts 16:11, Luke begins to use the pronoun "we."

Greeks and not a few prominent women."[2] Jealous of Paul's influence in the city, some Jews recruited a gang of thugs and started a riot. So intense was the opposition, the believers had Paul and Silas smuggled out of town (Acts 17:5–10).

Paul and Silas continued their evangelistic work further south, but after a time Paul sent Timothy back to Thessalonica because he was anxious about the state of the young church he had left prematurely and involuntarily. Timothy returned with a report after Paul had arrived in Corinth.[3] On the one hand, Timothy brought good news about the Thessalonians' faith and love, and their steadfastness under persecution (1 Thess 3:6–8). On the other hand, Timothy reported Paul's reputation was being undermined. He was being criticized for insincerity and ulterior motives, and also for abandoning the fledgling church because he hadn't returned to Thessalonica. Timothy also reported on some issues that needed to be addressed in the church—sexual immorality, idleness, and confusion about the second coming of Christ. It is in the context of answering specific criticisms of his ministry that Paul articulates some characteristics of ethical evangelism. In the excerpt quoted above, Paul begins his defense after recounting the opposition he faced during his first evangelistic efforts in Thessalonica.

The overall theme of the above passage is that integrity is essential to ethical evangelism. Paul keeps stressing his evangelistic work in Thessalonica had been done openly before God and before human beings. Again and again in his epistle, Paul uses phrases like "you know," or "you remember," or "you are witnesses."[4] Twice he appeals to God as his witness. Paul also reminds the Thessalonians he and his coworkers "dared" to share the gospel despite strong opposition. The verb translated "dared" is *parrēsiazomai*, which means to speak freely, openly, and fearlessly. Ethical evangelism is done openly and publicly. There are no hidden agendas or hidden identities. Ethical evangelism is also willing to endure opposition, and even persecution. This requires courage, another ethical virtue.

Paul also maintains their evangelistic appeal did not spring from error. Ethical evangelism is truthful. It does not resort to trickery or flattery. There was nothing devious about the methods used by Paul and his coworkers. "They made no attempt to induce conversions, for example, either

---

2. Acts 17:2–3. Stott suggests Paul's mission to the Jews was followed by a Gentile mission (see the reference to idolatry in 1 Thess 1:9), and he stayed in Thessalonica for a few months, rather than just the three weeks that are mentioned in Acts 17. Stott, *Message of Thessalonians*, 18.

3. Acts 18:5; 1 Thess 3:6.

4. 1 Thess 1:5; 2:1, 2, 5, 9, 10.

by concealing the cost of discipleship or by offering fraudulent blessings."[5] They also did not use flattery as a means of persuasion. Again, truthfulness and integrity characterize ethical evangelism.

Paul goes on to point out his evangelistic work was not done from impure motives. The Greek term is *akatharsia*, which means impurity or uncleanness, often associated with sexual immorality, as it is later in this letter (1 Thess 4:7). It is possible that Paul's critics were hinting at this meaning, since sexual immorality wasn't uncommon for traveling teachers. His critics might even be insinuating there was something suspicious about the "prominent women" who had been converted during Paul's stay in Thessalonica.[6] Other impure motives are also ruled out by Paul—greed and the praise from men. Successful evangelism can easily inflate one's ego. Paul is not motivated by fame or fortune. Instead, he seeks only to honor God, who tests our hearts.

Although Paul is not looking for *praise* from men or women, his work is motivated by *love* for men and women. Here we have a pure motive that underlies ethical evangelism. Paul uses the metaphor of "a mother caring for her little children" to describe his evangelistic work (I Thess 2:7). Indeed, in his rather long defense against the accusation he had abandoned or even forgotten the Thessalonians, Paul uses a variety of images to describe his love for them (1 Thess 2:17—3:13). His sudden departure is compared to parents reluctantly "torn away" from their children. Out of "intense longing" he had tried again and again to return to Thessalonica to visit them. When he could stand it no longer, he sent Timothy to encourage them in the faith and to bring back a report, and Paul was indeed "encouraged" and overjoyed to receive Timothy's positive report. The defense ends with a moving prayer for the church at Thessalonica. Paul reminds them he often prays for them. Ethical evangelism is motivated by a deep love of people.

Paul's ongoing care and concern for new converts highlights one other important feature of ethical evangelism. Paul has difficulty separating his work as an evangelist and his work as a pastor. In the first three chapters of his first letter to the Thessalonians, Paul repeatedly recounts his initial efforts at bringing them the gospel. But as we have already seen, interspersed in these reminders, there are also frequent prayers and expressions of concern and encouragements about growing in the faith. Just after Paul's response to various criticisms of his evangelistic efforts, Paul gives this positive description of his work as an evangelist. "We loved you so much that we were delighted to share with you not only the gospel of God but our lives as

---

5. Stott, *Message of Thessalonians*, 50.
6. Ibid., 49.

well, because you had become so dear to us" (1 Thess 2:8). Then Paul moves right on to describe his concerns about them as new believers. "For you know that we dealt with each of you as a father deals with his own children, encouraging, comforting and urging you to live lives worthy of God who calls you into his kingdom and glory" (1 Thess 2:11-12).

Ethical evangelism follows Paul's example in balancing evangelistic and pastoral concerns. Paul is not satisfied with just getting reports about how the Thessalonians had "turned to God from idols to serve the loving and true God," conversion reports that were spreading throughout Macedonia and Achaia (1 Thess 1:8-9). Paul also thanks God that the Thessalonians are "standing firm in the Lord," and he prays they will grow in faith and love and holiness (1 Thess 3:8, 12-13). Ethical evangelism is not only concerned about saving souls, it moves on to provide nurture and to make disciples of those who have been newly converted.

EPISTLES OR STORIES

Before proceeding any further with a treatment of Paul's epistles, it might be well to stop and explain how this chapter differs from the preceding chapters. We have already encountered Paul in our study of Acts. Paul liked to introduce himself as an apostle, though he admits his apostleship is unique in that it was based on a special revelation of the risen Christ on the Damascus road (1 Cor 15:7-10). Here is how the Lord describes Paul when he commanded Ananias to visit Paul after his Damascus experience: "This man is my chosen instrument to carry my name before the Gentiles and their kings and before the people of Israel" (Acts 9:15). Paul's many letters to churches he had founded on his three missionary journeys represent communications of a caring missionary and pastor to often fledgling congregations. In many cases, the membership will have involved recent adult Gentile converts, "mere infants in Christ" (1 Cor 3:1). They needed teaching of the basic doctrines of the Christian faith, exhortation, and sometimes even admonition. Often Paul is addressing specific problems in these mission outposts. Sometimes we need to do some reconstruction in order to understand what problems Paul was addressing in his letters.

The epistles differ from the Gospels and from the book of Acts in that they are not primarily concerned with telling stories. So, our exploration of the ethics of evangelism in these epistles will be somewhat different from that found in the previous chapters. The focus will be on the articulation of ethical principles that should govern evangelism. Sometimes these principles will emerge out of concrete situations Paul is addressing. At other times these principles will grow out of a systematic treatment of theology, which in turn is closely related to the shaping of a biblical worldview. Paul's letters frequently move from theology to ethics.[7] In this chapter I will at most hint at the theological and worldview grounding of ethical principles. Instead, as I have already illustrated, I am focusing on specific ethical principles and exhortations that relate to the way in which we should do evangelism.

In chapter 2, I outlined five different modes of ethical discourse in the Bible—specific rules or commandments, broader principles or frameworks, stories, narrative of the Bible as a whole, and a biblical worldview. In this chapter, the focus will be on the first and second of these modes of ethical discourse. I will be examining passages in the epistles that articulate rules or principles of ethical evangelism.

It is not possible in one chapter to do an in-depth treatment of the theme of the ethics of evangelism in all of Paul's epistles. Instead, I will examine a few important representative paragraphs in the epistles that articulate some principles governing the ethics of evangelism. References to other passages of Scripture that treat similar themes and principles will for the most part be found in the footnotes.

PAUL'S LETTERS TO THE CHURCH IN CORINTH

The Corinthian church had its origin in Paul's first visit to Corinth in the autumn of AD 50, as part of his second missionary journey after his visit to Thessalonica (Acts 18). Paul will no doubt have appreciated the strategic importance of Corinth for spreading the gospel. Corinth was one of the three leading cities of the Roman Empire at the time. It was a major commercial center, situated along some major trade routes by land and sea, and was a provincial capital. But in everybody's minds, Corinth was also associated with immorality. It was, after all, a seaport! Thus, it is not too surprising to discover that the emerging church in Corinth, which was predominantly Gentile and ex-pagan in character, would face a number of problems having to do with behavior. "You are still worldly," Paul suggests at the beginning of his first letter (1 Cor 3:3).

The problems in the Corinthian church led to a number of letters and visits from Paul, including an earlier letter that has not survived, where Paul

---

7. Some New Testament scholars have suggested there is no direct connection between Paul's ethical prescriptions and his theological proclamation. Hays objects and argues a close reading of Paul's letters will reveal a tight connection between theology and ethics. Hays, *Moral Vision of the New Testament*, 17–18. This is very clearly seen in Romans.

addresses the failure of some of the Corinthian believers to separate from people within the church who were sexually immoral.[8] The first canonical Epistle to the Corinthians was probably written AD 55 toward the end of Paul's stay in Ephesus. This letter deals with the fragmentation of the Corinthian church into factions, continuing gross immorality, litigation among members, irregularities at congregational meetings, and doubts about the resurrection of the dead.[9] Then follows a "painful visit" from Paul, and a "Severe Letter" now lost to us.[10] The second canonical Epistle, about which I will say more shortly, was probably written about a year later.

In order to see what these letters say about the ethics of evangelism, we first need to provide some context about a significant problem Paul was facing in his relationship with the Corinthian church. Paul's reputation was being undermined, and there were a number of factors contributing to this. Paul was being unfavorably compared to Apollos who had visited the church and who was probably superior to Paul in his abilities in teaching and preaching.[11] Paul's painful visit and his severe letter dealing with some serious moral problems in the church will no doubt have contributed to a worsening of relationships.[12] Then there was Paul's failure to follow up his severe letter with a visit he had promised (2 Cor 1:15–23). Some were also unhappy over Paul's refusal to be supported financially even accusing him of secretly getting financial support from the Corinthians through his coworkers.[13] But the biggest problem for Paul was the recent arrival of "false apostles" or "super-apostles" in Corinth who were not only challenging Paul's teaching but also attacking him personally.[14] In the six years of Paul's

8. Paul refers to this earlier in his letter, in 1 Cor 5:9–13.

9. See 1 Cor 3:3–4; 5:1; 6:1; 11:17–18; 14:26–36; 15:12.

10. See 2 Cor 2:1–4; 7:8 for references to the "painful visit" and the "Severe Letter." The latter formal title is suggested by Paul Barnett, *Second Epistle to the Corinthians*, 12.

11. Paul's defensive remarks about his unrhetorical preaching (1 Cor 2:1–5) may be contrasted with the glowing account of Apollos' rhetoric (Acts 18:24–28). In describing the problem of divisions in the church, Apollos is mentioned as one of the people around whom people were developing cliques (1 Cor 1:12). Paul specifically identifies some people who said that while his letters are "weighty and forceful," his speaking "amounts to nothing" (2 Cor 10:1, 10; 11:6).

12. 2 Cor 2:1–4; 7:8–12.

13. 1 Cor 9:15–18; 2 Cor 6:8; 7:2; 11:7–12; 12:13–18.

14. 2 Cor 11:1–13; 12:11. There is considerable debate among scholars as to the identity of these opponents of Paul. For an analysis of this debate, see Barnett, *Second Epistle to the Corinthians*, 32–40. It seems these "false apostles" or "super-apostles" (Barnett equates the two) were a fairly large group of men (2 Cor 2:17; 11:18) who had come to Corinth from outside and therefore required letters of commendation (2 Cor 3:1). They were probably Greek-speaking Jews and ministers of Christ who had come from Jerusalem (2 Cor 11:22–23). They were Judaizers, rejecting Paul's claim the old covenant had been

association with the Corinthian church, this was by far the most serious problem that had arisen.

It is these attempts to undermine Paul's status, teaching, and reputation that prompted Paul to defend himself. Indeed, there is a defensive tone in much of Paul's second canonical letter to the Corinthians.[15] It is within this context of Paul defending himself against a variety of criticisms that he also touches on the ethics of pastoral ministry and the ethics of evangelism. I will focus on the latter in what follows.[16]

ELOQUENCE AND WISDOM

After dealing with the problem of divisions in the Corinthian church, Paul moves on to develop a theme that keeps recurring in his letters. Paul highlights the foolishness of the message of the cross and he challenges the wisdom of this world (1 Cor 1:18—2:16). Inserted into the middle of this discourse Paul gives us a normative description of his early efforts of evangelism in the city of Corinth.

> When I came to you, brothers, I did not come with eloquence or superior wisdom as I proclaimed to you the testimony about God. For I resolved to know nothing while I was with you except Jesus Christ and him crucified. I came to you in weakness and fear, and with much trembling. My message and my preaching were not with wise and persuasive words, but with a demonstration of the Spirit's power, so that your faith might not rest on men's wisdom, but on God's power. (1 Cor 2:1–5)

Paul is here reminding his readers that in his initial missionary endeavors in Corinth, he did not rely on his rhetorical skills or his abilities as a learned rabbi to impress potential converts with his wisdom. Now this

---

superseded by the coming of Christ. They liked to boast of their achievements by contrasting their strengths with Paul's perceived weaknesses (2 Cor 10:12—12:3).

15. At one point Paul even asks a rhetorical question: "Have you been thinking all along that we have been defending ourselves to you" (2 Cor 12:19)?

16. For those who might argue Paul is primarily concerned about the ethics of pastoral ministry, I would respond as follows. First, it can be argued there is little or no difference between the ethical principles that should govern preaching and the ethical principles that should govern evangelism. Second, many of the members of the church of Corinth had become believers because of Paul's evangelistic endeavors. Thus, in his letters, Paul slips easily from pastoral admonitions to reminding the believers of his initial work among them as an evangelist (2 Cor 1:19; 2:12; 1 Cor 3:6; 15:1). So, Paul is often hearkening back to his work as an evangelist, and when he does so he sometimes explicitly articulates principles of ethical evangelism.

might seem a little odd, because as we have already seen in Acts, and as we see in his writings, Paul was rather good at debating and constructing a systematic theological argument. So what is Paul saying here? To answer this question, we need to examine the broader context in which these words are found.

Paul is contrasting the wisdom of the world and the wisdom of God. The word "wisdom," or *sophia*, occurs twenty times in these two chapters. It is Paul's overriding concern. But exactly what does he mean when he says that from the perspective of Greek wisdom, or the wisdom of the world, the message of the cross is foolishness? Paul Gooch suggests that while we cannot be entirely sure, there are some clues in the text which suggest Paul is addressing four concerns.[17] First, Paul is concerned about a certain approach to rhetoric that the Greek sophists were famous for. Rhetoric isn't bad in itself, but it is all too easy for rhetoric to degenerate into showmanship, into trying to impress people with your eloquence. Secondly, the Greeks were known for their endless arguing and debating, and this too was a concern for Paul. Hence the question, "Where is the philosopher (debator) of this age?"[18] Thirdly, Paul is concerned about pretensions in our abilities to know God, when there are obvious limits to human knowledge.[19] But the primary concern of Paul is the conceit of human wisdom. Again and again in these chapters Paul comes back to the theme of boasting,[20] and that is why he keeps talking about the foolishness and weakness of God, even to the point of exaggeration. It is a way of shaming the proud pretensions of human wisdom.

Jews too found the message of Christ crucified to be a stumbling block (1 Cor 1:23). The notion of a Messiah hanging on a cross was "scandalous" for the Jew, because as we read in the Old Testament, "anyone who is hung on a tree is under God's curse."[21] A crucified Messiah was a contradiction in

---

17. Gooch, *Partial Knowledge,* chap. 2.

18. 1 Cor 1:20. In fact Paul has quite a lot to say about pointless arguing in his other letters (see 1 Tim 6:4; 2 Tim. 2:23; 3:7).

19. This concern comes out especially in the second chapter. "[N]o one knows the thoughts of God" (1 Cor 2:12). "For who has known the mind of the Lord" (1 Cor 2:16)?

20. 1 Cor 1:29, 31; 3:21; 4:7; 9:16. The theme of boasting is also prominent in 2 Corinthians. Here it is significant that although Paul is often boasting, he is embarrassed about doing so. It is because of all the attacks against him that he is forced to engage in "foolish boasting" (see esp. 2 Cor 10–13). Paul is very much aware he is ultimately answerable to God, and here there is little room for boasting (2 Cor 1:12; 4:2; 5:12). See Barnett, *Second Epistle to the Corinthians,* 94–95.

21. Deut. 21:23; cf. Gal 3:13–14. The Greek word used for "stumbling block is "*skandalon,*" from which the English word "scandalous" is derived.

terms, from their point of view. So again, the message of the cross doesn't make sense from the point of view of human wisdom.

So, what does all this entail for the ethics of evangelism? Ethical evangelism acknowledges the apparent foolishness of the gospel of Jesus Christ. There are limits to our attempts to make the gospel seem reasonable. I would suggest we also need to be cautious about apologetics as an ingredient in evangelism. There are limits as to what can be accomplished by argument and persuasion. As Paul says elsewhere, "the god of this age has blinded the minds of unbelievers."[22] So we need some divine help in doing apologetics and evangelism. Ethical evangelism recognizes that ultimately it is God's Spirit who must open minds and hearts to the gospel of Jesus Christ. Faith (and coming to faith) doesn't rest on human wisdom, but on God's power and on the work of God's Spirit (1 Cor 2:6–16). It doesn't all depend on us. This of course entails that prayer should accompany all attempts at evangelism. A further implication is that evangelism should always be done with a humble spirit. Ultimately, any success in evangelism depends on God's Spirit. Our own rhetoric plays a secondary role. Hence, there should be no boasting about our rhetorical abilities or our success in doing evangelism.

In his second canonical letter to the Corinthians, Paul returns to the above themes, this time addressing the issue of demolishing arguments against the faith. Here he reminds the reader, "the weapons we fight with are not the weapons of the world."[23] Instead, we rely on "divine power." All this is prefaced with a telling description of Paul's approach to rhetoric and argument—he appeals to people "by the meekness and gentleness of Christ" (2 Cor 10:1). Ethical evangelism should reflect the meekness and gentleness of Jesus Christ.

INTEGRITY IN EVANGELISM

There is another important summary statement on the ethics of evangelism early in the second canonical Epistle to the Corinthians:

> Therefore, since through God's mercy we have this ministry, we do not lose heart. Rather, we have renounced secret and shameful ways; we do not use deception, nor do we distort the word

---

22. 2 Cor 4:4. The hiddenness of the gospel is a common theme in Paul's writings. See 1 Cor 2:8–10, 14; 3:19. See also Paul's description of people "who suppress the truth by their wickedness." Because of this, "their thinking became futile and their foolish hearts were darkened" (Rom 1:18, 21). Only God's Spirit can open such hearts.

23. 2 Cor 10:4. See also Paul's description of "the full armor of God" in Ephesians 6:10–20, an analysis of which would yield similar principles for ethical evangelism.

of God. On the contrary, by setting forth the truth plainly we commend ourselves to every man's conscience in the sight of God. (2 Cor 4:1–2)

The immediate context of these verses is a discussion of Paul and his coworkers as ministers of the new covenant (2 Cor 3:12–18). That ministry includes preaching the gospel of Jesus Christ (2 Cor 2:12; cf. 4:5). The Greek word for "preaching" is *keryssein*, which means being a herald, a person who brings important announcements from a king or emperor to people scattered throughout his kingdom. So what is Paul saying here about the ethics of the proclamation of the gospel or evangelism?

First he talks of having renounced secret and shameful ways. Paul is responding to some critics who were accusing him of being devious and dishonest. As we have already seen, although Paul made it a point not to be supported financially by the Corinthians, he was being accused of secretly getting payment from them through his coworkers. Paul meets the charge head-on. There is nothing secretive or shameful about what he is doing. In fact, earlier in this section Paul compares what he does with the behavior of his critics. "Unlike so many, we do not peddle the word of God for profit. On the contrary, in Christ we speak before God with sincerity, like men sent from God" (2 Cor 2:17). Evangelism must not be done for financial gain. It must avoid even the hint of devious ways to benefit oneself.

Instead, there should be a transparency about everything that is done in the name of evangelism. Paul and his coworkers "do not use deception." They are quite open about what they are doing. They "speak before God with sincerity."[24] Their testimonial: "by setting forth the truth plainly we commend ourselves to every man's conscience in the sight of God."[25] Note the two prongs to this transparency—it involves transparency both before God and man. Paul appeals to everyone's conscience to check him out with regard to his motives, and when they do so, they will find that his motives are pure. Evangelism must not create even the hint of suspicion regarding our motives. We are also accountable to God, and so we engage in evangelism "with sincerity" before God. We don't engage in evangelism to make ourselves feel good. Our motivation in evangelism should not be to grow our church and thus make a name for ourselves. We do evangelism "like men sent from God." It is because we ourselves have received "God's mercy" that we want to tell others about God's mercy.

Paul goes on to give another characteristic of ethical evangelism. "[W]e do not use deception, nor do we distort the word of God." While

---

24. 2 Cor 2:17; cf. 2 Cor 1:12.
25. 2 Cor 4:2; cf. 2 Cor 5:11; Col 4:4.

deception might be linked here to the previous charge concerning economic underhandedness, I think it is better to link it with distorting the word of God. Here again, Paul is responding to false apostles who were in fact distorting the gospel of Jesus Christ. The broader context of these verses suggests the false apostles were trying to combine the gospel of Jesus Christ with elements of the old Mosaic covenant. They were trying to persuade Gentile Christians to live like Jews.[26] Later in this letter, Paul chastises the Corinthians for even listening to these people who preach "a Jesus other than the Jesus we preached," or who present "a different gospel" from the one they had accepted (2 Cor 11:3–4). By contrast, Paul is concerned about "setting forth the truth plainly."[27]

Ethical evangelism is careful not to distort the word of God. It is careful to always portray the gospel of Jesus Christ truthfully. Sadly, distortions of the word of God and the gospel of Jesus Christ also exist today. This happens when we water down the gospel, when we fail to present all of the gospel, when we fail to present to the potential believer the full costs of following Jesus, when we present a simplistic version of the gospel, and when we cheapen grace by forgetting about Jesus' words that remind unbelievers they have to take up their cross and follow him if they want to become a Christian.

POWER IN WEAKNESS

The theme of servanthood relates to another emphasis in Paul's writings that bears on the ethics of evangelism—the motif of weakness and suffering. In a paragraph immediately following the verses that have been my primary focus in the last section, Paul highlights his own weakness and the sufferings he has endured as a minister of the gospel (2 Cor 4:7–12).[28] Paul

---

26. See Barnett, *Second Epistle to the Corinthians*, 35.

27. See also Paul's description of his work as an evangelist in terms of "truthful speech" (2 Cor 6:7). Paul also likes to describe the gospel as "the word of truth" (Eph 1:13; Col 1:5; 2 Tim 2:15; cf. 1 Tim 2:7). Paul also asks for prayer on his behalf: "Pray that I may proclaim it (the mystery of Christ) clearly, as I should" (Col 4:4).

28. This passage is only one of several so-called *peristasis*, "catalogues of circumstances," often found in the literature of the Hellenistic period, and used by Paul to describe the difficulties surrounding his work as a missionary (Barnett, *Second Epistle to the Corinthians*, 228–29). See also 2 Cor 6:3–10; 11:16–33; 12:1–10; cf. 1:5–11; 2:14–17. In each case, Paul highlights the power in weakness theme. See also Paul's earlier description of his state of mind during his first evangelistic efforts in Corinth: "I came to you in weakness and fear, and with much trembling" (1 Cor 1:2–3). Although Paul was convinced of the power of the gospel, he felt somewhat intimidated as he began his mission in Corinth, "the most populated, wealthy, commercial-minded, and sex-obsessed

and his coworkers, servants of Jesus Christ, are described as nothing more than fragile "jars of clay" (v. 7). They are subject to opposition on every side, bewilderment, and persecution. They are in fact sharing in the sufferings of Jesus Christ. But there is a paradox here. If Paul and his fellow workers are merely fragile jars of clay, they at the same time "show that this all-surpassing power is from God and not from us" (v. 7). While facing opposition, they are "not crushed," while perplexed, they are "not in despair," while persecuted, they are "not abandoned" (vv. 8–9). While suffering for Christ, the resurrected life of Jesus is "revealed in our body" (v. 10). This is the power in weakness paradox.

This same theme of power in weakness is found earlier in a parallel section to the verses which have been our focus in the last while (2 Cor 2:14–17). Here Paul uses the metaphor of a triumphal procession in which a conquering general would be followed by captives marching to their execution. The prisoners in the procession would often be forced to spread incense as they marched along in humiliation. Hence Paul's reference to spreading the fragrance of the knowledge of Christ—to some the smell of death, and to others the fragrance of life. And then comes a question: "And who is equal to such a task?" The raising of this question would suggest Paul is in fact once again answering his critics who were insinuating he was physically and even spiritually weak. Paul's answer: "Not that we are competent to claim anything for ourselves, but our competence comes from God" (2 Cor 3:5). Later in this letter, Paul returns to the power in weakness theme when discussing some ailment he is facing. The Lord's response to his repeated pleas to be delivered from the "thorn in my flesh," is simply: "My grace is sufficient for you, for my power is made perfect in weakness."[29]

What does this power in weakness emphasis entail for the ethics of evangelism? Ethical evangelists are willing to acknowledge their own weakness and frailty. We are not up to the task. Any competence we might have is in fact a gift from God. Ultimately, any success we might have in evangelism is the work of God's Spirit, and not the result of our own abilities. We should also not be surprised that evangelism is often accompanied by suffering and even persecution. Here we also need to keep in mind there is such a thing as

---

city of eastern Europe." Prior, *Message of 1 Corinthians*, 13.

29. 2 Cor 12:8. Another version of the power in weakness theme is introduced at the end of this letter when Paul defends himself against the super-apostles who thought of themselves as superior to Paul in rhetorical skills (2 Cor 11:5). Paul engages in some "foolish boasting" in defending himself in this regard, but he does so reluctantly, and once again he concludes by boasting of his weakness (2 Cor 11:29–30). We have also encountered this version of the power in weakness theme in our treatment of "Eloquence and Wisdom" earlier in this chapter.

mental suffering that results from a society repeatedly telling us our beliefs are naïve. Ethical evangelism accepts suffering as part of the cost of being a witness for Jesus Christ.

DOES THE END JUSTIFY THE MEANS?

Before leaving Paul's Epistles, we need to consider two troublesome passages that on the surface seem to involve a betrayal of an ethical approach to evangelism. The first deals with an important principle of communication—to evangelize, one needs to adapt to one's audience.

> To the Jews I became like a Jew, to win the Jews. To those under the law I became like one under the law (though I myself am not under the law), so as to win those under the law. To those not having the law I became like one not having the law (though I am not free from God's law but am under Christ's law), so as to win those not having the law. To the weak I became weak, to win the weak. I have become all things to all men so that by all possible means I might save some. (1 Cor 9:20-22)

This is a difficult text to interpret. Indeed, I believe it is often misinterpreted, leading to many distortions as to how we should evangelize. Exactly what does Paul mean when he talks about adapting to the Jew, or the Gentile, or the weak, so as to win each of these groups for Christ? Note the parallelism of the verse that sums up this paragraph. "I have become *all* things to *all* men so that by *all* possible means I might save some." Paul can't *literally* mean he becomes all things to all men in order to win them for Christ, because it is simply impossible. Paul was a Jew and it was impossible for him to become a Gentile. Paul was rather intelligent, and it was impossible for him to become a simpleton in order to win simpletons for Christ.

It is further impossible to take Paul literally when he says he has used "all possible means" to save men and women. We have already seen that Paul is very careful to rule out some means of evangelism, like the use of deception, or distorting the word of God, or the use of underhanded ways to win converts. The end simply does not justify any means when doing evangelism.

Paul is in fact careful to qualify his claims when describing how he reaches out to Jews and Gentiles. When speaking to Jews Paul became like one under the law, but then he adds a qualification (in brackets), "though I myself am not under the law." So again, Paul does not literally mean one needs to become like a Jew in every way possible in order to win them for

Christ. There are limits to such adaptation. Paul argues in a similar fashion with regard to reaching out to Gentiles who don't have the law. If you carried the idea of becoming like those who don't have the law too far, you would become lawless, and so, Paul adds a qualification, "though I am not free from God's law." Again, there are limits to becoming like those who don't have the law. Paul is not saying, "To the worldly, I become like a worldly person, in order to win the worldly."

So far, I have been focusing on what this passage does not mean. To understand what Paul is really saying, we need to examine more carefully the context of these verses. Paul is in fact hinting at this context when he provides another application of his principle of accommodation: "To the weak I became weak, to win the weak." Paul is referring here to the previous chapter where he talks about the need for Christians to accommodate themselves to the weaker brother or sister so they don't fall back into sin (chap. 8). In chapter 9, Paul goes on to give another example of accommodation, this time having to do with giving up his right as an apostle to be supported financially. Paul chose to be financially self-supporting, because he felt this would further the cause of his ministry.

Paul then gives us a summary statement. "Though I am free and belong to no man, I make myself a slave to everyone" (1 Cor 9:19). Here we have a general principle that also underlies the verses that follow regarding evangelism. As Christians, we are not the sort of people who keep demanding our rights or insisting on our freedom. Instead, we see ourselves as servants of others, as Jesus himself taught us (Mark 10:43–45). So, when Paul goes on to talk about becoming like a Jew, or a Gentile, or like a weak person, he is simply applying this general principle of servanthood. He is illustrating what it means for him as an educated, religious Jew, and a Pharisee, to make himself a servant of all in order to win as many as possible to Christ.[30]

Servanthood—that is what this passage is all about. Ethical evangelism is characterized by a servantlike attitude. We as Christians will try to identify with non-Christians, try to understand them, try to be sensitive to their

---

30. See Prior, *Message of 1 Corinthians*, 159. cf. 1 Cor 4:5. In fact, Paul exemplified flexibility with regard to the observance of Jewish regulations. Sometimes he was careful to obey Jewish law in order to further the proclamation of the gospel. For example, in having Timothy circumcised (Acts 16:3), or in discharging a Nazirite vow in the temple of Jerusalem (Acts 21:23–26). At other times, he refused to bow to pressure from Judaizers who wanted Titus to be circumcised, for example (Gal 2:3). In the previous chapter we have also seen how Paul uses very different approaches in presenting the gospel when speaking to Gentiles in Athens (Acts 17:16–33) and when he speaks to Jews in Corinth (Acts 18:1–6). In fact, the Jews eventually took Paul to court charging him with "persuading the people to worship God in ways contrary to the law" (Acts 18:13).

MOTIVATION

There is a second troublesome passage in Paul's letters that seems once again to undermine the importance of an ethical approach to evangelism. This is found in his epistle to the church at Philippi, an epistle Paul probably wrote while he was a prisoner in Rome in the early 60s AD.[31] There is no need to delve further into the background of this epistle, since our focus will be on Paul's description of his situation in Rome.

After his usual greeting and then a prayer for the saints at Philippi, Paul describes his current situation as being a prisoner in chains. Paul's trial has probably already taken place and he is waiting for the verdict.[32] Paul describes his being in chains as having opened the door to a very unique opportunity to advance the gospel (Phil 1:12–14). During his two-year imprisonment, Paul was allowed to entertain visitors, and quite in character, he welcomed all who came to him, "boldly" proclaiming the kingdom of God and teaching them about Jesus Christ (Acts 28:30–31). The soldiers who were always present would have had to listen to these conversations, and no doubt, Paul also would have dialogued with these soldiers. So, one by one, the members of the palace guard heard the gospel, and they would have told their families and friends. Paul then goes on to describe two very different responses to his evangelistic efforts.

> It is true that some preach Christ out of envy and rivalry, but others out of good will. The latter do so in love, knowing that I am put here for the defense of the gospel. The former preach Christ out of selfish ambition, not sincerely, supposing that they can stir up trouble for me while I am in chains. But what does it matter? The important thing is that in every way, whether from false motives or true, Christ is preached. And because of this I rejoice. (Phil 1:15–18)

What is troublesome here is that Paul seems to be unconcerned about the motivation behind evangelism. It doesn't matter whether Christ is proclaimed out of envy or rivalry, Paul says, as long as Christ is proclaimed. But, shouldn't we be concerned about motives when doing evangelism? Don't

---

31. Some scholars have suggested Paul may be referring to his earlier imprisonment in Caesarea or Ephesus, but I am following the traditional interpretation. See Fee, *Paul's Letter to the Philippians*, 34–37.

32. See Philippians 1:19, 23, 24 for some hints that would suggest this scenario.

motives matter to God? These are questions that call for some answers. I believe it is all too easy to misinterpret the above passage of Scripture, and this happens if we disregard the context and forget what the rest of Scripture teaches on the subject of motivation.

In fact, we are reminded repeatedly in Scripture that God is very concerned about the motives that underlie what we say and do.[33] Indeed, even in the Epistle to the Philippians, Paul calls on the saints to be one in spirit and purpose, "doing nothing from selfishness or conceit" (Phil 2:2–3). Selfishness and conceit surely have to do with motivation. Earlier in this chapter we have already seen that Paul quite specifically addresses the question of motivation when he describes his evangelistic work in Thessalonica as not springing "from error or impure motives . . . We are not trying to please men but God, who tests our hearts" (1 Thess 2:3–4). We have also seen that Paul objects to peddling the word of God for profit. By contrast, Paul and his coworkers "speak before God with sincerity" (2 Cor 2:16), and have "renounced secret and shameful ways" (2 Cor 4:2).

So why does Paul seem to dismiss the importance of motivation in doing evangelism in the above passage from Philippians? We need to keep in mind that there was a church in Rome before Paul arrived there as a prisoner. Paul was not the founder of this church.[34] So there will have been leaders, preachers, and evangelists, who had already attained a degree of prominence within the church. Small wonder that some of these established leaders and evangelists will have been tempted to feel a bit jealous when Paul arrived, a missionary statesman who had already written a letter to the church of Rome, and whose influence was growing over the two years he was in chains in Rome. They couldn't help but see Paul as a rival. So, it is not hard to imagine they will have used the pulpit "to make sly innuendoes and veiled attacks and concealed, damaging hints" against Paul.[35] Of course, I am adding some details here that are not found in the text, but I believe this reconstruction of events helps to explain why the motivation of these earlier evangelists was not entirely pure. They began to preach Christ "out of selfish ambition." They couldn't help but feel they were competing with Paul.

---

33. God is frequently described as testing our hearts, and this surely includes the testing of our motivation (see Ps 7:9; Prov 17:3; 1 Cor 4:5; 1 Thess 2:4; Rev 2:23). Paul, in giving us a theology of work, describes how slaves should serve their masters. He urges slaves to obey their masters not only to win their favor when they are watching, "but like slaves of Christ, doing the will of God from your heart" (Eph 6:6).

34. In his letter to the church at Rome, Paul talks about having "planned many times to come to you (but have been prevented from doing so until now)" (Rom 1:13).

35. Motyer, *Message of Philippians*, 76.

How does Paul respond to this rivalry? For one thing, Paul doesn't go into a lot of detail in describing this difficult situation.[36] It seems he wants to downplay the rivalry. Hence his seeming lack of concern about the impure motives of these preachers and evangelists. The important thing is that Christ is being proclaimed. We see here the generosity of Paul and also his exemplary self-denial. In fact, Paul was probably quite sensitive to the fact that through no fault of his own, he was breaking his general rule not to encroach on the territory of other workers for Christ.[37] So again, Paul generously doesn't worry about the seeming rivalry of the established evangelists and preachers in Rome. It may even be that Paul is using some exaggeration and hyperbole in his easy dismissal of impure motivation in doing evangelism. He wants to drive home the point that what really matters is that Christ is proclaimed.

There may be another aspect to Paul's downplaying of the importance of proper motivation in doing evangelism. Paul may also be saying this because he realizes our motivation is never entirely pure. We always have mixed motives in everything that we do.[38] If we waited until our motives were entirely pure, we would never get on with any job. The motives of these leaders who were competing with Paul weren't all bad. They wanted to serve Christ, and this is good. Unfortunately, this was mixed with impure motives. But again, the more important thing is that people hear the gospel message. Presumably, winning people for Christ is compatible with less-than-perfect evangelists.

I conclude that we misread the above passage if we interpret it as saying that motives are entirely irrelevant when we consider the ethics of evangelism. Motives do matter. In the above passage, Paul himself acknowledges that some motives are "false," such as preaching the gospel "out of envy and rivalry," or "out of selfish ambition." It is just that in this particular situation in Rome, where he is seen as a rival, he is willing to overlook these unethical motivations. Paul also says motives can (and should) be "true" or "sincere," and the gospel can (and should) be preached "out of good will." This prompts a further exploration as to what are some positive motivations for evangelism.

36. Ibid., 75. Motyer goes on to say, "There is great grace in Paul's silence, and great wisdom too."

37. At the end of his letter to the Romans, Paul describes his ambition in terms of preaching the gospel where Christ was not known, "so that I would not be building on someone else's foundation" (Rom 15:20).

38. This is no doubt why the Psalmist asks this question: "Who can discern his errors" (Ps 19:12)? David goes on to pray, "Forgive my hidden faults." Often, we are not even aware of our faults, particularly selfish motivations.

HEALTHY MOTIVATION

We have already begun to answer this question earlier in this chapter in our exposition of Paul's letters to the Thessalonians. Here Paul states his sharing of the gospel was motivated by love for men and women (1 Thess 2:7-8). We have also examined Paul's fundamental orientation in evangelism as making himself "a slave to everyone, to win as many as possible" (1 Cor 9:19). Paul is also very much aware of the command, "Love your neighbor as yourself" (Rom 13:9). God's ideal is that his love will so fill our hearts that we will, out of this overflowing, love our neighbors so as to win them for Christ. Ethical evangelism is motivated by love for our neighbors.

Paul keeps coming back to the theme of motivation in his letters. Twice Paul talks about being compelled to preach the gospel. "Yet when I preach the gospel, I cannot boast, for I am compelled to preach. Woe to me, if I do not preach the gospel . . . I am simply discharging the trust committed to me" (1 Cor 9:16-17). Then in the second canonical letter to the Corinthians, Paul speaks on behalf of his coworkers, "For Christ's love compels us" (2 Cor 5:14). Paul is not evangelizing out of a sense of duty or because of guilt. Instead, he has been so gripped by the mercy and love of Jesus Christ that preaching the gospel simply flows spontaneously from his very being. Ethical evangelism is motivated by our experience of Christ's love and mercy.

Paul is also very much aware of the fact that he has been entrusted with the office of being an evangelist.[39] He sees himself as one of Christ's "ambassadors" (2 Cor 5:20). He and his coworkers "know what it is to fear the Lord," and therefore "we try to persuade men."[40] Ethical evangelism is motivated by obedience to God. But again, Paul is not discharging this trust as a burdensome duty. Rather, he is motivated by gratitude for all that Christ has done for him. Paul is even more explicit about being motivated by thankfulness in his later letter to the Corinthians. "Thanks be to God, who always leads us in triumphal procession in Christ and through us spreads everywhere the fragrance of the knowledge of him."[41] Ethical evangelism is motivated by thankfulness.

---

39. See 1 Thess 2:4 and also the words God gave to Ananias when he asked him to visit Saul and give him his commission (Acts 9:15).

40. 2 Cor 5:11. See also Romans 1:14-15. "I am obligated both to Greeks and non-Greeks, both to the wise and the foolish. That is why I am so eager to preach the gospel also to you who are at Rome." In 1 Thess 2:4, Paul talks about pleasing God as his motivation for evangelism.

41. 2 Cor 2:14. We see this same theme of thankfulness come up with regard to another commandment in the New Testament, regarding being generous in our giving (2 Cor 8:1-2, 8-11; 9:7, 12, 15). The Old Testament also associates the telling of the wonderful news of God with thankfulness (Ps 75:1).

Paul is clearly very concerned about the ethics of evangelism. That is why he found it necessary to defend himself again and again against a variety of criticisms against his own person. One way to summarize Paul's many reflections on the ethics of evangelism is to introduce the notion of personal integrity. Paul knew the verbal witness of the followers of Jesus must be undergirded by Christian character and lifestyle.[42] Christian character and lifestyle are necessary ingredients of embodied ethical witness.

---

42. See also 2 Cor 3:2; Phil 2:14–16; and Ewert, "Evangelism by Lifestyle."

Chapter 6

General Epistles and Revelation

AUGUSTINE, TOWARDS THE END of his famous *Confessions*, gives a moving tribute to his mother after her death. In the excerpt that follows, Augustine describes the faithful witness of his Christian mother, Monica, to his pagan father, Patricius.

She was thus nurtured in an atmosphere of purity and temperance, and was subjected by you to the authority of her parents rather than by them to yours. When she attained full marriageable age she was entrusted to a husband; she served him as her lord, but she made it her business to win him for you by preaching you to him through her way of life, for by her conduct you made her beautiful in her husband's eyes, as a person to be respected, loved and admired. So gently did she put up with his marital infidelities that no quarrel ever broke out between them on this score, for she looked to you to show him mercy, knowing that once he came to believe he would become chaste. . . .

Eventually she won even her husband for you, toward the end of his life on earth, and she had no cause for complaint about anything in him after his baptism that she had tolerated in him while unbaptized. Moreover she was the servant of your servants. Every one of them who knew her found ample reason to praise, honor and love you as he sensed your presence in her heart, attested by the fruits of her holy way of life. She had been married to one man only, had loyally repaid what she owed to her parents, had governed her household in the fear of God, and earned a reputation for good works. She had brought up children, in labor anew with them each time she saw them straying away from you.[1]

---

1. Augustine, *Confessions*, 185, 187.

We come to the final chapter of our survey of the New Testament in relation to the ethics of evangelism. Beyond the Gospels and the Acts of the apostles, Paul's Epistles take up a good portion of the New Testament. But the apostles Peter and John also wrote epistles, as well as James, the half-brother of Jesus.[2] These epistles are often referred to as "General Epistles," because they are not addressed to specific churches as are the letters of Paul. They are also referred to as "Catholic Epistles," because they were accepted as canonical by the entire early church, in contrast to many other letters that were not recognized in this way. In addition, there is Jude, and the book of Hebrews whose authorship is in dispute. Then of course there is the final book of Revelation, also traditionally thought to be authored by the apostle John. These remaining writings of the New Testament contain fewer references to the ethics of evangelism. But there are a few significant treatments of the topic in some of these writings.

PETER'S FIRST EPISTLE

Although there has been some dispute about the authorship of 1 Peter, it is generally agreed that the author is Peter, a disciple of Jesus Christ, and one of the apostles. There is also general agreement that the first epistle was written about AD 62–64, to Christians scattered in Asia Minor (present-day Turkey). A dominant theme of the first epistle is encouraging Christians in the face of persecution.[3] Peter reminds Christians of their status as "aliens and strangers in the world," so it should come as no surprise that they are suffering for their faith.[4]

Another central theme of the first letter of Peter has to do with ethics. Peter repeatedly urges his readers to live good lives and to continue doing good deeds.[5] It is not easy to do so within an hostile environment. Indeed, lat-

---

2. I am here assuming the traditional interpretation of the authorship of these books, even though these are disputed by some scholars.

3. For references to persecution and suffering in 1 Peter, see 1:6; 2:12; 3:9, 14, 16–18; 4:1, 12–19; 5:10. Some writers have suggested this epistle was written immediately after the first outbreak of intense persecution by Nero in the 60s AD. More probably, Peter is anticipating a period of increasing widespread persecution in Asia Minor, which had already begun in Rome, which is probably where Peter wrote the letter prior to his own martyrdom. Many scholars assume the reference to Babylon (5:13) is figurative for Rome. See Green, *1 Peter*, 4–11.

4. See 1 Peter 1:1, 17; 2:11.

5. See 1 Peter 2:12, 15, 20; 3:6, 11, 13, 16, 17.

er in this epistle Peter reminds his readers, who were mainly Gentile converts, of their former way of life, "living in debauchery, lust, drunkenness, orgies, carousing and detestable idolatry" (1 Pet 4:3). Peter goes on to point out their friends "think it strange that you do not plunge with them into the same flood of dissipation," and that is why "they heap abuse on you" (4:4). This in turn leads to surprise that these converts to Christianity have the courage to continue living good lives and doing good deeds, even in the face of opposition and slander. It is in this context that Peter gives us one of the most explicit exhortations regarding ethical evangelism found in the New Testament:

> Who is going to harm you if you are eager to do good? But even if you should suffer for what is right, you are blessed. Do not fear what they fear; do not be frightened. But in your hearts set apart Christ as Lord. Always be prepared to give an answer to everyone who asks you to give the reason for the hope that you have. But do this with gentleness and respect, keeping a clear conscience, so that those who speak maliciously against your good behavior in Christ may be ashamed of their slander. It is better, if it is God's will, to suffer for doing good than for doing evil. (1 Pet 3:13–17)

In the above passage Peter links the two themes we have already identified as central to this letter, suffering and doing good, with evangelism. The lifestyle of these new Christians, and the good deeds they continue to do even in the face of opposition, prompts their pagan friends to ask them why they are living the way they do. Their behavior calls for some kind of an explanation.

Peter is urging Christians, then and now, to always be ready to provide an answer to those who ask for an explanation for the hope we have. "Hope" is here probably used to refer both to the Christian hope of the resurrection and more generally to the new life Christians have in Jesus Christ.[6] Christians are always to be ready to give an answer or a defense of the gospel. The Greek word used here is *apologia*, and is usually used in the New Testament to describe a defense in a formal or courtroom context.[7] Peter, however, is not thinking of a formal courtroom scene here, but rather of the

---

6. See 1 Peter 1:3, 13, 21; 3:5. Kreider and Kreider remind us that in our contemporary culture of fear, hope is profoundly countercultural (*Worship and Mission*, 182). Indeed, perhaps evangelism is better seen as "hope-sharing" than "faith-sharing" (186).

7. See Acts 22:1; 25:16; Phil 1:7; 2 Tim 4:16; cf. Jesus' instructions to his disciples in Luke 12:11–12; 21:12–14.

give-and-take of informal social settings. "Peter sees his readers as being 'on trial' every day as they live for Christ in a pagan society."[8]

I wish to highlight three important contextual features in the above passage that bear on the ethics of evangelism. First, Peter is highlighting the power of doing what is right and doing good deeds. Earlier in the epistle, Peter introduces eschatological considerations to underscore the power of exemplary living. "Live such good lives among the pagans that, though they accuse you of doing wrong, they may see your good deeds and glorify God on the day he visits us."[9] Peter may also have in mind Jesus' words in the Sermon on the Mount. "[L]et your light shine before men, that they may see your good deeds and praise your Father in heaven."[10] The early church followed these admonitions. Indeed, as various studies of the growth of early Christianity have shown, by AD 303, when the "Great Persecution" began, at least 10 percent of the whole Roman Empire had become Christian, and Christians probably were a majority in the major cities of the empire.[11] And this happened despite disincentives, the scorn of the powerful, and waves of intense persecutions. Indeed, the post-apostolic church didn't have evangelism programs and their worship services were largely closed to the public because of persecution. The church grew because there was something deeply attractive about the early Christian movement.[12]

There is a second thing to note about Peter's description of evangelism. Peter is deliberately highlighting a connection between doing good and evangelism. People are asking Christians for an explanation as to why they live the way they do.[13] Evangelism as verbal proclamation grows out of what various writers have called "lifestyle evangelism" or "evangelism by

---

8. Green, *1 Peter*, 117.

9. 1 Pet 2:12. Ewert draws attention to the unusual verb "to see" (*epopteuo*) which speaks of an observation over a period of time. The reference to "the day of visitation" (RSV) may be understood eschatologically, but it may also refer to the day when the unbeliever is converted (Ewert, "Lifestyle Evangelism," 23).

10. Matt 5:16. Jesus' and Peter's words also reflect the Old Testament image of the people of God being a light to the nations, so attractive that people from all nations stream to the mountain of the Lord to be taught the ways of the Lord (Isa 2:2–3; see chap. 2, pp. 31–32).

11. Stark, *Triumph of Christianity*, 147. Stark estimates Christianity grew at the rate of 3.4 percent a year in the first three centuries of the church (164).

12. Kreider, *Change of Conversion*, chap. 2, "The Intriguing Attraction of Early Christianity." On the attractiveness of early Christians, see also Stark, *Triumph of Christianity*, chapters 6 & 7.

13. Paul would seem to be making this same point when he highlights the importance of knowing "how to answer everyone" (Col 4:6).

attraction."[14] While I believe such expressions are misleading, there is still something to be said for using them. Peter is calling for evangelism that is backed by an exemplary lifestyle and good deeds. There needs to be a match between word and deed. The proclamation of the gospel needs to be done by good people who specialize in doing good.[15] Ethical evangelism grows out of personal integrity. So, while "evangelism by attraction" and "lifestyle evangelism" aren't really evangelism *per se* (because they do not involve verbal proclamation of the gospel), lifestyle and good deeds are nonetheless essential accompanying characteristics of ethical evangelism.

Third, Peter is envisaging evangelism as occurring in response to people asking questions. There is obviously no coercion involved here because Christians are being invited to give an explanation for their way of life. Christians are being given permission to speak. Indeed, Christians have earned the right to speak in this situation—their lives are distinctive enough to have prompted inquiries as to why they live the way they do. This highlights another important criterion of ethical evangelism. Ethical evangelism is not coercive.

I am not suggesting the above scenario represents the only way in which evangelism can avoid being coercive. Clearly there are times when the gospel can be proclaimed without the express permission of the hearers. For example, an ordinary conversation between friends might lead to a casual comment about how Jesus is significant for the Christian. This cannot be considered coercive, as conversations between friends often take unusual turns. But if a non-Christian friend should suggest he or she does not want to follow up this train of thought, it is incumbent on the Christian to drop the subject. Ethical evangelism will respect the right of those being evangelized to say they don't want to hear the gospel. To persist in sharing the good news after recipients have explicitly said they don't want to hear more is unethical.

---

14. See Ewert, "Lifestyle Evangelism." I put "lifestyle evangelism" and "evangelism by attraction" in quotation marks because good lifestyle and good deeds are not in themselves evangelism, given my definition of evangelism as verbal proclamation (see chap. 1, p. 17.

15. North African apologist Minucius Felix illustrates this point when he highlights the fact that in the third century, it was the Christians' chaste lives that spoke to a need in contemporary culture, encouraging people to investigate Christianity. His famous statement that "beauty of life encourages . . . strangers to join the ranks," had to do with Christians' reputation for sexual discipline, which he saw as having implications for church growth (quoted in Kreider, *Patient Ferment of the Early Church*, 101–2, 123).

RESPONDING TO QUESTIONS ETHICALLY

Peter goes on to identify three important characteristics of evangelism that grow out of the exemplary lives and good deeds of Christians. Here he is addressing the question of how we should speak, once we have been invited to give an answer for the hope we have. First, speaking about your faith should be done "with gentleness" (3:16). The Greek word used here is *prautēs*, which also has the connotation of meekness. Meekness is "the quality of not being overly impressed by a sense of one's self-importance, instead committing one's life and sense of justice to God."[16] This exhortation needs to be understood in context. Peter is addressing Christians who are being slandered and persecuted for their faith. The invitation to give a reason for the hope you have probably has a cutting edge to it. The person inviting you to speak may in fact have been speaking maliciously against you behind your back. You may even be aware of this. And that is why it is so important to respond with gentleness or meekness. Your gentle and considerate response might even lead them to become "ashamed of their slander" against you. Of course, Peter has in mind the example of Jesus Christ, who was abused, but did not return abuse. Instead he entrusted himself to the one who judges justly (2:23). We need to do likewise.

Gentleness and meekness go hand in hand with humility.[17] Ethical evangelism speaks with gentleness and humility. No defensiveness. No bombastic, self-righteous proclamation of the gospel. No arrogant attacking of the other person's beliefs. But a gentle, kind, and sensitive response to the deeper hunger that might lie behind the invitation to give a reason for the hope within you. Here it needs to be stressed that this does not mean we cannot express our disagreement with what the other person believes. This is the myth that is perpetuated by contemporary relativism. Disagreement can be stated respectfully. Indeed, giving reasons for our disagreeing with someone can be the highest respect one can show to the other person. But it matters a lot how this disagreement is expressed. It can and should be expressed with gentleness and with humility.

Peter goes on to highlight a second component of ethical evangelism. When you are invited to give a defense of the hope within you, you should do so with "respect" (3:16). The NIV use of the word "respect" begs the question as to who is to be respected. The context would suggest it is Christ who is to be respected. Hence the NRSV use of the word "reverence" which

---

16. Green, *1 Peter*, 118.

17. Peter specifically addresses the importance of humility later in his epistle (1 Pet 5:5–6).

is probably a better translation of the Greek *phobos* in this context.[18] Reverence speaks to one's basic attitude toward God. Peter has in fact given us a description of what reverence means in the preface to the statement under consideration: "But in your hearts set apart Christ as Lord" (3:15). Here we have a fundamental confession of Christian faith, "Christ is Lord," combined with an inward attitude of respectful awe of Christ as Lord. So, it is respect for Christ as Lord that is to accompany our giving an answer to those who ask us to provide a reason for the hope that we have.

Ethical evangelism speaks out of a sense of reverence for the Christ who has become Lord of the Christian's life. It is this reverence for Christ that helps the Christian to respond to hostile questioning without fear. Indeed, just prior to the verses under consideration, Peter addresses the problem of feeling frightened and intimidated (3:19). "It is this 'holy fear' or respectful awe, focused on Christ, that drives out other fears, and makes possible an honest and effective response to interrogation."[19] Reverence for Christ will also ensure we do evangelism in an ethical manner.

Finally, Peter links witnessing to our faith with "keeping a clear conscience" (3:16). A few verses later, Peter talks of "the pledge of a good conscience toward God" (3:21). What he has in mind here is when we give witness to our faith in a hostile environment where we are being maligned for good conduct, we will need to keep focused on pleasing God to whom we are ultimately accountable. "A clear conscience gives stamina and faithfulness to a Christian's witness. He knows that the malicious slander that he hears is untrue. He can therefore wait patiently for the truth to win out. His detractors may be ashamed sooner than he thinks."[20] What this speaks to also is the importance of integrity in our witness, as was highlighted earlier. "The witness of a good conscience is crucial for the witness of a good word."[21] Ethical evangelism must be backed up with a life lived in obedience to God. There must be integrity in our lives which will then translate into power to witness effectively.

I return again to the overall context of this exhortation for ethical witness. As we have already seen, Peter is trying to help Christians in Asia Minor who are facing suffering and persecution. Again and again, he reminds them of the sufferings of Christ. Indeed, Christ is seen as an example of how

---

18. The word *phobos* is used differently in 1 Peter 3:14, where it refers to the fear of men. Peter is here drawing on Isaiah 8:12–13 where it is very clear the fear of the Lord Almighty is an antidote to fearing what men fear. Hence Peter's admonition not to fear (*phobos*) those who are causing us to suffer for doing what is right.

19. Michaels, *1 Peter*, 187.

20. Clowny, *Message of 1 Peter*, 152–53.

21. Ibid., 152.

we should respond to unjust treatment. "When they hurled their insults at him, he did not retaliate; when he suffered he made no threats. Instead he entrusted himself to him who judges justly" (2:23). Christ loved even the enemies of the gospel. Therefore, "rid yourselves of all malice," Peter urges his readers earlier in his epistle (2:1). "Do not repay evil with evil, or insult with insult, but with blessing" (3:9). And then this generalization: "Show proper respect to everyone" (2:17). Christians, of all people, should know the importance of showing proper respect to all persons, even enemies of the gospel. After all, each person is created in the image of God. God loves each and every individual, even those who are antagonistic to the gospel. Ethical evangelism upholds the dignity and respect of those being evangelized. We are to love enemies of the gospel.

CASE STUDIES

The story of Augustine's mother at the beginning of this chapter gives us an interesting and concrete application of the general guidelines for ethical evangelism we have just considered. Peter speaks to a similar situation earlier in his first epistle, within the context of a discussion of household codes.[22] It follows the counsel given to slaves to accept the authority of their masters, even those who are harsh (2:18–20), which in turn is followed by a general call not to return evil for evil (3:9). Indeed, these exhortations color the entire discussion of the household codes. In the example under consideration, Peter is addressing a very particular problem, a marriage in which the wife has become a believer, and the husband is still an unbeliever.[23] Unfortunately, this specific context is often not taken into account, leading to a misinterpretation and misuse of this passage:

> Wives, in the same way be submissive to your husbands so that, if any of them do not believe the word, they may be won over without talk by the behavior of their wives, when they see the purity and reverence of your lives. (1 Pet 3:1)[24]

22. These household codes (*Haustafeln*) are also found in several of Paul's Epistles, and so would seem to be part of the standard catechism of new Christians in the early church. See Eph 6:1–9; Col 3:18—4:1.

23. The description of unbelieving husbands as those "who do not believe the word," occurs elsewhere in Peter's Epistle. For example, the same expression is used in 2:8 where those who disbelieve are portrayed as persons who reject the Messiah (cf. 3:20; 4:17). "This suggests not simply 'unbeliever,' but persons who have actively rejected the gospel and, in the context of 1 Peter, would likely be numbered among those casting aspersion on followers of Jesus" (Green, *1 Peter*, 94).

24. Paul addresses a very similar situation in 1 Cor 7:12–16, though interestingly

The opening phrase "in the same way" has a number of possible antecedents.[25] It could refer to following the example of Christ in suffering, which immediately precedes these verses (2:21–25). Or it might be linked to Peter's earlier advice to slaves to accept the authority of their masters (2:18). Peter is addressing a cultural context in which slavery was accepted, and also where it was expected that wives would accept the religious authority of their husbands and worship the gods of their husbands.[26]

So how does a Christian wife exercise her new freedom in Christ within the context of a religiously mixed marriage? Verbal witness would probably not be tolerated and would in any case be counterproductive. Peter counsels Christian wives not to give "way to fear" (3:6), but to remain in their marriages and to accept their husbands' authority, although not to the extent of renouncing their Christian faith. Instead, they are to try to win over their husbands by living lives of purity and reverent obedience to Christ as Lord. Peter also warns against extravagant outward adornment. Instead, Christian wives should focus on the inner self and cultivate "the unfading beauty of a gentle and quiet spirit" (3:4). Here Peter uses some of the same words we have already encountered in his general advice about defending the faith within the context of a hostile environment. Speak with gentleness and humility and reverence.

Peter's exhortation to wives clearly recognizes that unbelieving husbands "may be won over without talk." He may be "countering a temptation to use argument or nagging or a manipulative method of persuasion to bring about a change in their husbands."[27] Instead, they are counseled to live chastely and faithfully, doing what is right without fear. This does not entail that verbal proclamation of the gospel is unimportant. It is just that sometimes open declaration of faith is not possible, and then the focus should be on exemplary character and deed, not words. Ethical evangelism is sensitive to situations where open proclamation of the gospel is inadvisable.

---

he includes the scenario of either the husband or the wife becoming a believer and the other partner not being a believer. He encourages the believing partner to keep the marriage intact, if possible. He suggests that the unbelieving partner is "sanctified" in some way by the believing partner. Paul concludes with an ambiguous question: "How do you know, wife, whether you will save your husband? Or, how do you know, husband, whether you will save your wife?"

25. Green, *1 Peter*, 91.

26. In his "Advice to Bride and Groom," Plutarch wrote: "A woman ought not to make friends of her own, but to enjoy her husband's friends in common with him. The gods are the first and most important friends. Hence, it is becoming for a wife to worship and to know only the gods that her husband believes in, and to shut the door tight upon all strange rituals and outlandish superstitions" (quoted in Green, *1 Peter*, 92).

27. Waltner, *1 Peter* 96.

Peter's advice might have more general application. Open witness and proclamation of the gospel is not always possible. Institutions and governments sometimes prohibit explicit evangelism. How should Christians respond to such edicts? There may be a place for submission to such authority. That would seem to be the advice Peter gives to Christian wives within the context of the institution of a marriage. Similar advice is found earlier in Peter's Epistle where he addresses the relation of citizens to government: "Submit yourselves for the Lord's sake to every authority instituted among men," including kings and governors (2:13). Here again this is combined with a call to do good, which might have the effect of silencing the ignorant talk of foolish men (2:15). Of course, this advice needs to be balanced with the example of Peter and the apostles who at times did disobey the authorities who tried to stop them from proclaiming the gospel.[28] There is a tension here that is not easily resolved. But again, it would seem ethical evangelism sometimes submits to authorities that make open proclamation of the gospel impossible.

PETER'S SECOND EPISTLE

Peter touches on the subject of ethical evangelism again in his second epistle. Peter's second epistle is a short homily encouraging Christian growth, but set within a context of threats to Christian stability from a type of destructive and heretical teaching (2 Pet 2:1). Peter recognizes he will soon be leaving the earthly scene (1:13, 15), so there is urgency in his warnings to guard against doctrinal and moral perversions that are infiltrating the churches. Although the congregations "are firmly established in the truth," Peter wants to refresh their memory concerning the authentic message of the apostles and prophets (1:12; 3:1). It is within this context that Peter highlights another point about ethical evangelism:

> We did not follow cleverly invented stories when we told you about the power and coming of our Lord Jesus Christ, but we were eyewitnesses of his majesty. (2 Pet 1:16)

Peter then recounts the events on the "sacred mountain," the Mount of Transfiguration, where he and James and John saw Jesus in a breathtaking display of his majesty, and then heard a voice from heaven affirming him as the very Son of God (1:17–18). This experience confirmed for the apostles the witness of "the word of the prophets," or the Old Testament, which pointed to Jesus' coming as "a light shining in a dark place" (1:19–21).

---

28. See Acts 5:29. See my treatment of this defiance of authorities in chapter 4, pages 70–73.

The false teachers in the church at the time were accusing Peter and his fellow apostles of being quack doctors, serving up cleverly invented stories or "myths."[29] Peter counters this by reminding his readers that he and the apostles were in fact accurately reporting what they had seen and heard. Peter also asserts the apostolic teaching is in continuity with that of the Old Testament prophets (1:19), whose words were supernaturally inspired by the Spirit of God (1:20–21). This defense of the apostles and prophets as authentic teachers is rounded out by a direct attack on false teachers. Indeed, it is these false teachers who are in fact exploiting their listeners "with stories they have made up."[30] Given this overall emphasis on truth and being authentic witnesses, I think it is fair to apply all this to evangelism.

Ethical evangelism is truthful. It seeks to remain faithful to the gospel. It does not fabricate truth, nor does it embellish truth. It is very careful not to distort the gospel. In contrast to the false teachers who are "bold and arrogant" (2:10), Jesus' followers bear humble witness to the truth they have received as a precious gift. Like the prophets of the Old Testament, we cannot but speak of the message God himself has given to us.

JOHN'S FIRST EPISTLE

Most scholars agree that 1 John was written by the Apostle John who was also the author of the fourth gospel. After Jesus' resurrection, John remained in Jerusalem for some time and was one of the pillars of the church (Gal 2:9). John followed many other Christians who fled from Jerusalem in the mid-60s AD because of persecution under the Roman emperor Nero after the destruction of Jerusalem. John probably fled to Ephesus and it is here where he wrote 1 John, an epistle sent to the congregations of Asia Minor which were under the apostle's special care. The epistle was written towards the end of the first century. A key concern of this epistle is to combat false teaching, generally identified as gnosticism, together with its resulting distorted behavior.

The letter opens with an abrupt summary statement of the gospel message that John and his fellow apostles were proclaiming. Although the letter

---

29. The Greek word for "stories" is *mythoi*. This term always occurs in the plural in the New Testament, and generally has a pejorative connotation (see also 1 Tim 1:4; 4:7; 2 Tim 4:4; Tit 1:14). "'Myths' were far-fetched stories usually about the gods, and the plural form of the term here is meant to contrast with the singularity of the gospel." Harvey & Towner, *2 Peter & Jude*, 61.

30. 2 Pet 2:1–3. The Greek words used for "made-up stories" is *plastois logois*, and implies deceit, pretense, forgery and so suggest the intention to cheat, lie and deceive (Harvey and Towner, *2 Peter & Jude*, 80).

is addressed to churches in Asia Minor, I think it is fair to extrapolate John's comments and apply them to the context of evangelism.

> That which was from the beginning, which we have heard, which we have seen with our eyes, which we have looked at and our hands have touched—this we proclaim concerning the Word of life. The life appeared, we have seen it and testify to it, and we proclaim to you the eternal life, which was with the Father and has appeared to us. We proclaim to you what we have seen and heard, so that you also may have fellowship with us. (1 John 1:1–3)

The above passage contains a curious mix of neutral pronouns ("that which") and a masculine noun translated "Word" (*logos*). Clearly John's reference to "the Word of life" which was "from the beginning" echoes the beginning of the Gospel of John. Here John moves easily from the Word made flesh to the *message* about the Word made flesh, and hence the mix of neutral and masculine pronouns.

What might this introduction to the letter say about the ethics of evangelism? John, like Peter, is clearly concerned about establishing the credentials of the apostles as eyewitnesses to the life, death, and resurrection of Jesus. What they proclaimed was true because they were proclaiming what they had seen and heard. Ethical evangelism is careful about proclaiming the truth. John is equally concerned about believers holding on to the teaching of the apostles and not being misled by false teachers (2:24–27; 4:1–6). Again by extrapolation we can assume John would be concerned about all Christians speaking the truth as they bear witness to the gospel of Jesus Christ. John is also concerned about new believers growing in the faith and remaining true to their new-found faith. Ethical evangelism cares about what happens to new believers after conversion.

REVELATION

The final book of the Bible presents an interpretive challenge. There are preachers—past and present—who interpret Revelation as giving us a blueprint for the end of history. I'm not sure this preoccupation with mapping out the end times is always that healthy. It can lead to escapism and endless speculation, but there is also a danger we will overreact to these excesses and neglect the book of Revelation. Perhaps there is another way of reading the book beyond its alleged purpose of telling us about the "furniture of heaven and the temperature of hell."[31] Eugene Peterson's delightful treatment of the

---

31. Reinhold Niebuhr, quoted in Peterson, *Reversed Thunder,* xiii.

book of Revelation, entitled *Reversed Thunder*, argues the real purpose of Revelation is to fire the imagination of ordinary believers so they will be able to live the Christian life in the thick and thin of everyday affairs.[32]

We need to remember that the traditionally assumed author of Revelation—John, the apostle—had been a pastor in the early church. He wrote the book of Revelation near the end of his life after he had been exiled on the island of Patmos. He couldn't forget his many parishioners in various churches in which he had ministered, people who were trying to make sense out of the confusion of life, people who were suffering and were being persecuted. John was also a poet, and poetry is not the language of objective explanation but the language of imagination, according to Peterson.[33] And so John as pastor and poet is trying to help Christians, then and now, to cope with everyday life and to give us a vision that will help us to live life more fully, fruitfully, and hopefully.

Interestingly, this pastor/poet touches on evangelism in a few places in the book of Revelation. Given these specific references, and given the overall purpose of Revelation, I think it is fair to ask whether John's visions might have some relevance to the ethics of evangelism.[34] The first theme that emerges is the connection between evangelism and suffering. Already in the first chapter John introduces himself as "your brother and companion in the suffering and kingdom and patient endurance that are ours in Jesus" (Rev 1:9). John then informs us he is in exile on the island of Patmos "because of the word of God and the testimony of Jesus" (1:9). In other words, John is in exile because he has been a witness to Jesus Christ. Similarly, Antipas, from the church in Pergamum, lost his life because he was "my faithful witness" (2:13). It is dangerous to tell the truth about God. In the early church there was a direct link between being a witness and being a martyr.[35]

A few chapters later, after a vision of the Lamb who was slain (chapter 5), John reviews various kinds of evil that are part of history (chapter 6). He does this by using the figurative language of the Lamb opening seven seals:

> When he opened the fifth seal, I saw under the altar the souls of those who had been slain because of the word of God and the

---

32. Ibid., xi–xii.

33. Ibid., 5.

34. Peterson describes the relevance of the book of Revelation to evangelism in this way: "The contribution of the Revelation to the work of witness is not instruction, telling us how to make a coherent apology of the faith, but imagination, strengthening the spirit with images that keep us 'steadfast, immovable, always abounding in the work of the Lord' (1 Cor. 15:58)." Ibid., 112. The appeal to imagination might also have some relevance for apologetics. See Ordway, *Apologetics and the Christian Imagination*.

35. Peterson, *Reversed Thunder*, 102.

testimony they had maintained. They called out in a loud voice, "How long, Sovereign Lord, holy and true, until you judge the inhabitants of the earth and avenge our blood. Then each of them was given a white robe, and they were told to wait a little longer, until the number of their fellow servants and brothers who were to be killed as they had been was completed. (Rev 6:9–11)

You have here the cry of martyrs, the cry of those who have proclaimed the word of God, of those who have given testimony to the good news of Jesus Christ. They cry to their Sovereign Lord for judgment. Interestingly, this cry for justice is not condemned. Instead, each of these martyrs is given a white robe, a symbol of that which is right and good. And then they are told to be patient. They need to wait until history delivers the full number of Christian martyrs.

We have here another important lesson concerning evangelism, a lesson we have already encountered in other books of the New Testament. Ethical evangelism is prepared to experience suffering, and sometimes even martyrdom. What John's visions do is help Christians, then and now, cope with the suffering that comes with bearing testimony to Jesus Christ. John not only names the evils of history like persecution, but he also gives them meaning.[36] He helps us to reframe these evils in an imaginative picture that has God still firmly in control. Each of these martyrs is also given dignity by being clothed in a white robe. Indeed, in the following chapter, there is "a great multitude, from every nation, tribe, people and language, standing before the throne in front of the Lamb," crying in a loud voice, "Salvation belongs to our God, who sits on the throne" (7:9–10). They are joined by angels standing around the throne who fall down and worship God (7:11–12). And finally there is the promise of a time where suffering and persecution will be no more (7:13–17). Here indeed is an answer to the many who suffer because they are engaged in evangelism.

The reference to people from every nation, tribe, people, and language is repeated later in Revelation, and again is associated specifically with evangelism. Here we are introduced to an angelic evangelist.

Then I saw another angel flying in midair, and he had the eternal gospel to proclaim to those who live on the earth—to every nation, tribe, language and people. He said in a loud voice, "Fear God and give him glory, because the hour of his judgment has come. Worship him who made the heavens, the earth, the sea and the springs of water." (Rev 14:6–7)

---

36. Ibid., chap. 6.

This vision seems to suggest Christians need a bit of angelic help in the task of evangelism! The gospel proclaimed in this case is reduced to a bare minimum, perhaps because this vision comes in the middle of scenes of political conflict and judgment. Different circumstances call for different presentations of the gospel. We also learn that evangelism is meant to be universal in scope. The eternal gospel needs to be proclaimed to every nation, tribe, language, and people. Of course, all of us have limited influence. We need to be faithful in our sphere of influence, trusting that others are similarly faithful in their spheres of influence, but the aspiration in evangelism should always be to reach everyone with the gospel. To limit evangelism to just "our" people, or "our" tribe, or to limit evangelism just to growing "our" church is unethical.

There is a hint of another lesson to be learned from the particularities identified in describing the scope of the gospel. The gospel message needs to be translated into the language of every tribe and people in the world. The gospel message needs to be contextualized. Just as Paul speaking to philosophers on Mars Hill adjusted the gospel message to his audience of Stoics and Epicurean philosophers, so this angel too is adjusting the language of the eternal gospel to a context of political conflict and judgment. We too need to ensure the gospel is presented in such a way that the people we are talking to will really understand it and grasp how it might challenge the assumptions underlying their current worldview. This isn't just a strategy to ensure we are being understood. This is communication that really loves the other person. Loving communication is another characteristic of ethical evangelism.

There is another underlying theme in the passages I have underscored so far in Revelation—worship. Worship of the Lamb who was slain. Acknowledging the Sovereign Lord, holy and true. Worship of the Creator God. Indeed, Revelation begins with a description of Jesus Christ as "a Son of Man," a commanding, redeeming and glorious figure (Rev 1:12–16).[37] He is not "a pale Galilean, but a towering and furious figure who will not be managed."[38] So spectacular is this vision of Jesus that it causes John to fall at his feet in worshipful fear (1:17). It is this Jesus who is worshipped by elders and angels and living creatures, and finally even by those who have rejected him. All will finally proclaim him, "King of Kings and Lord of Lords" (19:16). Interspersed in all these scenes of worship are accounts of Christians and angels bearing testimony to Jesus Christ. We have here a

---

37. The phrase "son of man" originates in the vision of Daniel (7:13–14), and should be seen as "the most pretentious piece of self-description that any man in the ancient East could possibly have used" (Ethelbert Stauffer, quoted in Peterson, *Reversed Thunder*, 197n3).

38. Tom Howard, quoted in Peterson, *Reversed Thunder*, 29.

lesson we have already alluded to earlier in this chapter. Ethical evangelism grows out of respect and reverence for Jesus Christ as Lord.

I conclude with a picture of Christ, "the faithful and true witness, the ruler of God's creation," as described in one of the letters to the seven churches, early in the book of Revelation (3:14–22). The church at Laodicea is described as being lukewarm, and this would seem to be the worst condition possible. It is worse even than Sardis, where there is at least a glimmer of hope. Nothing positive is said about the church at Laodicea. But even this church is given a chance in the oft-repeated words of invitation:

> I stand at the door and knock. If anyone hears my voice and opens the door, I will go in and eat with him, and he with me. (Rev 3:20)

While these words are said within the context of rebuking a church, I think it is fair to apply them also to the context of evangelism. Christ is standing patiently at the door of each person's heart, knocking. It is only if a person opens the door that Christ will enter and a relationship with the eternal ruler of all creation can begin. Ethical evangelism waits patiently for people to freely respond to the gospel message. It is not coercive.

Chapter 7

Summary of Biblical Analysis: Guidelines for Ethical Evangelism

A group of dedicated Christians in a major city in America are serious about evangelism.[1] *They take as their model Jesus and the apostles who proclaimed the gospel in the public square. They sponsor training sessions which prepare Christians to do open-air and one-to-one evangelism on the streets and parks, and at festivals and parades in the city. Occasionally they do open-air preaching in front of a local license office in their city. The doors of the license office opens at 8:00 am, but a line begins to form around 7:15 am. Members of the evangelistic group preach to those who are in line and are waiting for the doors to open.*

They always preach in pairs: one person does the Bad News and preaches through the Ten Commandments, and the other person does the Good News and shares the gospel. They usually have a small step ladder that each person climbs to be better seen and heard. A sympathetic observer writes: "These guys are very courageous, and not afraid to talk about sin, death, judgment, and hell, terms which are increasingly falling out of vogue here in the States. They do not insult people and generally shy away from 'decisional' kinds of presentations. They do the preaching, and then afterward pass out Bibles, Gospels of John, and tracts."

WE HAVE COME TO the end of my survey of the New Testament canon. So far, my study has been inductive in nature. I have examined the

---

1. The details of this story are drawn from the group's website and from correspondence with a member of this group who has requested anonymity.

books of the New Testament to see if they have anything to say about the ethics of evangelism. It is now time to summarize what we have learned.

This chapter will attempt to synthesize my findings and also begin to apply them to the contemporary world. In order to do so, I will obviously have to condense the material covered so far. Drawing on Richard Hays, I argued in chapter 2 that there are a variety of modes of ethical discourse in the New Testament—rules, broader principles, stories, and the larger narrative or worldview of the Bible. In order to summarize the lessons of the previous chapters, it will be necessary to reduce this multi-level approach to the ethics of evangelism to a more singular focus. I will be transforming the lessons learned into guidelines, closer to the rules and broader principles of Hays's analysis. Obviously this takes away from the richness of the earlier treatment in the previous chapters which recognized different modes of ethical exhortation in the New Testament, but this is the nature of a summative chapter. Summaries have to simplify and will of necessity involve a kind of reductionism.

I will summarize what we have done so far by proposing thirty guidelines for ethical evangelism as found in the Bible, mainly the New Testament. I will organize these under headings that will hopefully make this overall summary more useful. At the same time, I will be collating the material of the previous chapters so as to avoid obvious repetition. Some repetition will remain when some of the lessons fall under several headings, or when there are slightly differing nuances within related guidelines. Each set of guidelines under a heading will be prefaced with an introduction. Given the summary nature of this chapter, there will be little by way of providing biblical references for the guidelines under consideration. The reader will need to return to the previous chapters to find detailed referencing and justification for the ethical guidelines being summarized here. For exact page references, the reader might also look up the key concepts of each guideline in the index.

A few qualifications are in order before I review the thirty guidelines for ethical evangelism that have emerged from our study. First, I use the label "guidelines" deliberately because I want to avoid these being read as ethical rules. There are dangers in treating ethics as though it is just a bunch of rules. It can lead to legalism. Abstract rules also fail to take into account context and circumstances. Besides, ethics cannot be exhaustively described in terms of rules. Ethics also includes dispositions and character.

So how do ethical guidelines differ from ethical rules? Ethical guidelines aren't as crisp and well-defined as rules. As will be seen in this chapter, the guidelines for ethical evangelism are most often not stated in short sentences, giving specific commands. Guidelines are rough around the edges. Guidelines might be described as "soft rules." They acknowledge the messiness of real life and might even acknowledge exceptions. They require some thinking when applied to concrete situations. I would hasten to add there are limits to guideline-oriented ethics as well, but despite these limits, I believe articulating some guidelines for ethical evangelism still has some merit. People need guidelines to help them discern what is ethical.

Secondly, it should be noted the guidelines I am proposing vary in degrees of generality. In order to solve complex moral problems, we need a gradation of moral principles, ranging from the very broad and abstract to the more specific and concrete.

Thirdly, no matter how specific the guidelines, this approach to the ethics of evangelism will remain somewhat abstract. In the end, ethical guidelines need to be contextualized. It is impossible to take into account all the unique features of concrete situations in everyday life. There will always, therefore, be a need for judgment in applying the ethical guidelines I am proposing. Indeed, in the New Testament, there are repeated calls for judgment and discernment, even though some ethical rules and principles are given to us by the various writers.[2] At the same time, we must avoid leaving it all up to individual judgment, and we must also avoid staying at a level of generality that will be of little help to the individual decision-maker.

A. FOUNDATIONAL GUIDELINES

I begin my summary by looking at five foundational guidelines for ethical evangelism. They are so named because they grow out of the very foundations of biblical or New Testament ethics. As such, they provide the foundation for the rest of the guidelines in this chapter.[3] These are the most important guidelines to be considered. They are also broad in scope, but even though these guidelines are rather general and abstract it will be seen they still carry some ethical punch.

In chapter 2, we began our biblical analysis of the ethics of evangelism by looking at the narrative of the Bible as a whole. The biblical narrative starts with creation. God created all things. God also ordered all of creation. The foundation of biblical ethics is grounded in God's creation laws

---

2. See, for example, Phil 1:9–11; Rom 12:1–2; Eph 5:8–10.

3. Jesus clearly defended a hierarchy of commandments when he described loving God with our whole being as "the greatest commandment." Loving your neighbor is like the first. "All the Law and the Prophets hang on these two commandments" (Matt 22:37–40). Paul too describes the second commandment as "summing" up the rest (Rom 13:9).

that govern all spheres of human existence, including the spheres of human interaction and evangelism. Ethical evangelism therefore starts by acknowledging God as the source of ethics.

1. God and Christ as Lord

> Ethical evangelism grows out of love, respect, and reverence for God and Christ as Lord. Evangelism becomes unethical when it fails to follows God's norms for relating to persons, and when it fails to follow the example of Jesus Christ when he proclaimed the good news of the kingdom of God.

The Gospel of John, reminiscent of the creation story, begins with "the Word" creating all things. John also tells us the Word who was made flesh is Christ, who lived for a while among us, "full of grace and truth" (John 1:14–15). Christ is the model for embodied witness. Ethical evangelism must embody grace and truth. This is why we talk about "proclamation in word and deed," or "evangelism by lifestyle."[4] I have chosen to define evangelism in terms of verbal proclamation of the good news, because this is the primary meaning given to evangelism in the New Testament. But this doesn't mean deeds or lifestyle aren't important. They are critical ingredients in ethical evangelism, as we found in our study of Jesus and the apostles. Our words must be backed up by Christian character, an exemplary lifestyle, and good deeds. Indeed, embodied witness will provide opportunities for verbal witness, as Peter reminds us (1 Pet 3:1). I wonder whether the ineffectiveness, or even the lack of evangelism in the church today is because our lives are not distinctive enough to call forth questions from our non-Christian colleagues and friends.

2. Incarnational Witness

> Ethical evangelism embodies the good news being proclaimed. Ethical evangelists are people of good character, living exemplary lives and doing good deeds. They speak and act with a clear conscience before God and man.

We are also told, in the creation story, God created man and woman in his own image. People therefore have dignity and worth. This theme also runs throughout the Scriptures, so here again we have a foundational

---

4. See chap. 1, p. 17 and n. 51, and Ewert, "Evangelism by Lifestyle."

principle for ethical evangelism. Evangelism must always be done in such a way as to protect the dignity and worth of those being evangelized.

It might seem this dignity principle is so broad that it is not useful in helping us to distinguish between ethical and unethical evangelism, but I suggest it has some teeth to it. Evangelicals would do well to pay heed to the frequent complaint heard from those whom they are trying to evangelize, namely that they feel like pawns in the evangelizing programs of churches or individuals.[5] Anthropologist and long-time Christian missionary Jacob Loewen, while acknowledging that establishing friendship with people is a positive way to develop a Christian witness, worries about this being subverted to become a "baited hook" approach to evangelism.[6] If a friendship is merely a way of luring the unsuspecting into the Christian fold, then the person being befriended is denied his or her dignity. Friendship evangelism is ethical if attempts at witnessing are spontaneous and grow naturally out of a genuine friendship. Indeed, a genuine friendship should endure even if the other person indicates clearly that he or she doesn't want to hear anything further about the Christian gospel.

3. Dignity

> Ethical evangelism is always done in such a way as to protect the dignity and worth of those being evangelized. Evangelism becomes unethical when it reduces the potential convert to the status of an object or a pawn in the evangelism program of any person, church, or church organization.

The Great Commandment is another foundational principle found in both the Old and New Testaments.[7] We are called to love God with our whole being and to love our neighbor as ourselves. Ethical evangelism is an expression of love to God and neighbor. Jesus, both in his teachings and by example, showed us what it means to love our neighbor. He healed the sick even while he was proclaiming the good news of the kingdom of God. Ethical evangelism must always be an expression of concern for the whole person. Our study of Paul also showed he was always careful to follow up his evangelistic work with pastoral care. To neglect the hard work of making

---

5. For some other examples of treating evangelism targets as pawns see Thiessen, *Ethics of Evangelism*, 162–64.

6. Loewen, *Educating Tiger*, 91–92.

7. See Deut 6:4–5; Lev 19:18; Mark 12:29–31; Gal 5:14.

disciples of new Christians is a failure in love and care. "Hit-and-run-evangelism" is simply unethical.[8]

4. Great Commandment

> Ethical evangelism is an expression of love for our neighbor. It cherishes the person being evangelized as someone loved by God. Ethical evangelism must always be an expression of concern for the whole person and all of his or her needs. To care only for the salvation of souls is unethical. Loving evangelism also entails that we engage in the hard work of helping new converts to grow and become faithful disciples of Jesus Christ.

Closely related to the Great Commandment is the Golden Rule, which Jesus describes as summing up the Law and the Prophets. "In everything, do to others what you would have them do to you" (Matt 7:12). The Golden Rule serves as a useful procedural principle to determine when evangelism is ethical. Ethical evangelism follows the Golden Rule. We need to think about how we would want others to evangelize us. This then should provide a useful guide for how we should evangelize others. Applying the Golden Rule also entails that Christians operate under the assumption that other religious groups or individuals have the right to evangelize as well. Sadly, the history of the church is littered with a refusal to extend this right to others, including atheists, Catholics, Muslims, Anabaptists, and dare I add, cults or new religious movements.[9]

5. Golden Rule

> Ethical evangelism follows the Golden Rule. Evangelize others as you yourself would like to be evangelized. The Golden Rule also entails that we protect and defend the right of others to evangelize. It is unethical to assume or work toward a monopoly in evangelism.

---

8. Thangaraj, "Evangelism Sans Proselytism," 345.

9. It is of course legitimate for Christians to object to unethical techniques used by cults to evangelize, but the rhetoric against cults often betrays another undercurrent—the assumption that it is right for Christians to evangelize, but not for cults or new religious movements. This violates the Golden Rule and is unethical. Lorne Dawson argues that our willingness to apply brainwashing theories to cults might betray a deeper polemic of denying them the very right to evangelize. Dawson, *Comprehending Cults*, 113.

B. GUIDELINES RELATING TO THE INTERFACE BETWEEN THE HUMAN AND THE DIVINE

The next set of guidelines relates to an interesting theological problem that is not easy to resolve. What is the relation between divine initiative and human effort? Paul gives us a succinct statement of the problem when in the same sentence he urges the saints at Philippi to "continue to work out your salvation with fear and trembling," and then goes on immediately to suggest "it is God who works in you to will and to act according to his good purpose" (Phil 2:12–13). Paul does not try to resolve the tension between these two claims. Nor should we. It is one of many mysteries of our Christian faith.

This same tension exists with regard to evangelism, as our survey of the New Testament has shown.[10] Jesus, before his ascension, tells the disciples to wait for the outpouring of the Holy Spirit, and at the same time he commissions them to be his witnesses. Success in evangelism is ultimately dependent on God. And yet, we as Christians are called to make every effort to find the lost and declare to them the good news of Jesus Christ. Further, as we have seen, only the Holy Spirit can open the hearts and minds of people to the truth of the gospel. And yet we as Christians should use the best tools available to "demolish arguments and every pretension that sets itself up against the knowledge of God" (2 Cor 10:4–5). Following the example of the apostles, when engaged in evangelism, we pray as though it all depends on God. And yet, we try to be faithful in doing our part in spreading the good news.

The focus of this book is on doing evangelism in an ethical manner. The human component of evangelism is being assumed. Thus, we need reminders of the divine component in evangelism.[11] This leads to three further guidelines for ethical evangelism.

6. God and Human Effort

> Ethical evangelism recognizes that ultimately it is God in Christ who calls people to himself. It recognizes the limits

---

10. For a classic treatment of the tension between God's sovereignty and human effort in evangelism, see Packer, *Evangelism and the Sovereignty of God*, especially chapters 1 & 2.

11. Bishop John V. Taylor issues this caution with respect to mission generally. "The chief actor in the historic mission of the Christian Church is the Holy Spirit. He is the director of the whole enterprise. . . . 'It all depends on me' is an attitude that is bedevilling both the practice and the theology of our mission in these days" (Taylor, *Go-between God*, 3–4).

of human effort. It doesn't try too hard. It doesn't strategize too much. It acknowledges a good harvest is ultimately God's doing. And yet it accepts human responsibility for the task of doing evangelism.

7. Holy Spirit and Conversion

Ethical evangelism recognizes the limitations of human reason, rhetoric, persuasion, and apologetics. Ultimately, success in evangelism rests on God's power and the work of the Holy Spirit to open minds and hearts to the truth of the gospel.

8. Prayer

Ethical evangelism is always accompanied by prayer and permeated with an attitude of humble dependence on God.

C. GUIDELINES RELATING TO FREEDOM AND COERCION

God created human beings with the ability to make choices. From Genesis to Revelation, we encounter challenges similar to the awesome choice God gave to the people of Israel (and to us) through Joshua, "Choose for yourselves this day whom you will serve" (Josh 24:15). Indeed, this ability to choose to obey or disobey God is central to the dignity of human beings (Guideline #A3). How this can be reconciled with the sovereignty of God is of course another mystery.

The issue of human freedom has also come to the fore in our study of the New Testament and evangelism. Again and again we have encountered some individuals who accepted the message of Jesus and the apostles, while others rejected it. Further, Jesus respected the right of individuals to accept or reject the good news that he and his disciples proclaimed. This kind of ethical sensitivity is also illustrated in Peter's first epistle, where we are encouraged to respond with gentleness when unbelievers ask us to give a reason for the hope we have. Note here that unbelievers are inviting believers to explain their faith, and so believers are being given the permission to evangelize. Responding with gentleness once again respects the freedom of the listener to either accept or reject the gospel. Ethical evangelism is careful to avoid coercion.[12]

This moral guideline seems straightforward enough. But difficulties quickly emerge when it comes to describing exactly what we mean by freedom or coercion. Vagueness surrounds these terms. Human beings aren't completely free. There are degrees of freedom and coercion. We can also identify different types of coercion—physical, emotional, psychological, sociological, and political. Evangelism that involves physical coercion is probably the easiest to deal with. Obviously, when a twelfth-century Christian crusader gave a Muslim an ultimatum to convert or die while holding a sword over him, this should be labeled as coercive evangelism. But even here, questions can be raised as to whether this is necessarily coercive. After all, there are many examples in history of persons who refused to convert even under these conditions, but such people are the exception rather than the rule. I give this example only to illustrate that the notion of coercion is not as clear-cut as we often assume. The problem of vagueness becomes even more pronounced when dealing with emotional, psychological, sociological, or political coercion. Defining what we mean by "freedom" and "coercion" is not easy and would require that we delve into the fields of philosophy, psychology, sociology, and propaganda theory. This is obviously beyond the scope of this chapter.[13] I will, however, add a word of caution: It would be unfair to criticize New Testament writers for not dealing with these questions using the insights of modern scholarship.

So far, I have been focusing on coercion generally. Jesus and the apostles also address a specific kind of coercion—the use and abuse of power. Jesus quite explicitly addresses the problem of power when he urges us not to lord it over others like the Gentiles do (Matt 20:24–28). Ethical evangelism is very sensitive to the abuse of power. We are servants, not power-brokers, when we evangelize. Ethical evangelists are very conscious of their own weakness and frailty, and their fallibility and sinfulness. We are, after all, all too human. Thus, as we have seen in chapter 5, Paul develops the theme of power in weakness.

---

12. The early church fathers frequently spoke to the issue of non-coercion. Clement of Alexandria wrote: "For God does not compel, since force is hateful to God, but He provides for those who seek." Irenaeus wrote: God works "by means of persuasion.... [God] does not use violent means to obtain what he desires." The Epistle to Diognetus states: "Compulsion is not God's way of working." Quoted in Kreider, *Patient Ferment of the Early Church*, 119.

13. I have addressed these questions in more detail in my earlier work on evangelism. See Thiessen, *Ethics of Evangelism*, chap. 4 & 7.

Here let me comment briefly on the example of evangelism given at the beginning of this chapter, as it provides a good illustration of the complexities surrounding the problem of coercion. There is much to admire about this missionary group and their approach to evangelism. They take evangelism seriously. There is surely nothing wrong with open-air preaching—Jesus and Paul did the same. Indeed, I believe Christians need to do more thinking about creative ways to do evangelism in the public square today. I appreciate that this evangelistic group doesn't work towards quick decisions, and there is follow-up in terms of literature and the giving of contact information. The one worrying element about the license office venue is they are preaching to a captive audience. Does this not involve coercion?

Here are some further comments about this evangelistic endeavor from my correspondent. "Most of the time, people don't seem to pay much attention, looking at (their) cell phones, reading etc. . . . Occasionally we get hecklers. What has concerned me the most are a few comments—not many—that they are forced to hear this while standing in line. The last time I actually did this we got seriously heckled by two folks who let it be known they did not want to hear this. One tattooed lady confronted me and said that we had no right to force this on her while she was waiting. It got so bad, that I just announced we were going to stop and go down the line and pass out literature . . . to which she responded 'now you're talking!'"

I think these comments illustrate a significant ethical problem with this approach to evangelism. The preachers are exploiting a situation in which they have a captive audience. This involves a form of coercion which is unethical. It would be quite different if this were a public space in which people would be free to leave if they didn't want to listen. There might still be people who would rather not have evangelists invade public space, but here we are dealing with another issue that is not necessarily ethical in nature.[14]

A final comment relates to the effectiveness of this approach to evangelism. My correspondent admits that the interest level of those listening was low (though some do listen). People didn't want to take time to talk while the evangelists were distributing the literature (though this might be a result of their immediate business), and he knew of few people being converted as a result of their efforts (though there may be others he just didn't know about). He also wondered how many were turned off with their approach. But, here we need to be careful—evaluating effectiveness is different from ethical evaluation. I believe we need to evaluate evangelism at both levels, but my focus in this book has to do with ethical evaluation, and

---

14. Elsewhere I distinguish between ethics and what is considered uncivil or bad etiquette. Ibid., 138–42.

here my concern with the above scenario is the problem of coercion when proclaiming the gospel to a captive audience.

The considerations of this section lead to two further important criteria for ethical evangelism. As already mentioned, vagueness surrounds the notions of freedom and coercion. The same applies to the notion of power. So, for now, we will need to be satisfied with some rough guidelines regarding coercion and power. I will deal with a specific type of coercion in chapter 10, where I treat the relation between evangelism and humanitarian aid.

9. Freedom and Coercion

> Ethical evangelism respects the freedom of those being evangelized. It doesn't insist on being heard. It avoids any kind of coercion.

10. Power in Weakness

> Ethical evangelism models itself after Jesus, coming in weakness and vulnerability. It is humble and servantlike. It avoids worldly patterns of lording it over others.

D. GUIDELINES REGARDING THE CONTENT OF EVANGELISM

If there is one ethical principle that is nearly universally accepted, it is the principle of telling the truth. Yes, there may be the occasional exception to this principle (e.g., a moral dilemma), but most of the time we should tell the truth. This ethical principle is affirmed in the Christian Scriptures. As noted in chapter 2, the principle of truth-telling is included in the Ten Commandments of the Old Testament. The importance of truth-telling is also underscored in the New Testament. As already noted in chapter 3, the notion of truth comes up repeatedly in the gospels. Clearly the ethical principle of truth-telling has implications for evangelism. Ethical evangelism is truthful. It is also careful not to speak falsely about neighbors, i.e., other religions.

We have also seen that the gospel writers and the apostles were concerned about being faithful in presenting the full truth of the gospel. For example, Luke prefaces his Gospel with a declaration of having taken great care to write an accurate and orderly account of the life of Jesus. As we have seen in our study of Acts and the Epistles, the apostles are frequently concerned about countering error and preserving the essential truths of the gospel. Ethical evangelism is therefore careful to convey the heart of the gospel—the story of the life, death, and resurrection of Jesus, as well as his teachings. Ethical evangelism includes a call to individuals to repent from sin and to change their lives to become obedient to Jesus Christ. It also includes a proclamation of the good news of the kingdom of God, where God's will is done in every sphere of human existence. It is unethical to proclaim an incomplete gospel. Of course, it would be unfair to demand that the "whole" gospel be proclaimed in every evangelistic endeavor, but I do worry about simplistic approaches to evangelism which reduce the good news to "four spiritual laws," or the "good news-bad news" approach described at the beginning of this chapter. I also worry about the gospel being reduced to a psychological panacea, where calls to conversion are presented in a "Things-go-better-with-Jesus wrapping."[15]

We have also seen that Paul is very concerned about integrity in proclaiming the gospel. He and the other apostles will have nothing to do with secret and shameful ways of doing evangelism (2 Cor 4:2). Again and again Paul declares his conscience to be clear before God and men.[16] Ethical evangelism is done with integrity. It is always transparent and open. There are no hidden agendas or hidden identities. Here let me express my concern about evangelistic endeavors that are described in misleading ways as entertainment or doing door-to-door surveys.[17]

11. Truthfulness

> Ethical evangelism is truthful. It does not fabricate or embellish the truth of the gospel. It is also careful to speak truthfully about other religions or worldviews. It does not misrepresent the religious or irreligious beliefs of others. Ethical evangelism is also careful to proclaim the whole gospel of Jesus Christ.

12. Integrity

> Ethical evangelism is done with integrity. It is always transparent and open. There are no hidden agendas or hidden identities. It does not resort to trickery or flattery. Ethical evangelists

---

15. Bosch, "Evangelism," 14–15.

16. See Acts 23:1, 9; 24:16; Rom 9:1; 2 Cor 1:12; 2 Tim 1:3; 1 Pet 3:16.

17. For a number of examples of underhandedness in advertising evangelistic events, see Thiessen, *Ethics of Evangelism*, 191, 194–95.

also guard against impure motives (see also #H—Motivational Guidelines).

E. GUIDELINES REGARDING THE DELIVERY OF CONTENT AND PERSUASION

In the previous section I have dealt with guidelines concerning the content of the gospel message. *What* we say is important, but perhaps of equal importance is *how* we say it. This distinction is made by Jesus when he sends the twelve disciples on their mission. After describing the risks involved, Jesus says, "But when they arrest you, do not worry about what to say or how to say it" (Matt 10:19). Thus we need to address not only the ethical guidelines concerning the content of evangelism, but also the ethical guidelines concerning delivery of the content of the gospel, including questions of rhetoric, persuasion, and apologetics.

We have already touched on one aspect of delivery in relation to coercion. Ethical evangelism must be sensitive to problems of the abuse of power. Instead of lording it over others, ethical evangelists adopt a servant-like attitude (Guideline #C10). Closely related to this is the biblical virtue of humility.[18] This is exemplified so well by John the Baptist, who didn't call attention to himself. As we have seen, Paul and Peter both specifically describe the task of evangelism as requiring meekness and humility. So, ethical evangelism is characterized by humility.

Evangelism, at its core, involves proclamation—telling the biblical story, especially the story of Jesus. But, as we have seen in the lives of the apostles, they did sometimes move explicitly to a more persuasive mode of speech. Significantly, this was done most often in response to invitations and questions from those outside the church. Further, when evangelism includes persuasion and apologetics, we must not forget some of the guidelines we have already considered. For example, we must not forget the limitations of human reason and argument (Guideline #B7). We have also seen that success in evangelism rests on God's power and the work of the Holy Spirit to open minds and hearts to the truths of the gospel. Persuasive ethical evangelism is therefore always accompanied by prayer and humble dependence on God. (Guideline #B8). Further, when evangelism includes persuasion and argument, it is always careful to allow for a free response on

---

18. Ps 25:9; Prov 3:34; 16:18–19; Isa 66:2; Mic 6:8; Matt 5:3; 18:2–4; John 13:1–17; Phil 2:3–11; Col 3:12; Jas 4:6.

the part of the hearer either to agree or to disagree with what is being said (Guideline #C9). We must also not forget about the principle of humility, discussed above. Persuasion and apologetics must be done in a manner that is humble and gentle and patient.[19] However, the principle of humility must not be interpreted as ruling out persuasion and even rigorous defense of the gospel, as is again illustrated in how Jesus and Paul responded to those who were objecting to the good news.

A consideration of the persuasive dimension of evangelism would be incomplete if we did not also consider the part that rhetoric and emotion play in proclamation and persuasion. There is very little said about rhetoric itself in the New Testament. Paul might be hinting at this when he describes his preaching as not involving "eloquence" or "persuasive words" (1 Cor 2:1, 4), but for the most part Paul and the apostles followed Jesus in focusing on the content of the gospel. Of course, most communication and persuasion includes some appeal to emotion. I am only objecting to the excessive or exclusive appeal to emotions in evangelism.[20] Sadly, the Christian church has all too often coupled evangelism with what one writer has labeled "emotional turbo-charging."[21] I have myself experienced lengthy emotional altar calls and appeals to fear in evangelistic crusades.[22] Then there is the mass-marketing of hell by various Christian evangelical churches in North America, first premiered in Colorado in 1995 as "Hell House."[23] Such excessive appeals to emotion in evangelism are simply unethical. Ethical evangelism focuses on the proclamation of content, not the manipulation of emotions or excessive appeals to fear.

All this leads to three rather lengthy guidelines for ethical evangelism.

13. Humility

> Ethical evangelism speaks with gentleness, meekness, and humility. Evangelism becomes unethical when it becomes arrogant, condescending, and dogmatic in the claims being made. Ethical evangelism does not quarrel or engage in loud and

---

19. See Stackhouse, *Humble Apologetics*.

20. For an analysis of the distinction between normal and excessive appeals to emotion, see Thiessen, *Ethics of Evangelism*, 90–91, 174–75. 185–87

21. Quoted in Pritchard, *Willow Creek Seeker Services*, 220.

22. The infamous fire-and-brimstone sermon delivered by American revivalist Jonathan Edwards in 1741, "Sinners in the Hands of an Angry God," is often given as an example of evangelism that makes an excessive appeal to emotions. See Thiessen, *Ethics of Evangelism*, 29, 90, 174–75.

23. For a description and an evaluation of this approach to evangelism, see Fletcher, *Preaching to Convert*, chapter 5, and Thiessen, *Ethics of Evangelism*, 174–76.

arrogant shouting of God's message. Ethical evangelism is also self-effacing. It focuses on Christ, not ourselves.

14. Persuasion and Apologetics

Ethical evangelism can include persuasion and apologetics, most appropriately when invited to do so. Persuasive evangelism is always careful to allow for a free response on the part of the hearer either to agree or disagree with what is being said. While evangelism can include a rigorous defense of the gospel, such a defense should still be done with gentleness, humility, and patience, all the while depending on the work of the Holy Spirit (see also Guideline #B7).

15. Rhetoric and Emotions

Ethical evangelism focuses on proclamation of the content of the gospel. It is careful to proclaim the essentials of the gospel, and to provide the information necessary to make a decision to become a Christian. It does not involve the manipulation of emotions or excessive appeals to fear.

F. RELATIONAL GUIDELINES

Evangelism is essentially a very personal endeavor. It involves persons relating to other persons. This gives rise to another set of ethical guidelines that govern relationships.

The first guideline is drawn from the many examples of Jesus mixing easily with tax collectors and sinners. Then there are Jesus' parables of finding the lost sheep or the lost coin or the lost son. Jesus loved people who were obviously sinners. So should we. Jesus was also very gentle with those who recognized their sinful condition. With such people he doesn't start out with judgment and criticism. "A bruised reed he will not break, and a smoldering wick he will not snuff out."[24]

---

24. Matt 12:20. This guideline might have exceptions. For example, Jonah's message in the Old Testament started with judgment. Here is one example of a tension that needs to be faced, and somehow resolved (see chap. 2, p. 24).

16. Seeking and Welcoming Sinners

> Ethical evangelism identifies with sinners and welcomes them. Indeed, it goes out of its way to find sinners and love them. It is not preoccupied with condemning those who only dimly follow the paths of justice and truth. Instead, it focuses on encouraging the feeble expressions of justice and truth that are already present. When a message of judgment is necessary, it is always followed by a call to repentance and the good news of forgiveness found in Jesus Christ.

Here we need to be careful not to over-extend the above ethical guideline. Jesus' response to self-righteous Pharisees was sometimes confrontational.[25] But, as we have seen in chapter 3, what is significant is that Jesus does not reject them entirely either. He continues to reach out to them. He accepts invitations to their homes. He even meets with Nicodemus secretly, in the dead of night. But Jesus always took care to speak the truth, even though it might make his listeners uncomfortable.[26] It becomes clear Jesus loved the Pharisees even while speaking uncomfortable truth to them.

17. Uncomfortable Truth

> Ethical evangelism does not shy away from speaking uncomfortable truth, though such truth needs to be spoken with love. This includes the proclamation of Jesus as the Way, the Truth and the Life.

I now want to introduce a relational guideline for ethical evangelism using a concept that is not part of the vocabulary of the New Testament—tolerance. I hesitate doing so for two reasons. First, there is a danger in imposing a modern category onto the biblical text. Secondly, the notion of tolerance can so easily be distorted. But I believe there is a desperate need for tolerance in today's world which seems to be dominated by a "clash of civilizations," and where even within one nation people have radically different religious beliefs and worldviews. In a world of religious pluralism, we need tolerance. I also believe ethical evangelism needs to be tolerant.

25. See, for example, Jesus' interchanges with the Pharisees when they accused him of associating with sinners, or of healing a demon-possessed man by the power of Beelzebub (Matt 9:9–13; 12:22–37). See also Jesus' parable of the Pharisee and the tax collector in prayer (Luke 18:9–14).

26. For other examples of speaking uncomfortable truth, see Jesus' repeated emphasis on the cost of following him (Matt 8:18–22; 10:21–25; 16:24–28).

What do I mean by tolerance? Unfortunately, the contemporary liberal notion of tolerance has been stretched beyond recognition.[27] Today tolerance is often understood as implying relativism. All beliefs are seen to be equally valid, and therefore any criticism of someone's belief makes you intolerant. Of course, this position is itself intolerant, and it makes genuine dialogue with people impossible. What we need is the old-fashioned notion of tolerance understood as "forbearance"—putting up with beliefs with which we disagree. This does not preclude criticism of the beliefs with which we disagree, but such criticism must be done respectfully. Above all, *the people holding beliefs* with which we disagree must be treated with love and respect.

Given this more defensible notion of tolerance as respectful forbearance, there is abundant evidence that tolerance is a biblical virtue. In the Old Testament, there are calls to love the neighbor, including the alien and the stranger.[28] Jesus and the apostles also exemplified the virtue of tolerance. They lived in a religiously pluralistic environment, a point that is all too often forgotten today.[29] And it is within this religiously pluralistic environment that they conversed with others, disagreed with others, but always did so while "speaking the truth with love," a phrase Paul uses within the context of the church, but which is surely also applicable to evangelism (Eph 4:15). Indeed, Paul uses the related notion of forbearance several times, though again within the context of the church.[30] Peter also exhorts us to "show proper respect to everyone," an exhortation found in the middle of an epistle that exhorts Christians to respond to hostility with love and gentleness when defending their faith (1 Pet 2:17). The ideal of tolerance is of course also rooted in one of the foundational guidelines we have already considered, namely treating people with dignity (Guideline #A3). I believe a reformulation of these exhortations in terms of tolerance is necessary for understanding what ethical evangelism means today.

Sadly, after the terrorist attacks of Sept. 11, 2001, some Christian evangelical leaders were at the forefront of using inflammatory language against the Islamic faith. For example, Franklin Graham is quoted as having said

---

27. For a more detailed treatment of tolerance see Thiessen, *Ethics of Evangelism*, 105–14.

28. See Ex 22:21; Lev 19:18, 33, 34; Deut 10:19.

29. Jesus, living in Palestine, will have been very much aware of Roman deities. Paul was evangelizing in cosmopolitan cities, and at times identifies other gods (e.g. Acts 17:23). See Tomko, "Missionary Challenges to the Theology of Salvation," 197.

30. The Greek word for "forbearance" is *anecho*, and occurs in Col 3:12–14; Rom 2:2–4; 15:1–2. See Davis, *Forbearance*.

that Islam is "a very evil and wicked religion."[31] Not only is this an unfair generalization but it exemplifies intolerance. How very different from Paul, who speaks respectfully and even tries to link his message to the religion of the Athenians (Acts 17:16–34). Paul's tolerance of other religions is confirmed again later in Ephesus after he and his associates are threatened by a mob, incited by tradesmen who saw their economic interests undermined by the proclamation of the Christian gospel. The city clerk, after quieting the crowd and tactfully acknowledging the importance of the temple of Artemis, reminds them that Paul and his associates "have neither robbed temples nor blasphemed our goddess" (Acts 19:37). Ethical evangelism does not blaspheme other religions. This does not preclude fair criticism, but even this must be done with love and respect.

18. Tolerance

> Ethical evangelism is tolerant. It treats *persons* holding beliefs differing from that of the evangelist with love and respect. While it does not preclude fair criticism of other religious or irreligious beliefs, it treats the same with respect, and avoids hostile attitudes or the use of insulting and abusive language against other religions and worldviews.

G. GUIDELINES FOR RESPONDING TO RESISTANCE AND REJECTION

Our study of the Gospels and Acts makes it abundantly clear that Jesus and the apostles encountered a variety of responses to their proclamation of the gospel. Some listeners became interested, some believed, some rejected the gospel, and some were openly hostile to the bearers of the good news. Those in authority also responded in various ways, sometimes inviting Jesus and the apostles to speak further about their faith, sometimes urging them to stop speaking about the gospel, sometimes using threats to put an end to their evangelistic efforts, and sometimes even resorting to killing the messenger in order to silence the message.

Our study has also revealed ethical guidelines on how to respond to these varying degrees of rejection and resistance to the gospel and its messengers. The first deals with our expectations when engaged with evangelism.

---

31. Buckley, "Onward, Christian Missionaries," 58. For some additional examples of evangelical intolerance, see Thiessen, *Ethics of Evangelism*, 112–13, 199.

Ethics doesn't only have to do with actions. Expectations can also come under ethical evaluation. Ethical evangelism expects mixed responses to the proclamation of the gospel. It accepts the possibility of resistance and rejection. There are two ethical responses to rejection. We have already dealt with the first. Ethical evangelism respects the freedom of those being evangelized (Guideline #C9). Secondly, ethical evangelism responds to rejection with gentleness, humility, grace, and love. When rejection moves on to persecution of those doing evangelism, ethical evangelism will again respond with gentleness, courage, and love. After all, we are called to love our enemies, and that includes enemies of the gospel. And, when persecution reaches intense levels that carry with them the possibility of martyrdom, ethical evangelists remember the cross of Jesus Christ, and entrust themselves to Christ, their heavenly advocate, standing at the right hand of God.

Here then are four guidelines for ethical evangelism relating to resistance, rejection, and even persecution.

19. Expectations

> Ethical evangelism expects mixed responses to the proclamation of the gospel. It accepts the possibility of rejection and resistance.

20. Gracious Acceptance of Rejection

> Ethical evangelism respects the right of those being evangelized to reject the good news, or even to refuse to listen to the proclamation of the good news. It never takes rejection personally. It responds to rejection with gentleness, humility, grace, and love.

21. Loving Enemies

> Ethical evangelists love even the enemies of the gospel.

22. Persecution

> Ethical evangelism recognizes that persecution and even martyrdom may follow evangelistic endeavors. Here ethical evangelists are inspired by the cross of Jesus Christ, accepting their own vulnerability and powerlessness. Persecution is accepted as a

> privilege, a way to share in Christ's suffering. Ethical evangelism responds to persecution with gentleness, courage, and grace. We are also called to extend forgiveness to those who persecute us.

Sometimes attempts are made to put an end to evangelism efforts via social sanctions, institutional policies, or raw political power. Our study has shown there are a variety of responses to attempts to prohibit evangelism. In chapter 6 we have seen how Peter addresses a domestic situation and exhorts wives to submit to unbelieving husbands who are strongly opposed to the gospel and who might in fact not allow for verbal witness in the home. Perhaps they "may be won over without talk," by the good behavior and winsome character of their wives (1 Pet 3:1-2). However, in chapter 4 we saw how Peter and the apostles directly challenged authorities that were trying to silence them. "We must obey God rather than men" (Acts 5:29). I would suggest there is not one single answer to social and political restrictions to evangelism. Sometimes one should defy authorities that prohibit evangelism. Sometimes open defiance might hurt gospel witness and it might be better to submit to government authorities that have legislated against evangelism. What is needed here is sensitive ethical discernment. This leads to a final guideline in this section.

23. Prohibitions against Evangelism

> Ethical evangelism will sometimes refuse to submit to social sanctions or legal prohibitions against the proclamation of the good news. At other times, it might be more appropriate to submit to authorities that make open proclamation of the gospel impossible. What is needed here is sensitive ethical and political discernment.

H. MOTIVATIONAL GUIDELINES

The issue of motivation has surfaced repeatedly in our study of the New Testament, especially in Paul's treatments of the ethics of evangelism. Ethics is not just about outward behavior. It is also concerned about why we do the things we do. Motivational guidelines can be stated both positively and negatively.

24. Primary Motivation

Ethical evangelism is motivated by our experience of God's love and mercy. It flows from a sense of gratitude for what Christ has done for us.

25. Love and Service

Ethical evangelism is outward-focused. It is motivated by faithfulness to Jesus Christ, love for and obedience to God, and love for humanity. Ethical evangelists see themselves as servants of God, Christ, and humanity.

26. Fear and Guilt

Ethical evangelism grows out of a sense of security in the grace of Jesus Christ. It is not prompted by fear. Nor is it motivated by trying to win God's favor. Ethical evangelism is also not done out of a sense of guilt.

27. Greed and Fame

Ethical evangelism is not done from impure motives such as greed and financial gain, or for the praise of men and fame.

I. GUIDELINES CONCERNING MEANS, ENDS, AND SUCCESS

Christian evangelism can be seen as beginning at Pentecost where, by the power of the Holy Spirit, the gospel was proclaimed in many languages. Ethical evangelism is universal in scope. It translates the gospel into the language of those being evangelized. In chapter 5 we saw how Paul contextualized the gospel message so it would be understood by philosophers and Jews and Gentiles. Paul saw himself as a servant of all, but there are limits to such adaptation and contextualization. The end does not justify any means in ethical evangelism, as we have seen throughout our study.

Jesus and the apostles did not seem to be preoccupied with results or success.[32] Ethical evangelism is more concerned about being faithful than about being effective. Sadly, evangelical churches in the last few decades have become very preoccupied with results, success, numbers of converts, and church growth, what with the church growth movement, seeker-sensitive services, and mass marketing.[33] But such preoccupations lead to manipulation and the engineering of conversions, and thus violate the coercion principle (Guideline #C9). The focus is on human effort and seems to leave God out of the picture (Guideline #B6).[34] Mass marketing is also based on worldly methods and worldly forms of power (Guideline #C10). A preoccupation with marketing success also fails to uphold the dignity and worth of persons (Guideline #A3). One critic sums it up: "Put through the meat grinder of market analysis, the gospel becomes a 'product,' the unchurched become 'consumers,' Christians become 'salesmen,' and the 'needs' of the unchurched become a potential tool of manipulation."[35] All this is surely not only a betrayal of the Christian gospel, but also a betrayal of ethics.

These considerations lead to three final guidelines for ethical evangelism.

28. Communication and Contextualization

> Ethical evangelism involves loving communication and is permeated by a servantlike attitude. It translates the gospel into the language and understanding of the listeners, regardless of their religious or irreligious commitments, or their cultural backgrounds. Ethical evangelism contextualizes the gospel and is careful not to impose a particular cultural expression of the gospel on other cultures. It is universal in scope.

---

32. This does not mean Jesus and the apostles or the gospel writers were not at all concerned about numbers. See, for example, Mark 2:2, 15; John 4:39, 41; Acts 2:41, 47; 4:4; 9:42; 17:12. But my point about their not being *preoccupied* with numbers still stands. See Matt 7:13-14.

33. For a careful analysis of the Church Growth Movement and its offshoot, the Church Marketing Movement, and the paradigmatic attractional worship productions shaped by this school of thought, the seeker-sensitive service, innovated by Rick Warren's Saddleback Church and Bill Hybels's Willow Creek Church, see Fletcher, *Preaching to Convert*, chapter 7. See also Pritchard, *Willow Creek Seeker Services*.

34. It should be noted Bill Hybels does at times recognize the dangers of the marketing emphasis at Willow Creek, and at one point very clearly affirms it is "God's job to do the conversion" (Quoted in Pritchard, *Willow Creek Seeker Services*, 220). Unfortunately, most everything that is done at Willow Creek would seem to suggest conversions are brought about mainly by human effort and effective marketing methods.

35. Pritchard, *Willow Creek Seeker Services*, 244.

29. Means and Ends

> The end simply does not justify any means in ethical evangelism.

30. Results and Success

> Ethical evangelism is not preoccupied with results, success, numbers of converts, or church growth. These should be seen as a by-product of ethical evangelism, not a motivating force. Ethical evangelism is even content with failure. It also does not compete with others.

Perhaps the last guideline merits some reinforcement, because all too often Christians are too preoccupied with success and results when dealing with evangelism. The late Richard John Neuhaus tells the story of a young priest, newly ordained, who had the chance to visit the legendary Archbishop Fulton J. Sheen, who lay in the hospital dying. Sheen was famed for, among other things, winning many converts to the Catholic Church. "Archbishop Sheen," Neuhaus's friend said, "I have come for your counsel. I want to be a convert-making priest like you. I've already won fifteen people to the faith. What is your advice?" Sheen pushed himself up on his elbows from his reclining position and looked Neuhaus's friend in the eye. "The first thing to do," he said, "is to stop counting."[36]

CONCLUDING OBSERVATIONS

This concludes my survey of guidelines for ethical evangelism. I want to stress again this is only one way to summarize what the New Testament says about the ethics of evangelism. Ethics is more than rules and principles and guidelines. Indeed, I believe ethics is better done by way of telling stories and ultimately must grow out of a consideration of the narrative and worldview of the Scriptures. I have provided this fuller and richer treatment of the ethics of evangelism in the New Testament in the previous chapters. I trust readers will not divorce this summary chapter from the preceding ones.

It should further be noted there is some arbitrariness in the classification of these guidelines. No doubt there will be readers who would like one or the other guideline to be highlighted or subsumed under another category. I have tried to do justice to all the lessons to be learned from our inductive study of

---

36. Neuhaus, "While We're at it," 74.

the New Testament canon, but there is obviously some subjectivity involved in assessing overlap and repetition. I trust the reader will move beyond issues of classification and the missing of nuances that could not be captured in a summary, to the essential points made under each guideline. What I hope this summary has done, at the very least, is stimulate continued discussion and reflection leading to possible modifications and revisions towards a more adequate biblical analysis of the ethics of evangelism.

PART II

Applied Topics

Chapter 8

Evangelism of Children

As in the previous chapters, I begin the first chapter of Part II of this book with a story. The story that prefaces this chapter is found in a recent collection of eleven essays written by philosophers who reflect critically on their religious upbringing.[1] A variety of mainly Christian family backgrounds are represented, and they vary in degrees of narrowness and strictness. Each of these philosophers, in one way or another, also broke free from the "restraint and oppression" of a religious upbringing that was "imposed" on them as a child.[2] What motivated the co-editors of this volume to collect these stories? They wanted to help others who were struggling to get "free of doctrinal entrapment." They recognized that one of the most "potent helps" in finding release from "childhood conditioning" is the double realization "that nonbelievers can be as humane and compassionate as believers—far more so in fact—and that there may be others out there who have escaped from the same or similar constraints."[3] What follows is an excerpt from the story of Stefani Jones, one of the co-editors of this anthology.

I do not think my parents set out to indoctrinate me or my siblings, nor did they wish to harm us in any sense of the word—the thought, I believe, would have been repugnant to them. They educated us, both religiously and otherwise, in accordance to what was known and familiar to them, how they themselves were both raised and educated. There was no other way to go about it, at least not one they were willing

1. Caws and Jones, *Religious Upbringing and the Costs of Freedom*.
2. Ibid., 1.
3. Ibid., vii.

to consider or accept. There was no need to teach us critical thinking skills, since they could conceive of no situation in which it would be necessary to question what we were being taught. Though my childhood indoctrination was unintentional, I do think it was nonetheless morally questionable. As a child, I was taught that obedience, reverence, respect, and silence were, in practice, synonymous terms imposed by God, the church, and my father. Being a female child didn't help matters—submission was that much more expected. While I doubted the beliefs I was taught as a child, I had very little space or opportunity to learn otherwise. I did not have a voice to express my doubts, nor did I have any person in particular to appeal to for understanding or encouragement. I did, however, have the curiosity and will eventually to explore my doubts and to desire something more in my life; but this was not without a great deal of pain and argument with my parents, which ultimately resulted in a rift in our relationship that to this day has not been bridged. It was through my somewhat accidental introduction to both feminism and philosophy that I was able to begin first to find that I had a voice, and second to learn that I deserved to be heard.[4]

Part I of this book has been concerned with a study of the ethics of evangelism in the New Testament. The primary focus was to derive some lessons about ethical evangelism from the rules, principles, stories, and the grand narrative or worldview of the New Testament. I turn now to the task of applying the lessons we have learned to some specific contexts we face in our contemporary world. The primary focus of Part II will be to ask how Christians can be obedient to the witness of the New Testament as we grapple with some contemporary problems in relation to evangelism. My approach in Part II is again inspired by Richard Hays, whose study of the moral vision of the New Testament has served as a model for my treatment of the ethics of evangelism.[5]

There are any number of contexts or issues that could be dealt with. I have chosen four—the evangelism of children, evangelism within the context of professional life with a focus on the academy, evangelism within the context of humanitarian aid, and the controversy surrounding evangelical evangelism in Orthodox or Roman Catholic domains. There is some arbitrariness in the selection of these four topics. In part, my choice grows out of invitations I have received to write papers or speak at a variety of

---

4. Jones, "Finding My Voice," 193–94. Permission to use this story granted by Pennsylvania State University Press.

5. Hays, *Moral Vision of the New Testament*. In Part Four of his book, Hays moves on to "The Pragmatic Task: Living Under the Word—Test Cases," where he applies his analysis of the ethics of the New Testament to five contemporary test cases.

international conferences after the publication of my 2011 book on the ethics of evangelism. My hope is that working through these four topics will begin to show how the church should be dealing with other questions that might arise with regard to doing evangelism in an ethical manner in today's world.[6] My hope also is that the manner in which the earlier developed guidelines of chapter 7 are applied to these four particular topics may be suggestive of the fruitfulness of their application to other topics.

Like Hays, I give this advice to the reader: Do not read Part II of this book without first having read Part I and the two introductory chapters. The analysis and the ethical judgments I am offering are meant to be read in the light of the earlier chapters dealing with a study of the Old and New New Testaments and what they have to say about the ethics of evangelism. I would also add that the chapters of Part II are offered somewhat tentatively. Some of the problems dealt with are controversial. All of them move us beyond the mid-eastern context within which the New Testament was written. We therefore need to engage in some imaginative reapplication of New Testament ethics and its treatment of the ethics of evangelism to our contemporary context.[7] My hope is that what I have to say about these topics will, at the very least, stimulate further conversation.

In this chapter, I explore the ethics of evangelizing children. My aim here is to apply the discussion of the ethics of evangelism in the previous chapters to the more specific context of evangelizing children. Keith White, in his introduction to a recent book entitled, *Theology, Mission and Child*, suggests while Christians have long been engaged with children in various ways, "these initiatives have often not been accompanied by rigorous biblical or theological reflection."[8] Fortunately, there have been some significant contributions to rethinking the theology of the child and our approach to mission to children in the last few decades.[9] It is not possible, in a short

---

6. Hays describes the approach of the final section of his book: "One of the purposes for treating a range of different issues is to show that the decisions reached are not based on ad hoc prooftexting; rather, they represent the coherent outworking of a considered set of judgments about the way in which the New Testament ought to form the life of the church." Ibid., 314.

7. Ibid., 5–6, 315. In encouraging us to adopt an attitude of prayerful humility as we consider applying New Testament ethics to contemporary problems, Hays reminds us of Paul's advice to the Corinthian church "concerning virgins": "I have no command of the Lord, but I give my opinion as one who by the Lord's mercy is trustworthy" (1 Cor 7:25; Ibid., 315).

8. Prevette et.al., *Theology, Mission and Child*, 3.

9. See for example the writings connected with the Child Theology Movement: Collier, *Toddling to the Kingdom*; Willmer and White, *Entry Point*; and Bakke, *When Children Became People*. The Prevette volume, *Theology, Mission and Child*, has been very

chapter, to do justice to this growing literature. Instead, I will focus on the link between evangelism and the education of children.

There are two very different contexts we need to consider as we deal with this topic. First, there is the context of children being evangelized within a Christian family and their supporting church community. The second context moves beyond the home and the church, to evangelizing children in the community and the world at large. Before considering these two contexts, I want to respond to the story highlighted in the introduction to this chapter, as well as the anthology in which this story is found.

EVANGELISM AND INDOCTRINATION

I have deliberately begun this chapter by referring to a story from a book which is in fact hostile to the very idea of Christian parents evangelizing their children. Doing so is viewed as indoctrination. It is described as narrow, patronizing, and coercive. Nearly all of the contributors to this anthology describe how they broke free from the effects of such evangelism, a journey that was most often very painful and for some incomplete. I believe this anthology is quite representative of the overall attitudes within Western societies toward a religious upbringing and its costs to the freedom of children. Christian parents cannot help but be influenced by these attitudes to a religious upbringing. Thus, if Christians want to grapple with the issues surrounding the ethics of evangelizing our children in today's world, we need to take these very negative attitudes into account. I therefore begin by responding briefly to the objections to the evangelism of children raised in this anthology.

Nearly all the contributors to the anthology under consideration use the word "indoctrination" to describe their religious upbringing, but what does this term mean? There is a lot of confusion surrounding the meaning of indoctrination, as the editors themselves admit in their introduction. Indeed, this confusion is also apparent in the extensive literature on the concept of indoctrination that has emerged over the years in the philosophy of education. I have argued elsewhere that critics of religious indoctrination have problems giving a coherent account of what they mean by indoctrination, and that the term is largely emotive in meaning.[10] Until critics give us

---

much influenced by the Child Theology Movement. See also the excellent article by Greener, "Children-at-Risk and the Whole Gospel." For other approaches to the topic, see Brennan, *Vocation of the Child*, and Brewster, *Child, Church and Mission*.

10. For a book-length treatment of indoctrination, see Thiessen, *Teaching for Commitment*. For a chapter-length treatment of indoctrination, see Thiessen, *In Defence of*

a coherent account of the meaning of indoctrination, it is hard to know how to respond.

Most of the contributors also share a more general skepticism about religion itself. It is therefore not surprising that a religious upbringing is seen as problematic. Listen to the negative overtones of the editors' description of religion. Unbelievers are "far more" humane and compassionate than believers. (Prove!) A religious upbringing leads to "doctrinal entrapment." (Strangely, all eleven of the contributors broke free from their childhood entrapment!) Religious parents are described as unreasonable and at the mercy of their own "childhood conditioning." (Some of the parents are in fact well educated and seem quite capable of independent thought!) Other questions come to mind in pondering these comments. Are people religious simply because of childhood conditioning? Might religious belief be rational after all? It is surely the height of arrogance to claim that religious parents can't think for themselves or that they accepted Christian doctrine because they are not quite as rational as their liberated children.

The issue of coercion is of course central to the objections against a religious upbringing that are raised in this anthology. Stefani Jones describes her own religious upbringing as "oppressive."[11] As noted earlier, the editors talk about the "constraints" of "childhood conditioning." They describe their early childhood faith as being "coerced as a condition of family and social acceptance."[12] So strong was this influence that it was very hard to give up their faith as they matured, they claim. Clearly there is something right about these concerns about coercion. Children are by their very nature dependent, vulnerable, and impressionable. They will by and large accept the religious beliefs of their parents.[13] The problem here is that this kind of "coercion" is inescapable. Indeed, as Jones herself admits, such "parental impinging" is not only inevitable, but also "absolutely necessary" for a child's healthy development towards maturity.[14] Indeed, as various psychologists and philosophers of education have argued, children need to grow up in a secure and stable primary culture in order to develop into autonomous individuals.[15] I would suggest it was precisely the stability and security of

---

Religious Schools and Colleges, chapter 8.

11. Jones, "Finding My Voice," 197.

12. Caws and Jones, *Religious Upbringing and the Costs of Freedom*, vii.

13. Here we must be careful not to exaggerate the vulnerability and dependence of children. Children are in fact quite capable of some independent and critical thinking, as Jones herself concedes in her story.

14. Jones, "Finding My Voice," 208.

15. For a review of some of this literature, see Thiessen, *Teaching for Commitment*, 142–43, 169–70, 269–72, 289n12.

the religious upbringing of the eleven contributors to this volume that culminated in them becoming philosophers who could think for themselves and who could think critically.[16]

It is considerations such as these that lead us to a more coherent account of indoctrination. As I have argued elsewhere, religious indoctrination, understood as a pejorative term, involves the failure of parents and their religious community to combine the initiation of their children into a religious tradition with encouraging and facilitating the growth of their children towards autonomy.[17] Initiating children into a religious tradition is not itself necessarily indoctrinatory. It is what happens alongside such initiation, and what happens as children mature that might give us grounds for making the charge of indoctrination. The key to avoiding indoctrination is to combine the nurturing of children into a religious faith with helping children to grow towards "normal autonomy." More on this later.

Stefani Jones concludes the telling of her personal story with a more general treatment of moral issues involved in giving children a religious upbringing. What is curious is that she is largely in agreement with my analysis of indoctrination and the possibility of avoiding it. I therefore have some problems with her very negative assessment of her religious upbringing. In reading her story, I am not so sure her upbringing was as narrow and oppressive as she claims. Perhaps, like many adults, she has trouble being entirely objective about her upbringing. I would also suggest Jones is being a little unrealistic about the nature of unconditional love. Parents cannot help but be disappointed when their children reject that which they hold to be very precious. Some distance and even estrangement is inevitable. But continuing love is probably never in question. Indeed, Jones is forced to admit her parents loved her and continue to love her deeply.[18]

I would suggest Jones might have something to learn about loving and honoring her parents despite their disagreement with her own atheistic leanings. In concluding her essay, Jones reflects on now being a mother of two young daughters. She concedes that like her parents she will make mistakes, but she is "confident that they will not be the same ones."[19] I'm not so sure! I wonder how she would feel if one of her daughters should become an evangelical Christian!

16. One of the contributors, Raymond Bradley, concedes that despite his objections to growing up in a fundamentalist Christian environment, it nonetheless "gave me something tough to chew on, something to cut my teeth on intellectually." Bradley, "From Fundamentalist to Freethinker," 50.

17. See Thiessen, *Teaching for Commitment*, chap. 8.

18. Jones, "Finding My Voice," 210.

19. Ibid., 212.

PARENTS EVANGELIZING THEIR CHILDREN

In Part I we have considered what the books of the New Testament say about the ethics of evangelism generally. The context most often being assumed in these discussions is the evangelism of adults. The New Testament in fact has little to say explicitly about the evangelism of children. So we will need to extrapolate from the lessons we have learned about the ethics of evangelism generally, and also take into account what the Bible teaches about children and their education.

There are a number of variables that make the ethics of evangelizing children more complex. Children are typically born into a family. They have a mother and a father. In the first few years of their lives, children are deeply dependent on their parents. They are very vulnerable, and need a lot of care. Young children learn nearly everything from their parents and their immediate surroundings. They generally trust their parents and other caring adults. They generally believe what they are told. Young children are not autonomous, to use a term very much in vogue in educational circles today. These features bring to the fore the problem of coercion. It would seem that a coercive learning environment is inescapable with regard to young children, as we have already seen earlier in this chapter.

The above variables make the evangelism of children very different from the evangelism of adults. Indeed, we tend to talk about nurturing children into the Christian faith, rather than evangelizing them. Given the immediacy and the power inherent in the structure of the family, young children are inescapably initiated into the beliefs, sentiments, imaginings, and practices of the Christian faith.[20] They can't help but absorb the faith of their parents and the church to which their parents belong. And thus, in the end they are "evangelized," if we still want to use this word. With young children, the concepts of evangelism, nurture, initiation, and even education, tend to blur into each other.[21]

This blurring is in fact reflected in the Old Testament. Genesis teaches us the family is foundational to a society.[22] Children are God's gift to parents

---

20. For some classic descriptions of education as initiation, see Peters, *Ethics and Education*, chapter 2;, and Oakeshott, "Education."

21. I suggest William Abraham's analysis of evangelism as initiation into the kingdom of God is particularly appropriate when talking about the evangelism of children (Abraham, *Logic of Evangelism*). Attfield draws on Abraham's analysis to integrate evangelism and the religious education of children. See Attfield, "Child-evangelism and Religious Education."

22. We have already seen, in chapter 2, that God created a structured world, not only physically, but also in terms of the way in which human beings should interrelate and fulfill their various tasks. This has led Christian thinkers of both Catholic

(Ps 127:3), and parents are given the primary responsibility to educate their children.[23] Moses, in his final instructions to the people of Israel, gives us one of the clearest expressions of this responsibility and how it is to be carried out:

> Hear, O Israel: The Lord our God, the Lord is one. Love the Lord your God with all your heart and with all your soul and with all your strength. These commandments that I give you today are to be on your hearts. Impress them on your children. Talk about them when you sit at home and when you walk along the road, when you lie down and when you get up. Tie them as symbols on your hands and bind them on your foreheads. Write them on the doorframes of your houses and on your gates. (Deut 6:4–9)[24]

Several features in this exhortation need to be highlighted. Parents, and the community they are a part of, are responsible for educating their children. Children are given an immersion program in the Ten Commandments. But Moses is not only talking about giving children an ethical education. A few verses down he anticipates sons and daughters asking their parents, "What is the meaning of the stipulations, decrees and laws the Lord our God has commanded you" (6:20)? Parents are then exhorted to tell their children the story of how the people of Israel were once slaves of Pharaoh in Egypt, and how the Lord brought them out of Egypt with a mighty hand (6:21).[25] In other words, children were also to be told the larger story, the story of the redemption of the people of Israel. This of course brings us closer to what we typically think of as evangelism. Similar exhortations concerning the educating and evangelizing of children are found elsewhere in the Old Testament.[26] As already argued earlier in this chapter, there is nothing inherently unethical about giving children an immersion program in ethical and godly living.

---

and Protestant orientation to adopt a social philosophy of structural pluralism which recognizes there are multiple spheres of social activity, one of which is the family. For a clear statement of the biblical foundations of structural pluralism, see McCarthy et al., *Society, State, and Schools*, chapter 6.

23. For a survey of a biblical and secular defense of parents as having the primary responsibility for educating their children, see Thiessen, "Vocation of the Child as a Learner," 397–405.

24. See also Deut 11:18–21; 31:12–13.

25. It should be noted the evangelism of children, like the evangelism of adults, is best accomplished in response to questions being asked (1 Pet 3:15). Brueggemann highlights this need for balance between "advocacy and receptivity" in his insightful treatment of Old Testament texts on the nurture and evangelism of children (Brueggemann, *Biblical Perspectives on Evangelism*, chap. 4). He also reminds us the telling of stories is key to ensuring the ethical instruction of children (and adults) does not become coercive (114).

26. See also Gen 18:19; Ps 78:1–8; Prov 4; 22:6.

The above Old Testament teachings are the background to New Testament exhortations regarding the education and evangelism of children. Take for example what scholars have come to refer to as *haustafeln,* or tables of household duties, that summarize the ethical teachings given to new Christians in the early church.[27] These include some specific instructions regarding the relationship between parents and children.

> Children, obey your parents in the Lord, for this is right. "Honor your father and mother"—which is the first commandment with a promise—"that it may go well with you and that you may enjoy long life on the earth." Fathers, do not exasperate your children; instead, bring them up in the training and instruction of the Lord. (Eph 6:1–4)

The first thing to note about this set of household rules governing parent-child relationships is its connection to the Old Testament. The exhortation for children to obey their parents is one of the Ten Commandments found in Deuteronomy. The passage from Deuteronomy that was quoted earlier follows a review of the Ten Commandments. The exhortation to fathers (and mothers) to bring up their children in the training and instruction of the Lord is really an abbreviated version of what we have already seen in Deuteronomy. So there is continuity between Old Testament and New Testament teaching about how to bring up children. Parents have a responsibility to discipline (*paideia*) and teach (*nouthesia*) their children in accordance with the way of Christ who is the chief teacher and administrator of discipline. So the hope is that children will themselves come to know and obey the Lord.[28] In other words, parents have a responsibility to evangelize their children. Christian parents don't have to make any excuses about initiating their children into the Christian faith.[29] And again, there is nothing inherently unethical about initiating children into the Christian faith.

Secondly, there is a special exhortation to fathers, who are no doubt in need of this reminder! Don't exasperate your children, as you bring them up in the training and instruction of the Lord. Here we have a specific ethical qualification applied to the way in which fathers give their children a religious upbringing. Paul is not at all condoning a military style of family heirarchy, with the father barking orders, and children responding, "Yes, sir." In fact, what Paul is saying is in stark contrast to the typical practices of the Roman family where the father had absolute authority over all members of the family.

---

27. The importance of these household tablets is illustrated by the fact that very similar versions are found in three epistles (Col 3:18—4:1; Eph 5:21—6:9; 1 Pet 2:13—3:7).

28. Stott, *Message of Ephesians,* 249–50.

29. See Thiessen, *Teaching for Commitment,* 244–55.

He could kill newborns, he could sell his children as slaves, he could make them work in fields, even in chains, he could punish them as he liked, even to the point of using the death penalty. Paul is painting a very different picture of the Christian father—a self-controlled, gentle, patient educator of his children. Indeed, the verb used here is *ektrephō*, which means literally to nourish or feed. Calvin's translation is, "Let them be fondly cherished . . . deal gently with them."[30] There is nothing here of oppressive parenthood. Indeed, the Christian gospel was wonderfully redemptive and liberating for both women and children of the time. The call to submission on the part of children, is balanced by a call to parents to fulfill their responsibilities under God, and to do this in such a way that reflects God's love for all his children (cf. Eph 3:14–15). This kind of love is also assumed in the Deuteronomy passage we considered earlier. The nurturing and evangelism of children by parents is done with love and tender care for their children (see Guidelines #A4 and #E13 of chapter 7). This is the assumed ethical context of a Christian upbringing.

The third thing to note about this passage is that children are addressed in their own right. They themselves are being asked to respond to their unique calling. Again, this will have been unusual for the society in which Paul lived, where children were most often viewed as chattel. In a Christian household children are seen as persons, able to respond to instructions from the Lord. This acknowledgement of children as in some way independent leads to the next set of suggestions with respect to the evangelism of children.

CHILDREN BECOMING ADULTS

Paul's countercultural instructions to parents and children no doubt have their origins in Jesus' teaching and treatment of children. Indeed, as already noted earlier in this chapter, various recent studies have highlighted the need for more theological reflection on the nature of children, including Jesus' interactions with children. Jesus chastised the disciples for discouraging parents who were bringing their children to him so he could bless them and pray for them.[31] "Let the little children come to me, and do not hinder them, for the kingdom of God belongs to such as these" (Mark 10:14). Jesus went on to suggest adults have something to learn from children about receiving the kingdom of God. Jesus thanked the Father for hiding eternal truths from the wise and learned and revealing them to little children (Luke 10:21). As

---

30. Quoted in Stott, *Message of Ephesians*, 247.

31. This story is found in all three Synoptic Gospels (Mark 10:13–16; Matt 19:13–15; Luke 18:15–17).

he neared the cross, Jesus acknowledged the children and infants who were praising him (Matt 21:15–16). Jesus clearly loved children and treated them as persons in their own right.

It is important, therefore, to understand that children are not simply passive recipients of the influence of others. Even as children, they have the capacity to be agents of God. They can be active participants in their own growth and development.[32] And yet, they are vulnerable and dependent on parents and other adults. Jesus therefore issued a warning about causing "one of these little ones who believe in me to sin" (Matt 18:6). Here Jesus is reminding us that children are still in some sense "little ones," dependent and vulnerable, and in need of instruction. There is a tension here that must not be overlooked when we consider the nature and nurture of children. Children are not "subhuman," or "almost human," or just "on their way to being human."[33] Their individuality and childlike independence must always be respected in ethical Christian nurture and evangelism. And yet, children do need to grow and they need help in this process. In what follows, I want to focus on one aspect of this growth that has significant ethical implications.

Children do not remain children. They grow and develop and eventually become mature adults. Already, as a twelve-year-old, Jesus showed remarkable intelligence and independence when he dialogued with the teachers at the temple courts, and he did so without the knowledge of his parents (Luke 2:41–50). After this incident, we are told Jesus returned home and "grew in wisdom and stature, and in favor with God and men."[34] Today, such growth to maturity would be described in terms of becoming autonomous. The following ingredients are generally seen as essential to the modern liberal notion of autonomy which has its roots in the Enlightenment: freedom, independence, rationality, and critical thinking. I believe the standard liberal ideal of autonomy fails to do justice to human interdependence and human finiteness. This ideal is also unrealistic as to the level of freedom, independence, rationality, and critical thinking that can be achieved by "normal" human beings. Hence my adding the qualifier "normal" to the notion of autonomy in order to distinguish it from the contemporary liberal ideal of autonomy.[35] I also believe normal autonomy is in keeping with the biblical ideal of growing towards maturity. As we have seen in previous chapters, the individual person is given value, dignity, and

32. Greener, "Children-at-Risk and the Whole Gospel," 159, 162.

33. Bunge, "Vocation of the Child," 43.

34. Luke 2:51–52. The language used here is very similar to that used to describe the boy Samuel (1 Sam 2:26).

35. See Thiessen, *Teaching for Commitment*, chapter 5, for a detailed discussion of autonomy.

worth. Individual persons are given freedom (though limited), including the freedom to respond to God.[36] Individuals are also called upon to grow in knowledge and critical discernment.[37]

Although, as we have already seen, children display autonomy in a minimal sense, they still need to grow towards fuller normal autonomy. One could even say they have a right to have their capacity for autonomy developed. Although children become more independent naturally, there are some aspects of growth towards autonomy in which they need help (e.g., growth in knowledge and critical discernment). Children are again dependent to some degree on adults to help them achieve maturity and normal autonomy. This gives rise to some additional ethical requirements with respect to evangelizing children.

Christian parents should have two goals in mind for their children: 1) They hope and pray their children will in the end affirm the Christian faith into which they have been initiated, and 2) that their children will become "autonomous," realizing this might mean their children might in the end reject the faith of their parents. Having these dual aims is not easy to do, but is an essential component of an ethical approach to evangelizing children.[38]

Not only should Christian parents have this dual goal; they also need to actively work towards achieving it for their children. This means Christian parents should boldly initiate their children into the Christian faith, as I have already argued in the previous section. But Christian parents should also actively encourage and facilitate their child's growth toward normal autonomy, independence, and thinking for themselves. This means that parents and the church should encourage and facilitate growth beyond a childlike understanding of the Christian faith. Christian parents should also welcome the questions children raise about the Christian faith. Healthy Christian nurture also fosters growth by helping children honestly grapple with doubts and even objections to the Christian faith. Children should be made aware of the fact that there are religious beliefs different from those held by the family. Christian parents should not shelter children from

---

36. See Deut 30:19; Josh 24:15; Ezekiel 3; Matthew 7:13–14; 16:24–28; Luke 9:5, 55.

37. See Phil 1:9–11; Col 1:10; 1 Thess 5:21; 2 Pet 3:18; 1 John 4:1.

38. Catholic philosopher Terry McLauglin distinguishes between the long-term and the short-term aims of religious parents. "Their long-term, or ultimate aim, is to place their children in a position where they can autonomously choose to accept or reject their religious faith—or religious faith in general . . . Their short-term aim is the development of faith; albeit a faith which is not closed off from future revision or rejection." So a coherent way of characterizing the intention of religious parents is "that they are aiming at autonomy via faith." McLaughlin, "Parental Rights and the Religious Upbringing of Children," 79.

exposure to other belief systems and worldviews. Again, these are requirements for an ethical approach to evangelizing children.

As should be evident, a delicate balance must be maintained in child-rearing between teaching for commitment and teaching for autonomy.[39] Children need the stability and security of a Christian environment. At the same time, children need to grow to become increasingly independent. Nurturing autonomy is very much a developmental process, and as the child matures, parents should gradually and increasingly allow the child to make his or her own decisions with regard to the Christian faith (see Guidelines #C9 and #G20). So, while children in a Christian home are brought up as "practicing Christians," they should be reminded repeatedly there will come a time when they will need to make an adult decision, either to accept or reject the Christian faith into which they were nurtured.[40] And when they choose to reject the Christian faith, Christian parents pray to a God who loves their children even more than they do (see Guideline #B8). Prayer will also help us avoid the sin of being manipulative with maturing adolescents.

Here a word about baptism might be in order. I do not want to take sides on the issue of infant baptism versus adult baptism.[41] I believe the differences here are sometimes exaggerated. Child dedication often bears "suspicious" resemblance to infant baptism! What is essential in either approach to baptism is that parents and the church acknowledge that children eventually need to make the faith into which they were nurtured their own. Further, a genuine commitment to the Christian faith supposes a considerable degree of maturity. I believe it is therefore unethical for churches practicing adult baptism to baptize pre-adolescents. And for churches practicing infant baptism, it is essential that children are not forced, explicitly or implicitly, to take confirmation classes. Ethical evangelism requires that we postpone

---

39. See Smedes, *Caring and Commitment*. Smedes devotes a chapter to the commitment of parents to children (chap. 9). While acknowledging that the commitments parents make put them in control, Smedes goes on to highlight the principle that "parents are committed to their children's freedom from their commitment"(156).

40. For a helpful distinction between "practicing Christians" and "committed Christians," as applied to maturing children, see Attfield, "Child-evangelism and Religious Education," 44. I am well aware my treatment of growth and development of children suffers from oversimplification. James Fowler has developed a more sophisticated treatment of faith development. For a collection of essays on Fowler's theory, see Dykstra and Parks, *Faith Development and Fowler*. See also McLaughlin, "Parental Rights and the Religious Upbringing of Children," for a good philosophical treatment of the tension between teaching for commitment and teaching for autonomy. For a wonderfully practical treatment of parents relating to maturing children, see Peterson, *Growing Up with Your Teenager*.

41. For an overview of three understandings of the child in relation to baptism, see Vischer, "Best Interests of the Child," 418–30.

expressions of full Christian commitment, such as baptism or confirmation, until children are mature enough to make a such a commitment.

EVANGELIZING OTHER CHILDREN

I now move on to consider the evangelism of children outside of the context of the Christian family and the Christian church.[42] For example, churches often have programs devoted to reaching out to non-churched children, and there are parachurch organizations who are dedicated to evangelizing children.[43] I will be brief here because there is obviously some overlap between this context and the one considered in the previous sections of this chapter. Insofar as we are still dealing with children, the ethical guidelines that have already been outlined in this chapter also apply to the context under discussion here. My focus in this section will be on those features that are unique to the context of evangelizing children who do not belong to Christian parents or to a Christian church.

First a few comments about the justification of child evangelism outside the context of the Christian family. As we have seen, the Bible teaches that Christian parents should nurture/evangelize their own children. But does this mandate apply more generally to the evangelism of children beyond the church and the Christian home? This question is not without controversy. From our study of the early church in the New Testament it would seem evangelism was primarily directed to adults. The assumption seems to be when parents become Christians it is their responsibility to evangelize their children.[44] But clearly Jesus did bless the children (Mark 10:13-16). He declared that welcoming a child is equivalent to welcoming him (Mark 9:37). The Great Commission surely extends to all people, including children.[45] An extrapolation of the Golden Rule would suggest we should love our neighbors' children as we love our own children, and so the mandate

---

42. This is also the main focus of the Lausanne Occasional Paper No. 47, "Evangelization of Children," edited by Strachan and Hood, and produced by the Issue Group on this topic at the 2004 Forum for World Evangelization, in Pattaya, Thailand, Sept. 29 to Oct 5, 2004.

43. For example, Child Evangelism Fellowship is an international organization dedicated to evangelizing children.

44. For example, Paul addressed the issue of a marriage where one spouse had become a Christian and the other was still an unbeliever. His hope was the believing spouse would be able to evangelize the unbelieving spouse as well as their children (1 Cor 7:14).

45. Matt 28:16-20. Peter's final appeal in his Pentecost sermon includes children when he calls on everyone to repent and be baptized and when he promises the gift of the Holy Spirit (Acts 2:38-39).

of evangelizing our own children extends beyond the home. As we have seen in chapter 4, Paul and Silas, after their release from prison in Philippi, spoke the word of the Lord to the entire household of the jailor, and the entire family came to believe in God. Presumably, this included children.[46] Further, if we as Christians don't evangelize children, others will! Indeed, the "evangelism" of children is inescapable.

It is considerations such as these that suggest there is a place for evangelizing children outside of the context of the Christian family and church. The question that needs to be addressed therefore is: How do we do so in an ethical manner? I believe there are several additional parameters of this context of the evangelism of children that merit some attention.

The first has to do with the obvious fact that children are being evangelized outside of the context of their immediate family. As has already been pointed out, a Christian understanding of the family gives parents the primary responsibility for the nurture of their children. Given this understanding, children should not be subjected to Christian teaching and evangelistic efforts without the knowledge and consent of their parents.[47] Another way to defend this ethical requirement would be to appeal to the Golden Rule (see Guideline #A5). Christian parents would be very upset over attempts to influence their children to accept another faith without their knowledge and consent. So, we should treat parents of other faiths or "no faith" in the same way as we would want to be treated.

Such parents also need to be given a clear idea of what is happening in the programs their children are attending. Ethical evangelism of children outside of the Christian family and the church requires complete transparency. There is no place for hidden agendas or hidden identities (see Guideline #D12). Parents need to know what is going on, and should even be invited to attend the educational or evangelistic venues their children are attending.

Obviously, there should be no coercion when evangelizing other children (see Guideline # C9). As we have already seen, the vulnerability of children and their heightened receptivity to teaching should cause us to be very sensitive to the danger of exploitation. We also need to be sensitive to the power imbalance inherent in the relationship between a Christian adult and a child, especially in certain contexts. For example, a teenager at a Christian youth camp probably cannot escape. Great care needs to be taken, therefore, not to misuse power when engaged in evangelism in this context. There also needs to be sensitivity to the dangers of psychological and emotional coercion (fire and brimstone preaching, intense and repeated emotional appeals

---

46. Acts 16:16–40. See also Acts 10:24, 44–48; 1 Cor 1:16.
47. Brewster, *Child, Church and Mission*, 165, 169.

to convert). The more recent phenomenon of mass-marketing of hell by various evangelical churches in North America, often directed specifically to young children, calls for some serious evaluation as to whether this approach is coercive.[48]

Additional ethical concerns arise with regard to the content of evangelistic messages when dealing with children (see Guideline #D11). Obviously, the Christian gospel needs to be told in such a way that children can understand the good news. Children love stories, and they can understand stories. The Christian gospel is a wonderful story that can be understood by children, but they are obviously not capable of understanding the rich complexity of a Christian worldview, and it would be wrong to foist this on young minds. But it is equally wrong to reduce the gospel to simplistic formulas or to portray God as a mean-spirited crank who likes to condemn disobedient children to hell.

Great care should also be exercised with regard to encouraging children to convert. As I have already argued in this chapter, young children are not in a position to make a mature commitment to the Christian faith. I would suggest it is inappropriate and unethical to foist an adult agenda onto young children. Yes, they are capable of expressing childlike trust in Jesus, and this needs to be respected, as Jesus himself demonstrated in his treatment of children. But children need to be told there will come a time when, as adults, they will need to reaffirm their childhood commitment. Even as children, their circumstances might be such that a commitment to Jesus will involve ostracism, rejection, and even suffering. In such cases, the consequences of making a commitment to Christ must be clearly presented in a manner commensurate with the understanding and maturity level of the child.[49]

CHILDREN-AT-RISK

Sadly, there is a special category of children that needs to be mentioned—children in need and children-at-risk—and there are many children in the world that belong to this category. There are children without parents, living in orphanages. There are abandoned children living on the streets. There are children living in extreme poverty or suffering because of malnutrition or

---

48. For a description of "Hell House Kits," see Thiessen, *Ethics of Evangelism*, 174–76. See also Fletcher, *Preaching to Convert*, chap. 5.

49. Brewster, *Child, Church and Mission*, 170. Brewster also suggests a child making a commitment should not be baptized until the parents are also ready to be baptized. This is to ensure the child who makes a commitment gets support and encouragement in his or her newfound faith (166). This advice might be appropriate for young children, but there surely comes a time in mature adolescence when this rule no longer applies.

preventable diseases. Then there are the many children who are suffering because of "violence, exploitation, slavery, trafficking, prostitution, gender and ethnic discrimination, commercial targeting and willful neglect."[50] What is the Christian response to children in need and children-at-risk? What does ethical evangelism look like for children in crisis?

These are not easy questions to answer. Unfortunately, all too often there is a tension between those who are committed to addressing the physical, psychological, and social needs of these children, and those addressing their spiritual needs.[51] Thankfully, there are a variety of international Christian agencies working with children in crisis.[52] In most cases, these agencies have adopted a holistic approach to addressing the needs of these children. Love demands that all the needs of children be addressed (Guideline #A4). We need a whole gospel for the whole child.[53] With children-at-risk we cannot focus only on personal salvation apart from addressing the other desperate physical, social, and developmental needs of such children. If ever there is a need for integral mission it is here.

Of course, when we apply the notion of integral mission to children we cannot avoid asking about the relation between evangelism and the meeting of their other needs. I won't say much about this question here as I will deal with the general problem of combining evangelism with humanitarian aid in chapter 10. But I do want to stress the importance of being especially careful in situations where children and/or their parents are very dependent on the financial and/or material support of Christians. Some examples include children in orphanages and refugee camps, social aid projects, and communities heavily sustained by Christian development efforts. Clearly it is ethically wrong to make the giving of financial or material support conditional on first becoming a Christian. I believe it is also wrong to make the giving of financial or material support conditional on first being exposed to an evangelistic message (Guideline #C9). But what about a holistic program where some biblical teaching is simply part of an all-round program to help children in need? Is this coercive? I hesitate ruling out such "evangelism"

---

50. Greener highlights the Cape Town Commitment of the Lausanne Movement, 2010, as addressing these issues (Greener, "Children-at-Risk and the Whole Gospel," 166).

51. For a good description of this tension as experienced in Romania, following the collapse of Nicolae Ceaușescu's socialist government in 1989, see Prevette, "Disturbance of God, Holistic Mission and Children in Crisis."

52. For example, Compassion International, World Vision International, and Tearfund.

53. For a good treatment of integral mission for children, see Brewster, *Child, Church and Mission*, and Greener, "Children-at-Risk and the Whole Gospel." Greener's essay is found in a recent issue of *Transformation*, all of which is devoted to children-at-risk.

as unethical. I believe more attention needs to be paid to sorting out what is and what is not ethically appropriate in delivering holistic child development programs.[54] However, I am more certain about suggesting that in situations of extreme physical need or in times of crisis, the agenda of evangelism should be completely dropped.[55] In situations of desperate need, only "indirect evangelism of compassion and care" is ethically appropriate.

Additional efforts must be made when giving holistic care for children who are subject to violence, exploitation, and willful neglect. Here Christians need to face the enemy and try to shield children from harm. Here we need to be advocating for these vulnerable children, using adult power and status to address the systemic issues that underlie these problems.[56] Addressing these systemic issues will involve exposing, resisting, and taking action to eliminate any form of abuse of children. Here again evangelism should take second place to dealing with the desperate needs of these at-risk children.

Children have God-given dignity and worth. Jesus loved children. Paul addresses children as persons in their own right. One might even say children have a unique calling and vocation.[57] Our job as Christian parents and adults is to help all children become all they were meant to become. We dare not do anything that undermines the dignity and worth of children. It is therefore incumbent on us to ensure that the evangelism of children is done in an ethical manner.

---

54. I have benefited from an extended email conversation on this question with Daniel Hillion. Prevette has helpfully suggested we need to embrace the ambiguity that seems unavoidable in sorting out these issues. Ambiguity "can be a gift of grace when it leads to greater discernment" in trying to serve Christ in such programs (Prevette, "Disturbance of God, Holistic Mission and Children in Crisis," 106).

55. I will develop this as a general principle in a later chapter (see p. 192).

56. See Greener, "Children-at-Risk and the Whole Gospel," 166; Brewster, *Child, Church and Mission*, chap. 12.

57. See Brennan, *Vocation of the Child*.

Chapter 9

Evangelism in Professional Life: The Academy[1]

Though retired, I (Elmer Thiessen) have been enjoying teaching a six-week course in a life-long learning program at Wilfrid Laurier University each fall for the past eight years. It is a wonderful program—there are no essays to grade, the students attend because they are interested in the subject, and there are no discipline problems (well, hardly ever)! Each year I get a wonderful variety of students, all retired from various professions, and invariably representing a variety worldviews—atheists, agnostics, Christians and occasionally some other religion. I recently offered a course on Plato's Republic, and was a little afraid that few if any people would register for the course. To my surprise, twenty students registered, and became very engaged in the study of Plato. In the last lecture, I was explaining and boldly defending Plato's notion of the Form of the Good as a transcendent standard of ethics. One student, I think he is a retired lawyer, asked this penetrating and serious question: If you believe in an objective standard of right and wrong, what do you do about guilt? What a teaching moment! I described three options: (a) destroy the absolute ethical standard—that is what many relativists do to overcome guilt; (b) just forgive yourself—the recourse of humanists; (c) or look to a religion like Christianity, where there is a God who wants to forgive.

―――◆―――

1. This chapter draws on a recent article of mine which has appeared in a number of venues. See Thiessen, "Evangelism in the Classroom." Reprinted in *Journal of Christian Education*, May 2012/2013. A shortened version of this article also appeared in Etherington, *Foundations of Education*, 104–18. Parts of the original essay are being used here by permission from the editors.

THIS CHAPTER WILL CONSIDER the ethics of evangelism in the academy, with a specific focus on teaching. I choose the academy as one example of professional life. There are any number of other professions that could be dealt with, but I have chosen the academy because this is the profession I am most familiar with. While each profession is unique, there are also some similarities between them. For example, the doctor-patient relationship in the medical profession is in some ways similar to the professor-student relationship in the academic profession. Issues of power-imbalance and vulnerability arise in each, and thus present similar challenges when considering the ethics of evangelism. My focus in this chapter is on the academic profession, and I leave it to the reader to extrapolate to other professions.

Since my life has been spent in the academy, this chapter will also be more personal than other chapters in this book. The above story gives you a glimpse into my approach to teaching. In my first lecture, I told the students that I am a Christian of a fairly orthodox variety. So, when I listed the three options for coping with guilt, all the students will have realized that my preferred option was (c). I didn't say more by way of defending this option at the time. Had there been more time, or had a student asked me to identify and defend my preferred choice, I would have done so. I believe in teaching from and for commitment. I even believe in evangelism in the classroom, though there are some ethical constraints as to what can be done within the context of a secular and pluralistic classroom. This chapter will attempt to defend the appropriateness of doing some evangelism in the classroom and then articulate the ethical constraints in doing so. While I will be focusing on the college and university setting, what I say can, with some modifications, be extrapolated to other teaching contexts, as well as other professions.

WORK, VOCATION, AND EVANGELISM

Before I consider the place of evangelism within the academy it will be helpful, first, to deal more generally with work, vocation, and the place of evangelism in the workplace. I grew up within a home and church environment that distinguished rather sharply between religious and secular work. Religious work was important, and secular work merely necessary for survival. A further expression of this dualism had to do with how one's secular work relates to evangelism. I was taught that work is only the context in which you fulfill your *real* calling, which is to evangelize.[2] Paul was often cited as a

---

2. I still have in my files an article in my own denominational paper, written long ago by a prominent Mennonite Brethren leader, entitled, "Brother, Your Work is not Your Calling" (Peters).

positive example of someone who saw his tent-making job as an "avocation" to support his real calling of being a missionary.

It was only until I was well into my career that I was able to identify problems with this kind of dualism. The sacred/secular divide is simply not biblical. Work needs to be seen as one way of honoring God. It is a mistake to develop a theology of work and vocation based only on the example of Paul. Paul may in fact just be a very special case of a "tent-making" missionary. For the beginnings of a theology of work we need to turn to the instructions Paul gives to slaves, who were at that time the "professional" workers of the Roman Empire—teachers, doctors, accountants, and administrators. "Serve wholeheartedly, as if you were serving the Lord, not men, because you know that the Lord will reward everyone for whatever good he does, whether he is slave or free."[3] Here we have a robust theology of work, suggesting that teaching philosophy can be a way of serving the Lord.

Thankfully, much has been written in the last while by way of advocating a healthier understanding of work as a calling or vocation.[4] Amy Sherman has written about "vocational stewardship," by which she means "the strategic and intentional deployment of all the dimensions of our vocational power to advance foretastes of the Kingdom of God."[5] She uses the term "foretastes" to refer to the marks of the future, consummated kingdom of God, as we see those described in the scriptural texts that give us some glimpses of the new heavens and new earth. Some examples of kingdom foretastes are beauty, justice, wholeness, and truth. Sherman encourages Christians to consider which kingdom foretastes they might have opportunities to advance in their particular vocation. This approach to work and vocation integrates the sacred and the secular and gives work eternal significance.

Ideally, our work should be in line with the abilities and gifts God has given us. It is then through our work that each of us is able to do his or her part in building God's kingdom here on earth. I believe God has gifted me and called me to be a philosopher and an educator. Thankfully, I found a job as a college teacher where I could use these God-given gifts, doing my

---

3. Eph 6:7; cf. Col 3:23. Paul generalizes: "And whatever you do, whether in word or deed, do it all in the name of the Lord Jesus, giving thanks to God the Father through him" (Col 3:17).

4. See, for example, Volf, *Work in the Spirit*; Schuurman, *Vocation*; Keller, *Every Good Endeavor*; Guinness, *The Call*. Guinness wisely reminds us the notion of calling requires a Caller. He also reminds us that our primary calling is to be a disciple of Jesus. Work therefore needs to be seen as a secondary calling, done to serve our Lord (Guinness, *The Call*, 31).

5. See Sherman, *Kingdom Calling*, 20.

little part, in my small sphere of influence, to build God's kingdom. What a challenging mission!

I believe it is appropriate to talk about the mission of a Christian philosophy professor at a college or a university.[6] Indeed, there is a desperate need for missional professors at our colleges and universities, which are surely the key culture-shaping institutions in the world.[7] Mission is of course a broad term, and in academia includes many activities. It entails upholding that which is in keeping with what God had originally intended for such institutions, and where this is not the case, being an agent of transformation, seeking to bring these institutions closer to God's ideal.[8] A Christian professor is committed to excellence in teaching and research. Both teaching and research involve the search for truth as well as discerning and exposing patterns of thought that distort the truth and are harmful to human well-being. All truth needs to be reconciled to Christ "in whom are hidden all the treasures of wisdom and knowledge" (Col 2:3). The mission of Christian philosophers also includes the cultivation of wonder and imagination in an age marked too much by suspicion and devotion to scientific fact. I want to argue that evangelism is part of the mission of a Christian philosopher at a secular college or university.[9]

This of course raises a number of questions. How does evangelism in the academy relate to the broader mission of a professor at a college or university? What does evangelism in the academy (or other professions) look like? Are there some constraints to evangelizing in professions like the academy? How do we ensure evangelism is done ethically within the context of professions like the academy? I now want to provide a more detailed description of how I have answered these questions, focusing on evangelism within the classroom. Space constraints prohibit my saying more about the other dimensions of being a missional professor.[10]

---

6. See Gould, *Outrageous Idea of the Missional Professor*.

7. Ibid., 40–51. In an inspiring essay that has been in my files a long time, Charles Malik says this: "Save the university and Western civilization is saved, and therewith the world." Malik, "Other Side of Evangelism," 40. For a series of essays on the mission of Christian philosophers in the secular academy, see Evangelical Philosophical Society, "Christian Philosophers in the 'Secular Academy.'"

8. Dallas Willard writes about making one's job a primary place of apprenticeship to Jesus and building God's kingdom. "A gentle but firm noncooperation with things that everyone knows to be wrong, together with a sensitive, nonofficious, nonintrusive, nonobsequious service to others, should be our usual overt manner" (Willard, *Divine Conspiracy*, 285).

9. This is also the thesis of Gould, *Outrageous Idea of the Missional Professor*, 22, 84–90.

10. Let me give one example of what the broader mission of being a Christian

EVANGELISM IN THE CLASSROOM: A PERSONAL NARRATIVE

I have spent most of my career teaching philosophy in a state-supported secular college. Since I like to practice what I preach—I have written a book about teaching from and for commitment—I have been very open about my own Christian commitment in the classroom.[11] I have experimented with different ways to declare my commitment. Sometimes I tell my students I am a Christian in the first lecture of a course. One problem with this approach is it puts some students who are very hostile to religion on guard, and it takes some time to win their trust. At other times I wait until well into the course to disclose my Christian identity. Whatever approach, at some point in time I openly declare my Christian commitment, and warn my students (with a smile) they are stuck with a Christian philosopher and that my Christian commitment will color everything I say in the classroom.

Do I evangelize in the college classroom? Clearly, declaring my Christian commitment is the beginning of evangelism. Teaching philosophy also allows me to gently break down the many artificial barriers that stop students from considering the Christian faith—what some writers have labeled "preevangelism."[12] From time to time I also make it a point to counter the secular and materialistic presuppositions that hold sway in much of our society. Early on in my career, I recall a student who came to my office and pointed out I had shattered his worldview in an earlier lecture. He felt like he was left adrift in a desert, and didn't know where to turn. Here in a private conversation in my office I was able to point him beyond the desert.

But I do more than preevangelism in the classroom. In response to student questions related to faith and religion, I am open about my own views.

---

professor has meant for me during my 36 years at Medicine Hat College in Alberta, Canada. The vice-president of the college sent me a note shortly after he had been appointed to that position, and after I had written him a letter of congratulation, in which I also expressed some concerns over a few matters I felt needed to be addressed at the college. He responded with a brief note: "I have always considered you to be the conscience of the college." Playing that role was not easy, and sadly sometimes I failed, but I believe being the conscience of whatever institutional setting we find ourselves in is part of our Christian calling. Our job description as Christians always includes a bit more than is found in the official contract. See also my essay, "A Philosopher's Journey with Christ."

11. Thiessen, *Teaching for Commitment*.

12. This of course raises the interesting question as to whether preevangelism is evangelism. I would suggest it should be seen as part of evangelism. Paul hints at different stages of evangelism when he describes himself as planting the seed, Apollos as watering, and God giving the increase (1 Cor 3:6). All three elements belong to evangelism.

Where appropriate and natural, I will even venture into an apologetic for the Christian faith. For example, in my introductory philosophy course, when dealing with epistemology I try to open students' minds to the possibility of God revealing himself. For many years I have concluded this course with some readings on the meaning of life, and here I contrast a secular materialistic answer and a religious/Christian answer, even going on to explain why I find the latter approach superior.

An introductory ethics course has always been my favorite. In this course I critique the rampant relativism in student attitudes toward ethics, and explore various foundations for objective universal ethical norms. I always include an exploration of a religious and Christian foundation for ethics, and point to some of the unique aspects and advantages of such a foundation. In the concluding lecture of this course, I issue a very personal challenge to students to live the moral life. In doing so, I also explore the difficulties inherent in accepting this challenge, including the problem of moral failure. And then, very briefly, I mention the need for forgiveness when we experience guilt as a result of moral failure. I then review a variety of options, including the idea of a super-cosmic Forgiver. You can usually hear a pin drop during this final lecture in my ethics courses.

One student, in an evaluation of one of my ethics courses wrote, "This was a great class, Dr. Thiessen. Unfortunately, you opened (up) my conscience; is there another class I could take so I can shut it off!" Unfortunately, I didn't offer such a course, because I believe in teaching from and for commitment.[13]

I hasten to add there are constraints as to what I can do by way of evangelism in the classroom. For one, my primary focus is on teaching philosophy, not doing evangelism. In a secular classroom, my occasional

---

13. In teaching ethics courses, I have been inspired by an essay I read some time ago by R. R. Reno, entitled "American Satyricon." Much of the article analyzes our postmodern culture. In an age where relativism reigns, where people want to be completely free to do their own thing, and where they resist any appeal to authority which challenges their free lifestyle and free-thinking ways, Reno suggests the most appropriate form of evangelism is to confront postmodern man and woman where it hurts the most—to challenge their faith in sexual freedom. "At this center point, the increasingly alien and ambitious teachings of Christianity must cut like a sharp and two-edged sword, or they cut not at all," the essay concludes (41). Of course, once this two-edged sword cuts to the heart, and postmodern man and woman begin to see themselves as rebelling against the authority of God, then they might just be more open to hear the wonderful news of the gospel—redemption and the possibility of genuine ordered freedom under the King of kings. In my ethics courses, I have often touched on sexual ethics, critiquing the reigning paradigm of free sex. I can't help but be a little amused at the horrified looks of my students as I confront them where it really hurts. What has surprised me is their attentiveness whenever I do so.

declarations of support for the Christian faith necessarily take place in the context of pluralism. A Christian foundation for ethics is therefore presented alongside Kantian and utilitarian approaches to ethics. I make it a point to critique a Christian foundation to ethics in the same way as I critique Kantian and utilitarianism theories of ethics.

To give another example, I am careful not to transform a Philosophy of Religion course into an apologetics course.[14] While I am open about my own religious commitment, I ensure that all students face squarely the best arguments of philosophers against God and religion. This often presents a challenge for students who are Christians, but students who are atheists and agnostics also find my course threatening when they encounter the best arguments in favor of God and religion. Philosophy is all about helping students to think carefully and critically about their present beliefs. I have even had students approach me at the end of a course expressing concerns about my being an atheist! This, for me, is a sign that I have been fair in presenting both sides of arguments for and against God.

I also tell my students repeatedly they can disagree with me in class discussions and on exams and still get an "A" grade in the course. Indeed, I welcome disagreement and argument. Sometimes, when it seems natural to do so, I will express my conviction that the Christian faith is the superior faith, but I try very hard to create an atmosphere in the classroom where students are free to challenge my own position. Occasionally students become more serious about investigating the Christian faith. This has led to further discussions in my office or even in our home. Here I feel quite free to make a personal appeal to such students to consider a commitment to Jesus Christ.

I will have more to say about my approach to teaching in what follows. But before I do so, I would like to examine some objections to the very idea of evangelism in the classroom.

OBJECTIONS TO EVANGELISM IN THE ACADEMY

Have I encountered opposition to my approach to being transparent about my Christian faith in the classroom? Very occasionally a student has expressed some concerns. I have also had the occasional expression of concern from one or two of my colleagues after they hear reports from their students as to what I do in the classroom. I am sure these concerns are shared by many in the secular academy. Concerns such as these are typically grounded in two basic assumptions about public and secular schooling generally.

---

14. My approach is similar to that of Davis, "How Christians Should Teach Philosophy at Secular Institutions."

The first is the assumption of neutrality. The ideal of neutrality has its roots in the Enlightenment and has shaped education in a profound way.[15] Teachers are expected to be neutral in the classroom. Closely related is the commonly made distinction between public and private values. Schools are concerned about teaching public knowledge and public values. And so teachers are urged to avoid trying "to promote their own personal opinions in school."[16] Typically, religion is considered to be a private and personal matter, and so it follows that evangelism is thought to be out of place in the classroom.

The fundamental problem with the above expressions of opposition to evangelism is that neutrality is impossible. The ideal of neutrality has been shown to be problematic, especially in light of the insights of a postmodern epistemology.[17] The public/private distinction is similarly problematic.[18] Teachers cannot help but influence their students to some degree, whatever their religious or non-religious position happens to be, and however hard they try to remain neutral.[19] More generally, we are always influencing others, and that influence often includes explicit persuasion or evangelism. It is in the nature of a human being to evangelize.[20] The classroom is one very important context in which evangelism occurs.[21] "Education is always in the business of changing belief," not only beliefs about the natural and human

---

15. The Enlightenment postulated an objective and universal reason unencumbered by religious assumptions. This concept of reason was applied to education in an influential book by Paul Hirst, called *Moral Education in a Secular Society*. Stanley Fish has recently argued the only legitimate role for the professor is that of teaching and research, devoid of any moral, religious, or political values (Fish, *Save the World on Your Own Time*). "If what you really want to do is preach," Fish argues, you should do this either on your own time, or if this is not enough, "you should resign from the academy" (81).

16. See for example the advice given to teachers by the Citizenship Foundation, "Teaching About Controversial Issues."

17. I develop this argument in Thiessen, *In Defence of Religious Schools and Colleges*, 196.

18. For a treatment of the problems underlying the public/private distinction, see ibid., 105–7.

19. For a critique of neutrality in education, see Cooling, *Doing God in Education*, and Sandsmark, *Is World View Neutral Education Possible and Desirable?*

20. As John Haughey has said, "it seems to be endemic to the way we are as human beings to promote with others what we ourselves have come to understand as true and good." Haughey, "Complex Accusation of Sheep-stealing," 266. Henry Johnstone defines a human being as, "among other things, a persuading and persuaded animal." Johnstone, "Towards an Ethics of Rhetoric," 306. For an expansion of this point, see Thiessen, *Ethics of Evangelism*, 142–45.

21. See Berner, "Persuasion in Education," 28–33.

world, but also beliefs about ultimate concerns and what to trust.[22] In other words, education inevitably involves some evangelism.

I have therefore been puzzled when, very occasionally, a colleague of mine has expressed concerns about my approach to teaching from and for commitment in the classroom. These same colleagues have no problem being very open about their atheist or Marxist leanings in the classroom. Surely it is inconsistent then to object to a Christian being open about his faith when teaching. Of course, my atheist and Marxist colleagues might not see this as an inconsistency because they view their positions as academically respectable, while my Christian commitment is seen as merely a personal belief. I would argue, however, that the notion of what is academically respectable is itself subjective (or controversial), and that a case can be made for giving a Christian worldview the same epistemological status as a Marxist or atheistic worldview.[23]

A second objection to my approach to teaching from and for commitment involves the frequently made charge of indoctrination. Since I have already dealt with the charge of indoctrination in relation to the nurture of children (chapter 8), I will be brief here. Let me be very clear: I believe indoctrination in schools and colleges is unethical. But when we charge someone with indoctrination we need to make sure we have a coherent understanding of the concept.[24] Indoctrination, properly understood, involves "the curtailment of a person's growth towards normal rational autonomy."[25] I believe my approach of teaching from and for commitment, if done in an ethical manner, encourages growth toward independent and critical thinking. I will have more to say on this when I deal with the concept of liberal education.

I conclude with a statement of concern. I worry about Christians who so easily dismiss the possibility of doing evangelism within the context of their professions, and who give as a reason for doing so that they must maintain neutrality in keeping with established practice of their professions.[26] I

---

22. Astley, "Evangelism in Education," 186.

23. I provide a justification for such an equalization of academic status in Thiessen, *Ethics of Evangelism*, 71–76.

24. See Thiessen, *Teaching for Commitment*, for a detailed examination of the confusions surrounding the notion of indoctrination.

25. Ibid., 233.

26. For example, a Christian physician was asked by a Christian colleague of his, "How do you do evangelism in your practice?" His response: "I don't believe it is the place of [a] doctor to evangelise. It is both unprofessional and unethical." Wood, "The Ethics of Evangelism in the Doctor-Patients Relationship," 14. For a contrary position, see DiSilvestro, "What's Wrong with Deliberately Proselytizing Patients?" and Salladay, "Christian Ethics."

fear that all too many Christian professionals, including teachers at colleges and universities, and teachers in state-maintained public schools, hide their light under a bushel using the myth of neutrality as a convenient cover for their hesitancy to even identify themselves as Christians, let alone be witnesses to the truth of the Christian gospel in their professions.

I have encountered other ways in which Christian professors have expressed their opposition to doing evangelism in the classroom. For example, Stephen Davis, in resolving to be "a competent and dedicated teacher," goes on to say this: "I was not going to proselytize in class or do anything that could be interpreted as treating Christian students better than other students."[27] My problem here is that Davis is simply assuming that proselytizing in the classroom is incompatible with being a competent teacher. It is further possible for a professor to be open about his or her Christian commitment and not be seen to favor Christian students, a possibility Davis himself admits in the next sentence. Of course, when professors do sometimes engage in evangelism in the classroom, they need to do this in an ethical manner, and I will have more to say about that shortly. Here I am only objecting to Christians who reject the very idea of doing evangelism in the classroom.[28]

CONTEXTUAL CONSTRAINTS OF THE ACADEMY

When we deal with the question of the ethics of evangelism, we need to pay close attention to the context in which evangelism occurs. Differing contexts might impose different constraints on doing evangelism.[29] I have

27. Davis, "How Christians Should Teach Philosophy at Secular Institutions," 2.

28. A previous essay of mine on the place of evangelism in public K–12 schooling resulted in a healthy exchange with two Christian scholars who seem to be opposed to evangelism in the classroom. See Thiessen, "Evangelism in the Classroom," Cooling, "Evangelism in the Classroom," and Hill, "Proselytizing in the State School." I realize now that the language I used to defend evangelism in the classroom was too general and not sufficiently nuanced in my original essay. I should have been clearer in stating my central objective was to defend the legitimacy of a Christian teacher identifying himself or herself as a Christian and then seeking occasional opportunities to witness to the truth of the gospel within the context of classroom lectures and discussions.

29. I believe Hill and Cooling do not pay enough attention to the individual and contextual nature of the question I was addressing in my original essay (see previous footnote). In our exchange, it becomes clear Cooling is assuming a context of church-related schools, whereas I am dealing with the context of secular schooling. (Cooling, "Evangelism in the Classroom," 260). Elsewhere, Cooling is addressing the question of evangelism within the context of religious education classes. Cooling, *Christian Vision for State Education*, 112. I agree the constraints for doing evangelism within the context of religious education are more stringent than in other subjects.

already considered evangelism within the general context of work. I have argued that the context of the workplace imposes some constraints on doing evangelism. A worker is first required to do his work. Indeed, the New Testament writers stress the importance of doing a job well. It would be wrong to be engaging in evangelism when you should be attending to your work!

I now want to focus specifically on the context of the college or university classroom. What is unique about this context? Here we find ourselves, first of all, in an *educational context*. This context puts some educational constraints on evangelism. A university lecture hall is not the same as an auditorium of an evangelistic crusade. At a crusade, people attend expecting an evangelistic appeal. Evangelism in this context can be direct and unidirectional. This does not mean there are not some constraints even in this context. It is just that the constraints are different, given the unique context of an evangelistic crusade.[30]

Within an educational context, the first priority of the teacher is to teach, not to do evangelism. This of course raises the question as to the nature of an educational context. What are the aims of education? Here I will simply assume a standard account of the ideal of liberal education. Of course, this ideal can itself be questioned, but this is not my purpose here.[31] Let's assume education is about searching for truth, expanding the horizons of students, giving them the tools to function within a society, and helping them to become independent critical thinkers.

What should be noted here is that there is some congruence between the aims of education and the aims of evangelism. It is simply a mistake to assume evangelism and education are necessarily incompatible. Indeed, as has been noted by Jeff Astley, "Education and evangelism may be closer neighbours than many suspect."[32] In both, there is a search for truth. The sharing of a teacher's religious convictions, if done in the right way, can lead to further learning on the part of students. It can expand horizons. It can help students to become rational and critical thinkers as they examine their own convictions about religion. It can also help students understand the nature of healthy commitment, especially with regard to beliefs that are controversial. With proper modeling, students also learn how to influence others in an ethical manner concerning the beliefs they hold dear.

Another important contextual feature of my own experience in the academy is that I teach *philosophy*. The discipline of philosophy has

30. For a consideration of some aspects of the ethics of evangelistic crusades, see Thiessen, *Ethics of Evangelism*, 163–64, 179–80, 191, 195–96.

31. I provide an analysis and evaluation of different ideals of liberal education in Thiessen, *Teaching for Commitment*, chapters 2, 7, 8.

32. Astley, "Evangelism in Education," 190.

traditionally included wrestling with the big questions of life, including the question of God's existence. Philosophy also involves arguing and evaluating arguments. Philosophy is therefore rather unique in providing natural opportunities for the Christian professor to give expression to his or her faith. Philosophy, more than other courses, lends itself to critically evaluating the faulty presuppositions underlying various worldviews. Different subject areas will provide different opportunities and might call for differing constraints to doing evangelism. For example, the opportunity and appropriateness of evangelism in the classroom will be less in the context of teaching certain disciplines like mathematics and physics, where the influence of one's worldview is more indirect. But even here there will be times, for example, when doing the philosophy of mathematics or physics, where the professor's worldview can come to the fore, and where it might be appropriate to show how a Christian engages with the discipline. I believe the constraints are fewer when teaching the humanities.

Of special significance is the fact that the context of my teaching experiences is *secular and pluralistic*. By "secular" I do not mean that religion is excluded from public discussion. Rather, an environment must be created that is equally hospitable to a variety of worldviews or religious and irreligious commitments. These constraints are essentially political in nature and thus reflect the kinds of concerns that underlie pragmatic and political liberalism, which stresses the importance of finding some principles that all will be able to accept and that will allow us to live together in harmony despite our deep differences.[33] However, I disagree with the tendency of liberalism to call for a bracketing of religious language in the public realm.[34] Instead, there should be a welcoming of a diversity of religious justifications, including the promotion of these religious justifications in the public sphere. This means taking opportunities to witness to one's faith should be allowed in the academy, though there are some political and ethical constraints given the pluralistic nature of the educational context.

Here let me return to my story at the beginning of this chapter. Given the secular and pluralistic context of my class, I made it a point to briefly explain several options with regard to coping with the guilt that follows from the admission that there are objective moral standards. Had I been in a church context, I could have dealt with the Christian response to guilt only. In fact, even in this context, I believe it is important sometimes to explain

---

33. See, for example, Rawls, *Political Liberalism*, and Rorty, *Consequences of Pragmatism*.

34. See my discussion of John Rawls and Stephen Macedo on the bracketing of religious language in developing civic virtues in Thiessen, *In Defence of Religious Schools and Colleges*, 235, 316 footnotes 36, 37, 38.

options other than the Christian one, but the purpose here would be to help the congregation understand and defend the faith within a pluralistic society. However, within the context of a secular and pluralistic university, I am politically and ethically obligated to present several options. Had there been time, or had I been asked, I could have presented justifications for all three options, together with a critical evaluation of each. I will have more to say about the ethical constraints of teaching within a pluralistic context in the next section.

The final contextual issue that needs to be dealt with has to do with the *teacher/pupil relationship in an educational setting*. The college or university professor is in a position of authority in a classroom. He or she is also an authority in the subject being taught. Students, however, are most often younger, less knowledgeable, and of course have their work evaluated by the professor. There is therefore the danger of the professor exploiting the vulnerability of the student. R. S. Peters has famously said, "the teacher has to learn to be in authority and to be an authority without being authoritarian."[35] This is not easy to do. This power imbalance between professor and student calls for great care when it comes to evangelizing in the classroom. More on this shortly.

The danger of exploiting the vulnerability of students becomes much greater as we consider the elementary and secondary school context. As a general rule, the younger the students, the less mature, the less capable of independent thought, and the more impressionable they are. A classroom of young children will therefore call for a more cautious approach to giving witness to the faith on the part of the teacher. Teachers will also need to be especially sensitive to the fact they are dealing with a "captive audience" of young children who by law are forced to be in school, and hence the greater danger of coercion when evangelizing.[36]

ETHICS OF EVANGELISM IN THE ACADEMIC CONTEXT

We are now in a position to look at the ethics of evangelism in the context of the academy. How do the biblical and ethical guidelines for doing evangelism that we summarized in chapter 7 apply to the academic context? I will limit myself to those that are particularly relevant.

Let me start with the foundational guidelines. Ethical evangelism in the classroom must uphold the dignity of each and every student and this

---

35. Peters, *Authority, Responsibility and Education*, 47, 54.

36. Lerner, "Proselytism, Change of Religion, and International Human Rights," 559. I give an example of a misuse of a teacher's authority in evangelism within the elementary school context in Thiessen, "Evangelism in the Classroom," 230–32.

needs to be coupled with a genuine care for students (Guidelines #A3 & #A4). Students must never be seen as mere objects of a teacher's evangelism program. Christian teachers care for their students, and insofar as is appropriate and possible, care for them as whole persons.[37] However, given the educational context of the classroom, teachers are committed to ensuring the educational needs of their students remain uppermost. Teachers also need to protect the dignity and worth of each student regardless of their religious or nonreligious beliefs. It is particularly important to treat with dignity and respect those who oppose the gospel. Remember, ethical evangelists even love enemies of the gospel (Guideline #G21).

Students will also be looking for personal integrity in the teacher (Guidelines #A2 & #D12). A teacher who does not practice what he/she preaches will not be very effective in doing evangelism, but more important, such a lack of integrity is unethical.

The avoidance of coercion is of course fundamental to protecting the dignity of students (Guideline #C9). Here the power imbalance between professor and student becomes an issue (Guideline #C10). I have tried to level the playing field by telling students that I too am a learner and have something to learn from them. I have also encouraged students to call me by my first name. Of course it is impossible to eradicate entirely the fact that the professor is in a position of authority in the classroom. Hence, caution is in order when a teacher is open about his/her religious or nonreligious beliefs. Students' beliefs need to be treated with respect. It is wrong for professors to engage in an arrogant deconstruction of student beliefs. Unfortunately this happens all too often in the academy.[38] Students must never feel pressured to agree with the religious (or nonreligious) beliefs of their teacher. When writing essays that might touch on religious themes, students should feel perfectly free to disagree with the beliefs expressed by the teacher in the classroom (Guideline #G20).

A key to mitigating the power imbalance of the professor/student relationship is the adoption of a servantlike attitude on the part of the professor (Guideline #C10). Humility is also an ethical requirement (Guideline

---

37. In the middle of my career I read Eugene Peterson's trilogy on the work of pastors in North America, and found the advice Peterson gives to pastors most relevant to my work as a philosophy professor in terms of caring for my students. See Peterson, *Five Smooth Stones for Pastoral Work*.

38. Richard Rorty, for example, maintains that college professors ought "to arrange things so that students who enter as bigoted, homophobic, religious fundamentalists will leave college, with views more like our own." With no hint of his usual irony, Rorty writes that "students are lucky to find themselves under the benevolent *Herrschaft* of people like me, and to have escaped the grip of their frightening, vicious, dangerous parents" (quoted in Boffetti, "How Richard Rorty Found Religion," 29).

#E13). Arrogance, a condescending attitude, and dogmatism have no place in proclaiming the truth of the gospel in the classroom. Christian teachers must confess with Paul that they only know in part, that they only see through a glass darkly (1 Cor 13:12). However, humility must not be seen to rule out evangelism. Indeed, even persuasion and apologetics are not ruled out, especially within the context of a philosophy course. But here again, we need to remember there is such a thing as "humble apologetics."[39] Persuasion in the classroom must be done in such a way that students feel free to disagree with what is said by the professor (Guideline #E14).

Ethical evangelism is truthful (Guideline #D11). Education is finally a search for truth, and therefore it is of utmost importance that truthfulness characterize all attempts at giving witness to the gospel within the classroom. What is said about the Christian faith must be true. Given the educational context, a Christian professor also needs to be truthful in exposing historical distortions of the Christian faith. Indeed, objections to the Christian faith need to be entertained and dealt with fairly. Care also needs to be taken to be truthful when talking about other religions or worldviews.

I also argued in chapter 7 that ethical evangelism is tolerant (Guideline #F18). Tolerance is particularly important within a secular and pluralistic educational context. But here we need to be very careful to avoid misconceptions about the nature of tolerance. Christian professors will exemplify tolerance when they treat students who disagree with them with love and respect, but this does not mean the teacher is not allowed to criticize other religious traditions or worldviews, and doing so should not in and of itself be equated with intolerance. It is only if such criticisms are made using insulting or abusive language, or if the teacher displays hostile attitudes to the religion being criticized, that the teacher should be accused of being intolerant and unethical.

RESEARCH AND WRITING

I conclude with a final aspect of life in the academy—doing research and publishing articles and books. For me as a Christian this has been another venue in which I feel called to do some evangelism. How? I have made it a point to identify myself as a Christian of a fairly orthodox variety in books directed to a secular readership. Thankfully it is much more common now for authors of articles and books to declare their starting point early on in their writing. Further, my aim in my writing is to uphold truth, and correct error, trying to "take captive every thought to make it obedient to Christ" (2

---

39. See Stackhouse, *Humble Apologetics*.

Cor 10:5). Of course, there is a need here to practice discernment as to when one engages in explicit evangelism, and obviously this must also be done in an ethical manner.

Here too I have encountered some resistance to my efforts to be an evangelist in the academy. Of course, this is part of the give-and-take of academic life, particularly in the field of philosophy, but at times I have felt there was a more sinister dimension to objections being made. For me this has come to the fore especially when applying for various kinds of research grants and fellowships. An essential part of this process is to have one's proposals for such awards vetted by referees. It is a good process, and generally it leads to helpful comments on one's work, but at times biases come to the fore as I have experienced on a number of occasions.

In one case a referee claimed to speak on behalf of other Canadian academics in my field, informing me that some scholars, both in philosophy and in religious studies, regarded me as "narrow in training and perspective." He went on: "It is true that in certain ways Thiessen marches to the beat of a different drummer than most of his colleagues in Canadian philosophy of religion and religious studies." Another referee expressed concern about my "consuming research interests and studies," which all seemed to focus on the defense of religion. And then this: "Could he overcome his own personal religious convictions and concentrate on developing philosophical arguments that could compel and stand against any critical inquiry simply because they represent philosophical thinking at its best?"[40] This very same comment appeared again in a later evaluation of an application for a major Social Sciences and Humanities Research Council grant. I suspect it was the same person.

Well, I didn't get that grant, nor the earlier fellowship. While I would be the first to admit there may have been some good academic reasons as to why I didn't get them, and while I am also prepared to admit that some of the criticisms made in these reports may have had some justification, I do have a problem with their cutting edge. There are anti-Christian biases out there, and they hurt. After reading these reports, I had to swallow hard a few times, pray a little, do some introspection, and ask myself the hard question as to whether there was some legitimacy to some of the criticisms. But, in the end, I needed to move on, still marching to the beat of a different drummer, and still writing on topics I felt called to write about.[41] I also had to

---

40. Here we see, once again, the ideal of neutrality coming to the fore. Philosophy is not and cannot be a neutral discipline, and therefore there is nothing wrong with basing philosophical arguments on religious presuppositions.

41. Thankfully, not all academic reviews of my work revealed the biases being highlighted in this section. And I did get some grants and fellowships over the course of my career. McGill-Queen's University Press also published two of my books which are

remind myself that insofar as these comments represented an anti-Christian bias, I needed to accept them as the inevitable consequences of my Christian commitment. After all, Christ has called us to share in his sufferings, and that includes philosophers who are followers of Jesus Christ.[42]

In conclusion, I return to the more general topic of work and vocation and mission. Our work matters to God. We are called to honor God in our work. This also applies to Christians in various professions. Professions represent a unique opportunity for vocational stewardship and mission. This mission is broader than just evangelism, but it does include evangelism. May God help us to be faithful in declaring Christ as Lord and Savior, and also in advancing his kingdom in our professional lives.

---

decidedly Christian and also rather anti-establishment in the area of education.

42. Matt 5:11; 1 Pet 2:21; see also Guideline #G22. Naugle, in his essay, "Traits of Christian Philosophers," suggests "the Christian philosophical vocation is cruciform in nature" (2–3).

Chapter 10

Evangelism and Humanitarian Aid[1]

Anand Nayak tells a story about a family living in his neighborhood in Mangalore, the chief port city of the Indian state of Karnataka:

Srimati Madhusudan, a Harijan, was living in a small shed with a thatched roof at the foot of a hill with his wife and six small children. They were living on their handicraft trade of making baskets. Their daily income three years ago was Rs.20 per day (about 45 USA cents or 27 British pence). When his wife was dying he came to a Catholic priest for help. The priest got his wife admitted in the hospital and gave some help to the family. When she recovered she found a job on the priest's compound. The children, who had never seen a school before, were admitted in the Catholic parish school. Madhusudan had by now come to know other Christian homes where he got regular jobs. One day the whole family decided to become Christian and the priest baptized them and lodged them in a simple home built by a cooperative society.

The focus of this chapter is on the ethics of doing evangelism within the context of delivering Christian humanitarian aid and development. For brevity's sake, I will most often refer only to "aid," by which I mean the provision of humanitarian aid including help for the poor, care for refugees, medical services,

1. This chapter has its origins in the fifth Global Triennial Consultation of the Micah Network, held in Thun, Switzerland, Sept. 10–14, 2012. I gave a lecture on "The Ethics of the Evangelism/Aid Interface," and a workshop on "Principles of Ethical Evangelisation: Code of Conduct and Integral Mission." My thanks to those who gave me some valuable feedback.

development assistance, and emergency help in times of disaster. The focus could be made broader to include the entire range of what we as Christians are called to do in order to build God's kingdom here on Earth, adding such items as advocacy, working for justice, and protecting the environment. I am limiting myself in the main to the context of aid as a way of making the problem to be dealt with more manageable. I leave it to the reader to extrapolate to other areas of Christian social and political involvement.

As in the other chapters of Part II, I am trying to apply the biblical analysis of the ethics of evangelism covered in Part I to some concrete contemporary problems. The problem of the ethics of evangelism within the context of Christian aid is complex, and it is impossible to provide a comprehensive treatment of this problem within the confines of a short chapter.[2] I can at most highlight some of the central issues that need to be dealt with.

RESPONDING TO CRITICS

The above story was first told in the context of an online academic discussion group, whose members were exchanging views on the topic of combining evangelism and humanitarian aid, as well as the danger of using aid as an inducement to convert.[3] Some members of the discussion group felt that Christian aid cannot help but put pressure on those receiving aid to convert.[4] Indeed, this is a charge frequently made by critics of Christian relief and development work. One writer has described this problem as "arguably the prickliest subject in the emerging field of religion and development."[5]

---

2. Matthew Clarke, in an introductory essay of a "significant" collection of recent research on the relation between development and religion, suggests this field of study is in its "infancy." He specifically calls attention to the need for more reflection on the difference between faith-based organizations (FBOs) and nongovernmental organizations. Clarke, "Understanding the Nexus Between Religion and Development," 11.

3. This contribution was made as part of a Hindu-Christian email discussion group prompted by a statement from the Dalai Lama in January of 2001 (hcs-l@lists.acusd.edu Jan. 26—Feb. 2, 2001). The Dalai Lama's statement, while condemning all evangelism, at the same time expressed opposition to "conversions by any religious tradition using various methods of enticement." Anand Nayak, who was then teaching at the University of Fribourg, told this story as part of his contribution to the discussion on Jan. 29, 2001. In what follows, I am drawing on my discussion of this case in Thiessen, *Ethics of Evangelism*, 91–93.

4. Rajiv Malhotra, one of the members of the discussion group, objected to "preying upon the prospective client's poverty" (Jan. 28, 2001). Dave Freedholm suggested missionary activity often uses the unethical method of providing material incentives for conversion (Jan. 29, 2001).

5. Fountain, "Proselytizing Development," 80.

After telling the story, Anand Nayak, a Catholic scholar, asked the members of the discussion group a question: Is the above story an example of enticement to convert? Of course, it is, he responds. But then he probes with another penetrating question: Or should the priest have left Srimati Madhusudan and the children to die out of fear of enticing them to convert? Surely dire medical and economic needs call for a caring response. And if people convert as a result of such care, is it really fair to criticize the initial response as an exploitation of need, or as providing a material inducement to convert? Besides, are we really in a position to assess what prompted the conversion in the first place? Nayak prefaces this case description by pointing out that conversion is a personal act of faith, and it is only the convert who can really tell what his or her motivation is. Indeed, perhaps motivational assessment is best left to God!

Here it might be well for the critics of Christian humanitarian aid efforts to do some introspection on what motivates them to criticize Christian aid workers and evangelists! Indeed, as has been pointed out in a recent salient essay by Cecelia Lynch and Tanya Schwartz, entitled "Humanitarian's Proselytism Problem," concerns about Christian aid and development tend to rely on "a secularized humanitarian narrative" which itself needs to be critically evaluated.[6] Various scholars and policy makers have recently been arguing that secular humanitarian organizations are not immune to the problem of furthering a particular political or religious standpoint.[7] The problem of "evangelism" within the context of humanitarian aid is therefore a two-edged sword that applies to both secular and religious organizations.

A cautionary note for Christians is perhaps in order. In chapter 1, I noted there are many Christians, including evangelical Christians, who make the same objections to evangelism as do atheists and agnostics who are very critical of evangelism. I suggested further that this is worrying because all too often the thinking of Christians is shaped too much by the world around them. I believe the same applies to the problem being considered in this chapter. I find it rather alarming that there are many Christians who join secular critics in condemning all evangelism within the context of Christian aid.[8] This leads me to wonder to what extent Christian thinking

---

6. Lynch and Schwartz, "Humanitarianism's Proselytism Problem," 641.

7. Ibid., 642. Lynch and Schwartz label this "donor proselytism," and suggest secular humanitarian organizations frequently impose both a neoliberal economic and a cultural/political agenda on aid. Such donor proselytism also discourages local governance and chips away at local cultures and customs (642). Lynch and Schwartz even suggest this neoliberal agenda is itself religious in nature (644).

8. For some examples of this position, see a treatment of "The Range of Christian FBO Ethics Regarding Proselytism," in Lynch and Schwartz, "Humanitarianism's

on the subject has been unduly shaped by the secularized humanitarian narrative which dominates development scholarship and government agencies.

In this chapter I will argue that rather than making blanket condemnations of hidden agendas behind Christian aid, we need to spend more time trying to distinguish between ethical and unethical forms of evangelism within the context of humanitarian aid.

DISTINCT YET RELATED

The title of this chapter and the discussion of the story told by Anand Nayak assume a distinction that needs to be dealt with before we proceed any further. I am assuming we can distinguish between evangelism and Christian aid. Indeed, already in chapter 1 I argued we need to distinguish between a broader concept of Christian mission and a variety of particular tasks that fall under this broader concept. I argued evangelism is a vital part of God's larger mission in the world, the *missio Dei*. Social action is also a vital part of God's larger mission in the world. But should we even distinguish between evangelism and social action? As already noted in the first chapter, this distinction has been the subject of "an extremely important and often sharp and divisive debate" among Christians.[9]

David Bosch, in responding to what he describes as "the bewildering variety of interpretations of evangelism," identifies what he sees as the key problem with attempts to distinguish between evangelism and social action.[10] The moment you separate the two, Bosch argues, "you have, in principle, admitted that each of the two components has a life of its own." "You are then suggesting that it is possible to have evangelism without a social dimension and Christian social action without an evangelistic dimension." Bosch goes so far as to suggest this kind of "dualism" is "dangerous."[11] So how do we deal with what Bosch elsewhere calls "one of the thorniest areas in the theology and practice of mission"?[12]

Efforts have been made to overcome this allegedly dangerous dualism. For example, the notion of "integral mission" has been central to the Micah Network, a loose global alliance of over 330 evangelical Christian relief, development, and justice organizations that until recently was headed

---

Proselytism Problem," 639–41.

9. Sider, "Evangelism, Salvation, and Social Justice," 185.

10. Bosch, "Evangelism," 5.

11. Ibid. Mark Oxbrow labels the distinction between evangelism and Christian social action a "false dichotomy" (Oxbrow, "Christian Mission," 58).

12. Bosch, *Transforming Mission*, 401.

by Latin American theologian, René Padilla. At its first global consultation, held in Oxford, UK, in September 2001, the network members crafted a "Declaration on Integral Mission," based on Micah 6:8:

> Integral mission or holistic transformation is the proclamation and demonstration of the gospel. It is not simply that evangelism and social involvement are to be done alongside each other. Rather, in integral mission our proclamation has social consequences as we call people to love and repentance in all areas of life. And our social involvement has evangelistic consequences as we bear witness to the transforming grace of Jesus Christ.[13]

While I agree that evangelism and social action do interpenetrate each other, I have concerns about calls to completely "overcome" the dichotomy between proclamation and demonstration of the gospel.[14] Vinoth Ramachandra has proposed "we understand 'integral mission' less in terms of the church's activities and more in terms of what the church is called to *be*."[15] Ramachandra continues: "The emphasis lies, then, not so much in the practical 'balancing' of our various activities, but rather in the firm refusal to draw unbiblical distinctions."[16]

Now I certainly don't want to draw unbiblical distinctions, but I'm not so sure making a distinction between evangelism and social action is unbiblical.[17] What is unbiblical is the failure to see that the mission of the church includes both evangelism and social action, and I suspect this is in part the original motivation behind introducing the notion of integral mission.

13. Micah Network, "Declaration on Integral Mission." This declaration is also found in Chester, *Justice, Mercy and Humility*, 17–23. For a description of the Micah Network, its mandate, and its definition of integral mission, see Bradbury, "Micah Mandate." For some essays tracing the earlier history of the notion of integral mission and related concepts, see Samuel and Hauser, *Proclaiming Christ in Christ's Way*.

14. For example, Rick Richardson suggests we need to "overcome" the dichotomies we have created between evangelism and social action, or word and deed. We need to embrace "an integrated holism in which the church lives its faith and shares its life instead of treating these two as though they were separable, dichotomized activities." Richardson, "Emerging Missional Movements," 134.

15. Ramachandra, "What is Integral Mission?," 1. For Ramachandra, "Integral mission flows out of an integral gospel and an integrated people" (10).

16. Ibid., 2.

17. Ramachandra tries to show this distinction is unbiblical by asking us to consider what Jesus was doing when he voluntarily engaged in a face-to-face conversation with a social outcast like the Samaritan woman (John 4). Was he doing evangelism, or was he challenging the political taboos of his society? It is hard to say, and so Ramachandra concludes we should not be so ready to distinguish between evangelism and social action (Ramachandra, "What is Integral Mission," 2). The problem here is that it is surely wrong to draw a general conclusion from just one example.

However, I object to attempts to blur this distinction, or later attempts to achieve an even greater integration that in effect erases the distinction between evangelism and social action entirely.[18] After all, Jesus defined his mission in terms of preaching the gospel *and* releasing the captives, healing the blind, *and* freeing the oppressed.[19] Jesus also called his disciples both to preach the good news *and* to heal the sick (Luke 9 & 10). The early believers prayed fervently for boldness in proclaiming the gospel, *and* also that God would give them the power to heal and to perform miraculous signs and wonders (Acts 4:29–30). Paul in his description of the "cosmic Christ" talks both about "reconciling" to himself "all things," *and* about reconciling individuals to Jesus Christ (Col 1:19–20, 22). I therefore suggest it is biblical to distinguish between evangelism and social action.

Saying evangelism and social action are distinct does not exclude the possibility they might be integrally related to some degree. Ron Sider reviews several aspects of their interrelationship.[20] In the first place, evangelism, as I have defined it, includes a call to repentance and a turning away from sin, but sin is both personal and structural. Zacchaeus's conversion surely included both a turning away from personal sin and a declaration of compensation for the structural evil of a system of tax collection he had been a part of (Luke 19:1–10). Jesus declared, "Today, salvation has come to this house." So here evangelism clearly had social implications.

Second, social action facilitates the task of evangelism. The story of Srimati Madhusudan at the beginning of this chapter illustrates this point. Identifying with people suffering under unjust social structures and working in the name of Jesus to improve socioeconomic conditions for the oppressed can help people to begin to understand the message of God's love in Christ. Indeed, there is historical evidence showing Christian involvement in social action leads to conversions and church growth.[21]

Third, an examination of the Great Commission and the Great Commandment will again reveal the interrelations between evangelism and social action. It is simply a mistake to assume the former is only concerned

---

18. For example, Justin Thacker, in an article reviewing attempts to overcome the ambiguities in the notion of integral mission, calls Ramachandra's model "a paradigm shift in our concept of integral mission," which achieves a "profound" and an even greater sense of integration than previous models. Thacker, "Holistic Gospel in a Developing Society," 217.

19. Luke 4:18–19. See also Sider, "Evangelism, Salvation, and Social Justice," 193.

20. Ibid., 201–3.

21. See, for example, studies concerning the "improbable rise of Christianity in the Roman Empire" (Kreider, *Patient Ferment of the Early Church*; and Stark, *Triumph of Christianity*). For some contemporary examples, see footnote 38 in this chapter.

with evangelism and the latter only with social ministry, as is so often done. When giving us the Great Commission, Jesus instructed his followers to make disciples of all nations, and this includes teaching them to observe all he had commanded them, i.e., feeding the hungry, welcoming the stranger, and looking after the sick (Matt 25:31–46). Similarly, obeying the Great Commandment of loving one's neighbor surely includes telling them the good news about Jesus Christ.

So, I agree evangelism and social action are interrelated. Insofar as this is what is being affirmed by notions of holistic or integral mission, I am fully in agreement. But to concede interrelations between evangelism and social action does not entail that they cannot be distinguished from each other. Indeed, the "Micah Network Declaration of Integral Mission" quoted above assumes as much. But holistic concepts like integral mission carry with them the temptation to overlook useful distinctions.[22] Unfortunately, this is what has happened to these concepts over time, what with attempts to overcome a supposedly dangerous dualism. It is possible and biblically necessary to distinguish between Christian aid/development/advocacy and evangelism/proclamation, both at a *conceptual* and at a *practical* level.

Of course, once we admit there is a distinction, an additional question comes to the fore: How do we do justice to both these aspects of Christian mission? To try to escape this question by defining it away is a mistake. We need to face this difficulty head-on. One question that arises is: Should evangelism and aid always occur together and at the same time?[23] Here again, a close examination of the practice of Jesus and the apostles gives a mixed answer. Sometimes they do both at the same time.[24] Sometimes they appear to focus on only one aspect of this dual mission. Sometimes it is hard to tell.[25] What is significant is that the overall mission of Jesus and the disciples included both proclamation and demonstration of the good news. As followers of Jesus Christ, we are therefore bound to do the same.

---

22. See Daniel Hillion's careful analysis of the dangers inherent in the notion of integral mission ("Does Integral Mission Include Everything that God Requires of Us?"). Hillion refers to the Lausanne Covenant, which though sympathetic to the ideal of "integral mission," nevertheless points to some necessary distinctions: "reconciliation with man is not reconciliation with God, nor is social action evangelism, nor is political liberation salvation" ("Lausanne Covenant," #5).

23. This is the question Ramachandra raises about the original notion of integral mission (Ramachandra, "What is Integral Mission?" 1). See also Bradbury, "Micah Mandate," 112–13.

24. See Mark 1:39; 3:14; 6:30–44; Matt 11:4–6.

25. See, for example, Jesus' interaction with the Samaritan woman (John 4). For some comments on this example, see footnote 17 above.

There are two reasons why, at a practical level, Christians might be justified at times in engaging in one and not the other of these two interrelated aspects of Christian mission.[26] In part this may be due to differing gifts within the Body of Christ.[27] Sometimes it is the existential demands of a particular situation that make us focus on one or the other aspect of this dual mandate of Christian mission. For example, during a tsunami, it is probably more important to focus on meeting the basic physical needs of the people than it is to preach the gospel. Indeed, preaching the gospel in these circumstances will not only be ineffective, but also displays a profound lack of love for the immediate and desperate needs of these people. What is important is that overall and in the long run, the church be faithful to both evangelism and social action. Both need to be respected and seen as essential elements of the mission that has been given to the church.

There is another important question that needs to be addressed here—the question of priorities—and here too there is sharp debate among Christians.[28] Some maintain evangelism should have priority over social action. Some maintain they are equally important. Still others give priority to deeds.[29] Here it is important, first of all, to recognize that all tasks falling under the broad concept of mission are important, as I argued in chapter 1. Given the goals of the *missio Dei*, it is important to call people to repentance and reconciliation with God. The work of reconciliation between humans is also important, and so is the work of reconciling humans with creation. All are important aspects of God's project of bringing about *shalom* or an all-encompassing wholeness.[30] Jesus himself spent time proclaiming the good news, healing the sick, and upsetting the social and religious boundaries of his time. The Gospels provide no indication, either theoretically or by the space devoted to each of these tasks, that Jesus considered one more important than the other. God in Christ invites his chosen people to collaborate with him in achieving all these important dimensions of his kingdom project.

Ron Sider, in a passionate plea for the equal importance of evangelism and social action, concludes with this suggestion: "The time has come for all

---

26. See Lausanne Occasional Paper #21, Section #4B.

27. Ibid. "Some are gifted to be 'evangelists' (Eph 4:11), while others are called to 'service' (Rom 12:7; 1 Pet 4:11) or to do 'acts of mercy' (Rom 12:8)."

28. See Sider, "Evangelism, Salvation, and Social Justice," 185–90; Bosch, "Evangelism," 6–8.

29. Peter Dyck, in an early essay on a Mennonite theology of service, reports that in many Dutch Mennonite homes a Delft blue plate graces the walls bearing an old Mennonite motto, the last phrase of which says, "deeds are above words." Dyck, "Theology of Service," 266.

30. Kreider and Kreider, *Worship and Mission*, 46, 54.

biblical Christians to refuse to use the sentence: 'The primary mission of the church is . . . '"[31] Evangelism, social action, fellowship, teaching, worship—all are important parts of the mission of the church. I would make one qualification to Sider's position, a qualification which I am sure he would agree with. In certain circumstances, it might be that one aspect of the mission of God might temporarily become more important than the other. But, overall and in the long run, evangelism and social action are equally important.[32]

What does this rather lengthy defense of "distinct but related" have to do with the ethics of evangelism and humanitarian aid? I believe a fully integrated notion of integral mission leads to a skirting of ethical problems involved in the interface between evangelism and social action. These problems need to be faced head-on, rather than trying to resolve them by arbitrary definition. So, this lengthy section should be seen as preparing the way for an ethics of evangelism within the context of aid. I also worry that a blurring of the distinction between evangelism and social action will in the end lead to a tendency to focus only on social action.[33] Of course, there is also the danger that Christians focus too much or even exclusively on evangelism, as has been the tendency among evangelical Christians in the past.[34] Either of these extremes is not only unbiblical, but also unethical. These extremes are unethical because they fail to address the needs of whole persons (see Guideline #A4 in chapter 7).

31. Sider, "Evangelism, Salvation, and Social Justice," 201.

32. For a defense of the need for a balance between evangelism and social action, and for examples of such a healthy balance, see Sider, *Doing Evangelism Jesus' Way*, *One-Sided Christianity?*, and *Cup of Water, Bread of Life*.

33. Bill Prevette gives some evidence in support of this assessment in summing up his study of the work of churches and FBOs with children in Romania (Prevette, "Disturbance of God, Holistic Mission and Children in Crisis," 99–100). See also Sider's comments about the National Council of Churches in the United States (Sider, *Doing Evangelism*, 77–78). A review of the Micah Network's triennial meetings will reveal that the predominant emphasis is on Christian aid/development/advocacy, not evangelism. Tim Chester warned about this very danger at the time when the "Micah Network Declaration on Integral Mission" was first formulated at the first international consultation of the Micah Network in 2001 (Chester, *Justice, Mercy and Humility*, 3). While Steve Bradbury, who was chair of the Micah Network from 1999–2009, and who participated in the writing of the "Declaration on Integral Mission," claims a passion for evangelism has always been a vital part of the identity of the Micah Network, he is forced to go on to qualify—"at least in theory if not always in practice" (Bradbury, "Micah Mandate," 113).

34. Prevette also gives evidence of this tendency (Prevette, "Disturbance of God, Holistic Mission and Children in Crisis," 94, 100). See also Bosch, *Transforming Mission* 403–4; and Sider, *Doing Evangelism Jesus' Way*, 76–77.

CHRISTIAN AID EQUALS EVANGELISM

In the previous section I have examined attempts to blur the distinction between evangelism and social action. There is a stronger version of this blurring that needs to be considered, if indeed it should even be described in terms of a blurring of the distinction. What I have in mind is a frequently made assumption that Christian aid is in fact the same as evangelism. How often have I read or heard that the proclamation of the gospel can occur by word and deed?[35] Then there is the frequently invoked statement attributed to Francis of Assisi: "Preach the gospel at all times; if necessary use words." The usual interpretation of this oft-quoted aphorism is that there is another way to preach the gospel—via good deeds. Indeed, there is an implicit suggestion this is in fact a better way to do evangelism. After all, actions speak louder than words.

We have already treated this equation of word and deed with regard to evangelism in chapter 1, but my concern there was with the definition of evangelism. The focus here is more practical, and of course I want to examine the implications of this position for the ethics of evangelism in the context of Christian aid. We are also in a better position to consider this equation and its ethical implications given our study of the New Testament in Part I.

There is obviously something right about an emphasis on preaching the gospel without words. Jesus describes his disciples as the salt of the earth, and the light of the world in the Sermon on the Mount.[36] In chapter 6, it was noted that the apostle Peter seems to be reflecting his Master's words when he encourages us to do good and to live such good lives among the pagans that they will be forced to glorify God on the day of judgment (1 Pet 2:12). Peter even gives a specific example of the importance of nonverbal witness

---

35. An important Study Document of the Joint Working Group of the World Council of Churches and the Roman Catholic Church, talks about the mission of God in terms of "proclaiming through word and action." Joint Working Group, "Challenge of Proselytism," 214. Orthodox theologian, Eric Tosi defines evangelism as "the witness in living out of the proclamation of the good news of the risen Christ" ("Koinonic Evangelism: The Community as The Evangelist," 164). Interestingly, the third-century North African theologian, Tertullian, gave expression to this view in describing the witness of early Christians who won disciples because they "teach by deeds." Quoted in Kreider & Kreider, *Worship and Mission*, 184. For additional examples of this equation, see chapter 1, page 17, and footnote 51.

36. Matt 5:13–16. Jesus, when he was asked by John whether he was the Messiah, replied, "Go back and report to John what you hear and see: The blind receive sight, the lame walk, those who have leprosy are cured, the deaf hear, the dead are raised, and the good news is preached to the poor" (Matt 11:2–6). Paul speaks to the witness of changed lives when he says, "You yourselves are our letter (of recommendation) . . . known and read by everybody" (2 Cor 3:2).

when he encourages believing wives who have an unbelieving husband to behave in such an exemplary way that "they may be won over without talk" (1 Pet 3:1). It is considerations such as this that lead various writers to talk about "lifestyle evangelism."[37] Even today, the humanitarian activities of mission agencies do lead to people being converted.[38]

What is misleading here is the failure to understand the nature of nonverbal witness. The silent witness of the early Christians was never really completely silent. Peter's advice assumes the Christian identity of the wife will have been known to the unbelieving husband. Some words will have been spoken at some earlier point in time. No further talk is needed. Given what has preceded, the wife can rely on the fact that her actions can speak louder than further words. Similarly, the humanitarian activities of a mission agency are always done within a particular context. The Christian identity of the mission that was helping Madhusudan, in the example given at the beginning of the chapter, will have been known to him. Words about the identity of the Christian hospital were probably written on the hospital entrance. Words are necessary!

Further, actions alone cannot speak unambiguously. Giving aid to a foreigner can be interpreted as an act of Christian love, but such an action could equally well be the work of a terrorist organization seeking to win your allegiance. So, actions by themselves can be variously interpreted. It is only if they are put into a particular context, only if they are interpreted using words, that they can begin to speak in a less ambiguous manner. Thus, as is noted by Lesslie Newbigin, Jesus instructed the twelve disciples to preach alongside their acts of healing and exorcism. "[T]he healings—marvelous as they are—do not explain themselves. They could be misinterpreted—as in fact they were by Jesus' enemies, who attributed his healing works to Satanic

---

37. Lynch and Schwartz identify several writers who use this expression ("Humanitarianism's Proselytism Problem," 640). See also Ewert, "Evangelism by Lifestyle," 18. It should be noted that Ewert, at the very outset, cautions against a misunderstanding of his position as ruling out the importance of words. As I point out in chapter 1, I prefer not to talk about "lifestyle evangelism," because it confuses word and deed. Hence the quotation marks.

38. For example, in a *Time* essay on "The New Missionary," by Richard Ostling, the work of Jesuit missionary Father John Dahlheimer and 366 other Christian workers in Nepal are described. Though evangelism is forbidden in this officially Hindu land, and although these missionaries obey this law, yet their example has inspired more than 3,000 Nepalese to convert since 1954. Additional contemporary examples are described in Sider, *Cup of Water*, and *Doing Evangelism*, 78–79. See also Daz, "God and Refugees," 9, 11, and examples in footnote 21 of this chapter.

power."³⁹ The works by themselves did not communicate the gospel. For that words were needed: "The kingdom of heaven is near" (Matt 10:7).

That is why clarity about the identity of Christian humanitarian agencies is so important. If that identity is not communicated in some way, we really don't have Christian humanitarian aid. All that is left is an essentially "secular" enterprise. Hence the repeated concerns about the work of Christian nongovernmental organizations (NGOs) becoming secularized.⁴⁰ The Mennonite Central Committee (MCC), a well-respected relief agency, once made it a practice to stamp on all bags of grain shipped to needy countries, "In the Name of Christ." This is no longer a uniform practice. Indeed, MCC sometimes distributes aid through secular organizations.⁴¹ I am sure MCC is not alone in this practice. My concern here is that there is really nothing left of a Christian witness when the identity of MCC and other Christian relief agencies remains hidden. After all, Jesus instructed us not to hide our light under a bowl or a bushel (Matt 5:14–15).

Finally, we also need to keep in mind that the gospel is a story, a wonderful story of God's actions to redeem a world that has been badly distorted by sin. This biblical story cannot be told by mere actions. It needs to be expressed in words. The church must never forget the importance of telling the story of Jesus in words, even while engaged in social ministries.⁴² Of course, a question still remains as to when those words need to be spoken, and I have already suggested there may be circumstances where we focus only on works. But at some point words are needed if we want to be faithful to what Paul and Jesus teach us about proclaiming the good news of Jesus Christ.

So, what should faith-based organizations (FBOs) do in situations of need where governments or funding agencies prohibit evangelism? First of

---

39. Newbigin, *Gospel in a Pluralist Society*, 132.

40. Several speakers at the 5th Global Triennial Consultation of the Micah Network, held in Thun, Switzerland, Sept. 10–14, 2012, expressed concerns about Christian relief and development work becoming secularized, in part due to organizations getting funding from governments.

41. In response to an inquiry regarding this practice by the author (July 6, 2016), Elizabeth Kessler, Interim Donor Relations Coordinator for the Global Family program of the Canadian MCC office, admitted that MCC does sometimes work through secular organizations. It should be noted that in its current statement of "Principles and Practices," several sentences clearly indicate the work of MCC is done "in the name of Christ" (Mennonite Central Committee). It would seem this is not always carried out in practice.

42. Peter Dyck quotes Veronique Laufer of the Christian French relief and service agency, CIMADE, who wonders whether "our efforts to commit ourselves in service (is) not an escape from the task of speaking out the Good News." He also confesses that many times when asked why they are involved in Christian service, they "are not ready to give an account of our faith." (Quoted in Dyck, "Theology of Service," 267).

all, there needs to be transparency about Christian identity. In seeking official entry to serve the needy in countries that restrict Christian activity, Christians should be very open about their Christian identity and motivation.[43]

I also believe it is possible for FBOs to accept the restrictions placed upon them by governments or funding agencies, prohibiting them from taking the *initiative* in sharing their faith with those they are serving. But governments or funding agencies do not have the authority to stop Christians from explaining their faith in response to questions that might be asked within the context of giving aid and doing development work. Here we must firmly say, "We must obey God rather than men" (Acts 5:29). If a recipient of aid asks why we are serving them, we should be able to explain that we are doing this out of obedience to Jesus Christ and in response to his love.[44] I will have more to say about this later when dealing with disaster relief.

A final brief comment on another practical matter. While there is a growing recognition within governments and the secular development establishment of the contribution made by FBOs to aid and development, nervousness and suspicion remain, particularly with regard to the danger of using aid and development as a cloak for evangelism.[45] Thus we find secular development organizations often demanding that FBOs clearly separate their aid and development work from evangelism, and insisting that funding given to them not be used for evangelistic or church-related endeavors.[46] Given my defense of evangelism and social action being distinct (though interrelated) activities, it would seem Christian agencies can agree to such government strictures. However, here again transparency is called for. Christian aid agencies can agree not to use government funding for explicit programs of evangelism, but they should insist on being transparent with regard to their Christian identity. They should also make it clear that it is impossible to completely separate aid from evangelism. And again, they should insist on the right to explain their motivation when asked.

---

43. For a positive example of this, see Steve Bradbury's moving description of clarity of Christian identity and motivation of the ten people who were tragically killed in a remote part of Afghanistan on August 5, 2010, while returning from an International Assistance Mission (IAM) health camp. Bradbury, "Micah Mandate," 107–9.

44. See Micah Network, "Proselytism," Statement #6. This paper is based on the work of a South Asian Micah Network Disaster Management Working Group (2007).

45. Lynch and Schwartz, "Humanitarianism's Proselytism Problem," 636. Bickley, *Problem of Proselytism*, 51–52.

46. For some examples of such demands on the part of secular government aid and development programs, see Bradbury, "Mission, Missionaries and Development" 422–24.

In concluding this section, I want to caution against a possible misinterpretation. I fear my argument in this section might be interpreted as undermining the importance of Christian aid. Christian involvement in relief, development, and advocacy is a very important part of the broader mission of the church. My primary concern in this section has been to ensure we don't equate social action with evangelism, or see it as a stand-alone substitute for the proclamation of the good news of Jesus Christ. I would remind the reader of a foundational guideline for ethical evangelism. Ethical evangelism is incarnational in nature (Guideline #A2). There must be integrity to our witness. There must be a match between the words proclaimed, and the character and deeds of the evangelist. So, deeds are important. Indeed, they are very important. Ethical evangelism requires that the proclamation of the good news is backed up by good character and good deeds, and of course, also worship of God.

OPPORTUNISM: AID FOR THE PURPOSE OF EVANGELISM

There is another dimension of the relation between aid and evangelism that deserves brief treatment. It has to do with the motivation behind providing humanitarian aid. Why do we provide aid to those in need? A proper understanding of the *missio Dei* would suggest caring for the needy is good because God cares for the poor and the needy and the vulnerable in the world.[47] Christians collaborate with God in caring for the poor and the vulnerable, and this has value because it reflects the mission of God. In chapter 3, we also looked at Jesus' concern for the poor and the oppressed. Jesus was concerned about helping the poor and freeing the oppressed because it was the will of God. So it should be with us. Jesus did not instruct his disciples to heal the sick *in order to enhance* the preaching of the good news.

We must also not forget the cross, as is so poignantly stated by Isaiah Majok Dau, a Sudanese preacher:

> The cross provides a real stimulus to alleviate the suffering of others because the suffering of any of God's people grieves His heart. By seeking to relieve the hardships of others, we are working to ease the suffering and pain of God. As we meet the practical needs of those who suffer, we demonstrate to them the message of the cross. Our presence with and provision for the needs of those who are hurting assure them that God has not

---

47. See Exod 22:22; Deut 10:18, 16:11, 14; Job 19:16; Ps 41:1, 68:5, 72:13; Isa 10:2; Matt 25:31–46; Rom 15:1; 1 Thess 5:14; James 1:27. See also Das, *Compassion and the Mission of God*.

abandoned them in their misery and pain. Any assistance that we extend to them speaks of God's presence and identification with them in their suffering.[48]

Helping others is good because it reflects God's presence among those who are suffering. Helping others is good because it reflects God's love for the poor and the needy. We give aid simply because God wants us to give aid and because this is an expression of love for our neighbor. "We are not involved in giving relief to the needy so that we can evangelize but because it is our Christian calling to give relief to the needy."[49]

Here let me express some concern about the motivation that all too often colors the giving of aid among evangelical Christians. For example, I hear of churches who are involved in teaching English to refugees or new immigrants, but it is all too evident the purpose behind this endeavor is really evangelistic. We should be involved in teaching English to refugees and new immigrants because it is right to help those in need. Our motivation behind doing good should be for the sake of the other and for the sake of God (see Guidelines #H24–27).

Having said this, I would urge some caution in assessing the motivation of others or even of ourselves when offering aid of various kinds. Ultimately, only God can test our motivation.

God wants us to help others and he also wants us to share the good news. Loving others entails both caring for their physical/psychological/social needs, and their spiritual needs (Guideline #A4). We care for people as whole persons and it is therefore difficult to separate the meeting of physical and spiritual needs. Holistic care also makes it difficult to distinguish between the motivations underlying these two activities that are in any case closely intertwined. Perhaps a way to test our motivation is to ask ourselves whether we would still be engaged in teaching English to refugees and new immigrants even if there were no opportunity to share the gospel.[50] That being said, there is nothing wrong with praying our helping others will be used by God to show his goodness and eventually lead people to honor him. And of course, our helping others might prompt the question, "Why are you doing this?" and then there is nothing wrong with sharing the story that motivates our actions.

---

48. Dau, *Suffering and God*, 222.

49. Micah Network, "Proselytism," Statement #5. See also Nichols, "Ethical Issues in Evangelism," 144–47.

50. A parallel introspective question should be asked by Christians who are very committed to aid and social action. Would you be willing to proclaim the gospel of Jesus Christ, even though it was not at all connected to any kind of aid or social action?

COERCION

The story of Madhusudan at the beginning of this chapter highlights the fundamental ethical issue that arises in offering Christian humanitarian aid: Aid can become a coercive tool in enhancing evangelism efforts. Christian aid can induce recipients to convert. The connection between Christian aid and inducement to convert seems nearly unavoidable, but as we have already seen in our study of the gospels in Part I, Jesus quite clearly rejects coercion in evangelism (see Guideline #C9). So how do we address this difficulty?

Before we navigate this difficult terrain, two points of clarification about the nature of freedom and coercion need to be dealt with. The first involves an assumption about human nature. As already noted in chapters 2 and 7, God created human beings with the ability to make choices. A biblical worldview rejects a deterministic view of human nature. Human beings have free will, though our freedom is always limited to some degree. The extent of freedom possessed by an individual varies in light of a person's background and context. For example, heredity and social environment limit the freedom of individuals, but these constraining forces, while they limit freedom, do not eliminate freedom as determinists maintain.[51] We must therefore allow for varying degrees of freedom of individuals, depending on their background, but all individuals have some degree of freedom. The admission that freedom is a matter of degrees leads to a second point of clarification regarding coercion. We cannot talk about freedom or coercion in all-or-nothing categories. There is an inescapable vagueness surrounding the notion of coercion. How does all this affect our discussion of Christian aid and the inducement to convert?

First, we should be aware that the frequently made charge of coercion in relation to the giving of Christian humanitarian aid might be based on a problematic assumption of a denial of human freedom. Obviously, if we start with the assumption that human beings are determined, then all Christian aid will be interpreted as a coercive inducement to convert, but this begs the question as to whether or not humans have free will. We must therefore allow for the possibility of noncoercive conversions following the giving of Christian aid.

Secondly, once we admit human beings have the freedom to make choices, but that this freedom is limited, we need to address the problem of vagueness in relation to inducements to convert. Thus, while there needs to be sensitivity to the danger of creating inducements to convert, we must not be too quick to label aid as coercive. Unless inducements to convert are obvious or become extreme, caution is in order in making the charge

---

51. My account of free will draws on Taylor, *Metaphysics*, 42–45. For a diagram illustrating this view of limited free will, see Thiessen, *Ethics of Evangelism*, 82.

of coercion and labeling a practice as unethical. Of course, this is not very precise. I will give some examples of obvious inducements to convert in the next section, but generally, caution is in order when making dogmatic assertions with regard to Christian aid leading to inducements to convert.

Let me apply all this to the questions raised by Anand Nayak and the story cited at the beginning of the chapter. Nayak is quick to admit there was some inducement to convert for the Srimati Madhusudan and his family. His decision, as that of all human decisions, is made within a certain context. His wife needed medical help and he was poor, and so any aid would be welcomed and couldn't help but bring about positive feelings towards the givers of this aid. The giving of aid would also create a community network for Madhusudan and his family. All this would of course also serve as a "mild" inducement to convert, but, there was still a degree of freedom involved in Madhusudan making a decision to convert.[52] So, did the priest who helped Madhusudan and his family do something unethical in creating a mild inducement to convert? Hardly. He reached out to someone in need. In the end this resulted in Madhusudan and his family being converted. I would suggest there is nothing unethical being done here.

CONDITIONAL CHRISTIAN AID

I have suggested, in the previous section, that because of the inescapable vagueness surrounding the notion of coercion, caution is in order when identifying Christian aid as an inducement to convert. However, inducements to convert can be taken to an extreme, and then there should be general agreement that something unethical is occurring. For example, giving someone $100 to induce him or her to convert to Christianity would clearly be unethical. The same would apply to a gift of equivalent monetary value. This is outright bribery and plainly unethical.

There is a way of delivering Christian humanitarian aid that comes very close to being a form of bribery. Anthropologist and longtime missionary Jacob Loewen reflects on his own experience as a missionary in the Chocó of Columbia in the late 1940's and early 1950s. In order to lure people to the mission station, he opened a dispensary to deal with medical problems. At first he adopted the following rule: "if you want to receive the 'Lord's

---

52. Bickley would remind us that Madhusudan is not just a passive recipient of aid, but a free agent who could have decided against converting (Bickley, *Problem of Proselytism*, 9, 55). While we need to acknowledge the problem of vulnerability, we must be careful not to "vulnerabilise" all persons and situations (11, 56).

medicine,' then you must be willing to first listen to the 'Lord's message.'"[53] Loewen confesses it took him more than a decade to realize "that honest-to-goodness missionary witness and the baited hook just don't go together."[54]

Generalizing, receiving humanitarian aid should not be conditional on converting or on listening to appeals to convert.[55] This involves a violation of the freedom and dignity of persons (see Guidelines #A3 & #C9). I believe most Christian relief and development agencies would fully endorse this ethical guideline. For example, World Vision, one of the world's largest nongovernmental organizations involved in relief and development, in its "Ministry Policy on Witness to Jesus Christ," notes that its "support of religious freedom requires that we do not proselytize." (The word "proselytize" is here used to refer to coercive evangelism.) The policy statement goes on to say "proselytism takes place whenever assistance is offered on condition that people must listen or respond to a message, or as an inducement to leave one and join another part of the Christian church and/or one religion to join another religion." The policy goes on to say that out of respect for "the dignity of those with whom we work" World Vision will "not exploit vulnerability or use the power of development and humanitarian programs to coerce conversion."[56] Except for the confusion surrounding the word "proselytize," I commend World Vision for a clear guideline prohibiting an unethical form of linking aid and evangelism.[57]

---

53. Loewen, *Educating Tiger*, 89.

54. Ibid., 90. Jayasinghe gives us a more recent example of an unethical combination of making the giving of humanitarian aid conditional on first converting, during the 2004 tsunami that hit a tiny Hindu village in India's southern Tamil Nadu state. I must confess to some doubts as to the authenticity of this report, because it simply does not jive with my impression of Catholic missionary work. Jayasinghe, "Faith-based NGOs and Health Care in Poor Countries."

55. This is in keeping with the Code of Conduct formulated by the International Federation of Red Cross and Red Crescent Societies and the ICRC, Section #3. "Humanitarian aid will be given according to the need of individuals, families and communities. Notwithstanding the right of NGHAs (Non Governmental Humanitarian Agencies) to espouse particular political or religious opinions, we affirm that assistance will not be dependent on the adherence of the recipients to those opinions. We will not tie the promise, delivery or distribution of assistance to the embracing or acceptance of a particular political or religious creed."

56. Quotations from World Vision are taken from Bradbury, "Mission, Missionaries and Development," 426.

57. As I argued in chapter 1, the word "proselytize" is sometimes used as a synonym of "evangelism," sometimes to refer to unethical coercive evangelism, and sometimes to refer to sheep-stealing. I believe the World Vision statement implicitly refers to all three meanings.

EXPLOITING VULNERABILITY AND POWER

The World Vision statement identifies two other ways in which the coercive component of combining evangelism and Christian aid has been described. First there is the problem of exploiting vulnerability in order to do evangelism. Steve Bradbury describes the danger in this way: "Clearly the abuse of development interventions and humanitarian aid in order to give greater leverage to an evangelistic agenda—sugar for the evangelistic pill—is utterly unacceptable."[58] Elsewhere, Bradbury highlights a second way to describe the coercive dimension of combining evangelism and Christian aid.

> All development and humanitarian programs necessarily involve transactions between people of greater or lesser dependence on the one side, and those who are the conduit for essential resources or services on the other. Within the context of these transactional relationships there is an inevitable imbalance of power, regardless of how much care is exercised and regardless of the humility or otherwise of the development or aid workers.[59]

Bradbury is here recognizing that an imbalance of power is inevitable in humanitarian programs. Responding to needs will of necessity involve some imbalance of power. This is further in keeping with my earlier comments about the nature of freedom and coercion, where I stressed that human beings are not absolutely free. Freedom is always circumscribed by contextual constraints. We therefore need to face the inevitability of some degree of power imbalance when giving aid. This would suggest that the presence of a small degree of power imbalance doesn't make the giving of humanitarian aid coercive.

The same applies to using aid to leverage an evangelistic agenda. As I have argued earlier, we cannot entirely avoid the "problem" of humanitarian aid helping the cause of evangelism. We must always keep before us the question raised in response to the story of Madhusudan: Do we let the fear of exploiting need stop us from giving Christian aid? Surely not. We have to accept the fact that Christian aid will enhance an evangelistic agenda to some degree. We must therefore allow for the possibility of a healthy

---

58. Ibid., 426. Another description of the same problem is given by Laura Thaut, who asks whether FBOs that integrate a notion of "Christian witness" into their mission may actually be "employ[ing] a thinly veiled form of religious imperialism by taking advantage of unfortunate situations of human suffering to spread the Christian message to a necessarily captive audience." Quoted in Lynch and Schwartz, "Humanitarianism's Proselytism Problem," 638.

59. Bradbury, "Micah Mandate," 113.

combination of aid and evangelism within the context of holistic programs of a church or Christian aid organization.[60]

We still want to say, however, that it is possible to "abuse" humanitarian aid in order to give greater leverage to an evangelistic agenda. But when does such abuse occur? Similarly, with regard to the power imbalance inherent in giving aid. Surely at some point a power imbalance does become coercive and unethical. The question now becomes one of identifying when we have crossed the line in a power imbalance becoming excessive within the context of giving aid. So, how do we address these questions?

An important first step is to be aware of the power imbalance in giving aid and the possibility of exploiting aid for evangelistic purposes.[61] Such awareness should lead to sensitivity to the possibility of abusing power and the danger of exploitation. We also need to keep Jesus' warning before us not to lord it over others, but to be a servant (Matt 20:25; cf. Guideline #C10). There are also frequent biblical admonitions about being especially sensitive to the weak and the vulnerable.[62] We must also always keep before us the biblical foundational principle of the dignity of persons (Guideline #A3).

Here let me suggest a tool to help us navigate these difficult waters.[63] When considering the relation between aid and evangelism, it is helpful to think of a sliding scale. At one end of the scale there is complete separation of aid and evangelism. At the other end, evangelism and aid occur at the same time. Different situations will call for different placements along this

---

60. For some examples of aid workers articulating a healthy combination of aid and evangelism within the context of holistic programs, see Lynch and Schwartz "Humanitarianism's Proselytism Problem," 639–41; Bickley, *Problem of Proselytism*, 55; Sider, *Doing Evangelism Jesus' Way*, and *Cup of Water, Bread of Life*.

61. Rachel Uthmann, Director of Church Training with the International Association for Refugees (IAFR), provides a helpful list of observable differences in power/influence/control in humanitarian aid situations. Copyright ©2016 International Association for Refugees. All Rights Reserved. www.iafr.org

Helper	Recipient
-Basic needs are met	-Basic needs NOT met
-Freedom and choice	-Low physical or economic resources
-Some influence on circumstances	-Few or difficult options for their future
-Language ability	-Unwanted-outside of culture
-Outside resources (financial & relationships/affiliations)	-Language barriers

62. See references in footnote 47 earlier in this chapter.

63. I am drawing here on a suggestion given to me by Rachel Uthmann. Used here by permission.

scale. Consider three scenarios related to helping refugees. The first scenario involves helping refugees when they have first arrived in a country of refuge. Here their physical/social/psychological needs are intense, and I would suggest that addressing these needs should be uppermost in the minds of Christians helping these refugees.[64] Here aid and overt evangelism should be kept separate. A second scenario would fall in the middle of this scale. Suppose we are dealing with an ongoing program of learning the language of the country of refuge. Here it might be appropriate to provide literature on a table at the side of the room, which a refugee could pick up if interested. Consider finally a situation where relationships have been established over a period of time and there is greater equality between helper and recipient. Here it might be appropriate to combine a carefully nuanced proclamation of the gospel with the provision of a banquet, for example, provided those attending are made aware this will happen.

As a general principle, I want to suggest that the greater the need, the more sensitive the person(s) engaged in providing aid must be to the danger of exploiting that need, and thus inducing to convert. In situations where physical needs are overwhelming, evangelism should be kept separate from the activity of responding to these physical needs.[65] Loving our neighbor in this situation requires the entire focus to be on meeting the overwhelming physical needs of the moment (see Guideline #A4). Evangelism might come at some later point, but even then aid workers or missionaries must make it clear they are not trading medical or humanitarian aid for conversion. The person or group being evangelized must therefore be given a clear sense that it is perfectly acceptable for them to accept aid or medical help, and yet refuse any persuasive appeals to convert.

Another way to avoid any exploitation of vulnerability in these situations is to wait for questions to be asked concerning what motivates the giving of Christian aid. Steve Bradbury distinguishes between "programmatic" evangelism and the informal sharing of our faith in Jesus Christ in response to questions being asked when giving aid.[66] This is in keeping with Peter's advice in 1 Peter 3:15, which we considered in chapter 6. It is quite

---

64. For a careful sociological and theological treatment of the profound need for place and rootedness felt by refugees, see Das, "God and Refugees."

65. Alan Nichols provides a telling example of an abuse of this principle (Nichols, "Ethical Issues in Evangelism," 146). In the week after the October 1993 earthquake in Maharashtra state of India, one Indian Christian agency printed and distributed to survivors of the earthquake, 50,000 tracts urging conversion to Christ. Nichols observes that not only did the people reject the message as irrelevant to their condition, but this distribution of tracts violated the dignity of these survivors.

66. Bradbury, "Micah Mandate," 117–18.

appropriate for Christian aid workers to respond to questions about why they are involved in Christian humanitarian efforts. Sharing the faith in response to questions asked puts the recipient of aid in control, and thus helps to overcome the power imbalance of the situation.[67] Another way in which to overcome the power imbalance of FBOs providing aid in countries of need is to work in partnership with local churches. Various writers have identified one of the great strengths of FBOs as the ability to draw on established relationships with national and local churches to extend their reach into local communities.[68] As a general rule, "the neighbor-to-neighbor evangelism of local congregations embedded within communities, (even when connected to the distribution of aid), is more likely to be respectful and less likely to be coercive."[69] However, the danger of exploiting vulnerability or abusing the power of development and aid still remains. Thus, sensitivity is still called for.

A final comment about the sliding scale introduced in this section. Complete separation of aid and evangelism is impossible. Aid is always inspired by some kind of a narrative, and that narrative will invariably shine through. As was pointed out earlier in this chapter, even so-called "secular" aid relies on "a secularized humanitarian narrative" which is not immune to the problem of furthering a particular political or religious standpoint. This leads me to a consideration of a very influential code of conduct, by way of a conclusion to this chapter.

CODE OF CONDUCT

The rapid increase of FBOs and NGOs since the mid-1990s prompted the development of a Code of Conduct sponsored by the International Federation of Red Cross and Red Crescent Societies and major nongovernmental organizations involved in disaster relief, including many prominent Christian organizations.[70] Here it needs to be stressed this Code of Conduct specifically addresses disaster relief. It is within this context of emergency aid that the code stresses the following points: "The humanitarian imperative comes first" (Section #1). "Aid is given regardless of the race, creed or na-

  67. Micah Network, "Proselytism," Statement #6.

  68. Lynch and Schwartz identify a number of authors making this point ("Humanitarianism's Proselytism Problem," 638–39). See also Das, "God and Refugees," 10–12.

  69. Bradbury, "Micah Mandate," 117–18.

  70. International Federation of the Red Cross and Red Crescent Societies and the ICRC, "Code of Conduct." As of Jan 22, 2015, over 500 NGOs have signed this Code of Conduct, written in 1994. Lynch and Schwartz, "Humanitarianism's Proselytism Problem," 638.

tionality of the recipients and without adverse distinction of any kind. Aid priorities are calculated on the basis of need alone" (Section #2). And then comes a stipulation that relates to the focus of this chapter. "Aid will not be used to further a particular political or religious standpoint" (Section #3).

There is much that is commendable in this Code of Conduct, but I do want to raise some cautions concerning the stipulation about aid not being used to further a particular religious standpoint. As should be evident from the previous section, I am sympathetic with what I think might be the essential thrust of this stipulation. There should be no *overt* evangelism when giving aid within the context of *disaster relief*. I do have a concern, however, with the terminology being used to describe the prohibited connection between aid and evangelism. What does it mean to "further a particular religious standpoint?" The stipulation is vague. Indeed, a survey of Christian aid organizations reveals they interpret this statement in quite different ways.[71] Further, as I have already pointed out, the giving of aid cannot help but make the recipient sympathetic to the religious standpoint of the aid-giver. So, Christian aid cannot help but further an evangelistic agenda, albeit indirectly. The story of Madhusudan at the beginning of this chapter illustrates this point. I would therefore encourage Christian aid organizations to reconsider their practice of fully endorsing the above Code of Conduct and then interpreting it in whatever way that suits their purposes.[72] More transparency is surely called for (see Guideline #D12).

I have tried, in this chapter, to begin to sort out what can and should be said about the ethics of evangelism within the context of Christian aid, but there is still work to be done.[73] In the meantime, we must be careful not to exaggerate the problem of coercion and inducement to convert when delivering humanitarian aid.[74] We must not let the fear of exploiting aid in

---

71. Ibid., 639–41.

72. The Micah Network policy statement on "Proselytism" expresses "unequivocal" affirmation of the Code of Conduct, including its stipulation against using aid to further a religious standpoint. See Micah Network, "Proselytism," Statement #4. Other evangelical statements similarly seem to accept the stipulation as applying to all situations. See Lynch and Schwartz, "Humanitarianism's Proselytism Problem," 639–41. Bradbury also gives examples of other Christian organizations accepting the stipulation. Bradbury, "Micah Mandate," 109, 114.

73. While it is relatively easy to identify broader guidelines, I concur with Steve Bradbury that "a lot more work needs to be done to determine what all this means in the nitty-gritty detail of day-to-day work in the development arena." Bradbury, "Mission, Missionaries and Development," 427–28.

74. Problems of definition make it very difficult to determine when coercion, exploiting vulnerability, and the abuse of power have occurred. Further, studies show most Christian aid agencies agree it is unethical to use humanitarian aid as a coercive tool to try and convert someone. See Lynch and Schwartz, "Humanitarianism's Proselytism

order to do evangelism stop us from doing either. Above all, we must make sure evangelism and humanitarian aid flow out of our love for our neighbor, and our love and worship of the triune God.[75]

Problem," 641; Bickley, *Problem of Proselytism*, 9, 53, 55.

75. This is the central challenge of Kreider and Kreider, *Worship and Mission*. For a practical treatment of the need for integrating worship, justice, and evangelism, see Pilavachi, *When Necessary Use Words*.

Chapter 11

Ethics of Proselytism[1]

Eric G. Tosi tells this story of "a providential encounter" in his parish.[2]

The parish was playing a softball game against another church, a sort of ecumenical friendly game. By chance, one of the other players was hit by a ball and my wife, being a nurse, ran onto the field to assist her. She was taken to the hospital where our parish sent her flowers. She and her husband asked to meet me and we had a wonderful talk. It seems that they were not happy with their current church and were much taken by our kindness. Our meeting became a weekly event and we began discussing many aspects of the Christian Faith. Soon thereafter, she had a difficult pregnancy which confined her to bedrest for the last trimester. During that time, I catechized her and her husband. A year after that initial meeting, she and her family were received into the Orthodox Church. I asked her what had prompted their journey to the Orthodox Church and she stated, "It was the Christian love that was shown us, the joy of being a part of a loving community and the desire to be sacramentally part of the Church."

---

1. This chapter is based on a presentation I made at the Orthodox-Evangelical Consultation, held at the St. Vlash Monastery in Albania, Sept. 15–19, 2014. My presentation was subsequently published. Thiessen, "Ethical Evangelism and Proselytizing, 117–34. As well, my reply to two responses to my paper by Danut Manastireanu and Metropolitan Yuhanon Mar Demetrios was published in the same volume: Thiessen, "Reply to Responses," 148–54. Permission to draw on these essays has been gratefully received from Mark Oxbrow and Tim Grass, and Regnum Books International.

2. Tosi, "Koinonic Evangelism: The Community as The Evangelist" 170.

In this final chapter of Part II, I want to examine another kind of evangelism which often falls under the label "proselytism." Here I would remind the reader I am not referring to another use of this word where it is understood to mean evangelistic malpractice, or coercive evangelism. The focus of this chapter will be on proselytism, understood in its special and narrow sense of attempts by Christians from a particular church tradition to attract, recruit, or evangelize, people from another church tradition.[3] Opponents to this kind of evangelism sometimes refer to it as sheep-stealing, i.e., stealing members (sheep) from someone else's church. Miroslav Volf has creatively described proselytism as "fishing in the neighbor's pond."[4]

In the last several decades the problem of proselytism in this narrow sense has been the special concern of ecumenically minded Protestant, Orthodox, and Roman Catholic leaders.[5] For example, in August 1992, the heads of the two most venerated Episcopal sees in Armenian Christianity issued a joint encyclical entitled "Fatherly Advice." The two patriarchs objected to the notion that Armenia was a field ripe for proselytism. "Armenia is not a mission-field for Christian evangelism," they insisted. They spoke of proselytism as "soul stealing," the illicit conversion of Christians from one confession to another within an already Christianized nation." This activity is "a threat to Christian unity . . . and to national unity," they maintained.[6]

Another region where the issue of proselytism in the narrow sense of sheep-stealing has been, and still is, festering is in Latin America. At a Latin American Catholic Bishops Conference, it was stated that some 8,000 Roman Catholics a day convert to other Christian bodies, most of them Pentecostal. It is this phenomenon that prompted Pope John Paul II to caricature the charismatic and neo-Pentecostal churches in Latin America as "rapacious wolves" in his opening address to the 1992 Conference of Latin American Bishops.[7]

---

3. For a list of some important essays on this narrower sense of proselytizing, see Appendix #2 of Thiessen, *Ethics of Evangelism*, 246–47. See also a recent collection of essays in Oxbrow and Grass, *Mission of God*, Section #2.

4. Volf, "Fishing in the Neighbor's Pond."

5. For a summation of the problem and a statement addressing this problem, see World Council of Churches, "Towards Common Witness," 463–73. See also Nichols, "Mission, Evangelism, and Proselytism," for a lengthy and helpful summary of evangelical, Roman Catholic, Orthodox, and ecumenical statements on evangelism, proselytism, and human rights.

6. Guroian, "Evangelism and Mission in the Orthodox Tradition," 231.

7. Kerr, "Christian Understandings of Proselytism," 12. Cecil Robeck, in an essay giving a helpful overview of the problem of proselytism, questions this interpretation of what the Pope said, but admits others have said as much. Robeck, "Mission and the Issue of Proselytism," 4. Again in 1996, during Pope John Paul II's visit to Latin America,

There is also a long history of the Orthodox hierarchy accusing the Roman Catholic Church of proselytism in its domains.[8] Another area of concern regarding this narrow sense of proselytism is the recruitment activities of cults or new religious movements who often recruit from people already affiliated with churches.[9]

The primary focus of this chapter is to deal with the ethics of proselytism, understood as sheep-stealing. In order to simplify the discussion, I will focus primarily on the tensions created by evangelicals or Pentecostals doing evangelism (or proselytism) in countries that are predominantly Orthodox. In part, this choice is based on my having participated in an Evangelical-Orthodox Consultation in 2014.[10] There is also a personal reason for choosing this focus. My grandfather, Jacob G. Thiessen, a Mennonite Brethren preacher in the early 1900s, in what is now the Ukraine, made it a point to evangelize in the Slavic villages surrounding the Mennonite Molotschna Colony. While officially there was religious freedom in Russia, the Orthodox Church strongly opposed any efforts at evangelism by non-Orthodox Christians. Many attempts on my grandfather's life failed because of the good will of his Russian neighbors. Often my grandmother and her children were left to shift for themselves for weeks and even months without ever hearing from their father and husband. In the end, the family emigrated to Canada in 1923, partly out of fear for my grandfather's life.[11]

CONCEPTUAL CONFUSION

One of the problems with the repeated condemnations of proselytism in this narrow sense of sheep-stealing is that it is invariably loaded with negative nuances, which then make it easy to condemn the practice. Indeed, it would seem that for many, proselytism is by definition a pejorative term, hence the frequent description of proselytism as sheep-stealing. Obviously, it is wrong to steal sheep, and therefore proselytism is by definition unethical.

Another way in which proselytism acquires pejorative overtones is to associate it with questionable methods. For example, in an important statement of the World Council of Churches, "Towards Common Witness,"

---

he highlighted the Catholic resentment towards evangelical "prosperity." Lerner, "Proselytism, Change of Religion, and International Human Rights," 479.

8. See Minnerath, "An Ethical/Catholic Perspective of Proselytism," 46–47.
9. See Dawson, *Comprehending Cults*.
10. See footnote 1 of this chapter for details.
11. These details have been gleaned from the life story of my uncle, Jacob Thiessen, "We are Pilgrims," esp. pp. 29–30, 45, 94. See also Toews, "Calm Before the Storm."

proselytism is defined as "the encouragement of Christians who belong to a church to change their denominational allegiance, through ways and means that contradict the spirit of Christian love, violate the freedom of the human person and diminish trust in the Christian witness of the church."[12] The statement goes on to list some characteristics of proselytism that distinguish it from authentic Christian witness:

> –Unfair criticism or caricaturing of the doctrines, beliefs, and practices of another church.
>
> –Offering humanitarian aid or educational opportunities as an inducement to join another church.
>
> –Taking advantage of lack of education or Christian instruction which makes people vulnerable to changing their church allegiance.
>
> –Using physical violence or moral and psychological pressure to induce people to change their church affiliation.
>
> –Exploiting people's loneliness, illness, distress, or even disillusionment with their own church in order to "convert" them.[13]

In a case study of a major ecumenical effort at evangelization in Russia, Vito Nicastro, Jr., concludes a discussion of definitions of proselytism with a synthetic definition: "aggressive targeting and winning of converts from their (recognized) church to one's own, especially through improper means."[14] In a similar vein, Archpriest Eric Tosi, the Secretary of the Orthodox Church in America, describes proselytism in terms of getting someone to change denominational loyalty through "questionable means."[15]

Descriptions and definitions such as these simply confuse the matter. We need to separate the issue of trying to convert someone already belonging to a church, from the issue of using aggressive, coercive, or improper means in doing so. Obviously, the use of questionable means such as coercion or the exploitation of peoples' vulnerabilities is immoral (see Guideline #C9 in chapter 7). But are attempts to get someone to change church affiliation when he or she already belongs to a church immoral? This question needs to be treated separately. Most Christians, including evangelical and Pentecostal Christians who are frequently the target of charges of proselytism in this narrow sense, acknowledge the wrongness of unjust means of

---

12. World Council of Churches, "Towards Common Witness," 467. See also the Joint Working Group between the World Council of Churches and the Roman Catholic Church, "Challenge of Proselytism and the Calling to Common Witness."
13. World Council of Churches, "Towards Common Witness," 468.
14. Nicastro, "Mission Volga," 226.
15. Tosi, "Koinonic Evangelism: Case Study," 30.

evangelism that violate the freedom of the human person.[16] But is winning adherents from other Christian communities in itself immoral?

Let me illustrate. After the late 1980s, when Gorbachev introduced *perestroika* and *glasnost,* Russia was flooded with Western missionaries. Perry Glanzer describes one important missionary endeavor that in the end led to the charge of proselytism being made by the Orthodox Church hierarchy in Russia.[17] In 1992, three officials from the Russian Ministry of Education recognized a moral vacuum in post-communist Russian education. So, they invited representatives of the CoMission, a group of sixty evangelical Christian organizations in North America to spearhead a program to instruct Russian public-school teachers on how to teach Christian ethics. However, throughout the implementation of this program there was a tension between offering education about Christian morals, and introducing students to the Christian faith with the hope of leading teachers and students towards conversion. One of the CoMission leaders had this to say about the curriculum used in the schools: "In my opinion, it is not a curriculum of ethics. It is more an introduction to Christianity. . . . To be honest, I think it is a little unethical."[18] Indeed, to offer a course in Christianity, when the request was for a course in ethics is to be dishonest. This violates the truthfulness criterion discussed in chapter 7 (Guideline #D11).

Glanzer also points to duplicity in recruiting the missionaries/educators for this project. In the main, the 1,500 people recruited to help train teachers in Russia were not educators and were not trained to teach Christian ethics, but were in fact evangelists and missionaries.[19] This violates the principle of integrity (Guideline #D12). Glanzer, in reviewing this experiment in mission and education, sums up: "The Orthodox Church had good reason to distrust Western missionaries who were using government schools to further their evangelistic and church planting aims without revealing this agenda."[20] I would concur with Glanzer's assessment. Here we have an example where evangelicals and Orthodox Christians agree on what is unethical. Both agree that evangelism which lacks integrity, is overly aggressive, and is based on unworthy motives, is unethical. But we are still left with the question as to whether or not it is possible for evangelicals to proselytize Orthodox Church adherents in an ethical manner.

16. Robeck. "Mission and the Issue of Proselytism," 7.
17. Glanzer, *Quest for Russia's Soul.*
18. Ibid., 42.
19. Ibid., 196.
20. Glanzer, "Teaching Christian Ethics in Russian Public Schools," 305.

HISTORICAL AND THEOLOGICAL CONSIDERATIONS

In order to answer this question it will be helpful, first of all, to identify some historical and theological considerations that underlie Orthodox resistance to evangelicals proselytizing in their domains. Vigen Guroian reminds us Orthodox resistance to foreign proselytism needs to be understood in light of centuries of Ottoman captivity.[21] Here survivalism was combined with ethnocentrism and later with full-blown nationalist ideologies, all of which narrowed the catholic vision of the Orthodox churches. Then there are the more recent wounds inflicted on Eastern European churches and nations by years of Communist rule. Ion Bria, a priest of the Romanian Orthodox Church, points to the failure to recognize this historical fact on the part of expatriate missionary agencies and evangelical groups who invaded Orthodox regions in Eastern Europe in the 1990s in order to engage in evangelization. Surely these groups should have given the Orthodox churches in these regions time to recover from communist oppression and develop their own resources for renewing the church and evangelizing their people.[22] One can hardly blame the Orthodox Church for being critical of the proselytism of Western Christians during a time when what they really needed was some time to recover from communist oppression, and also the good will and prayers of the rest of the worldwide church.

Perhaps of more significance to Orthodox resistance to evangelical proselytism in their domains are some theological considerations. I want to briefly identify four areas of theological differences between evangelical and Orthodox Christians that relate to proselytism and mission.

First, there are differences in the understanding of persons. Orthodoxy understands the human person as belonging to a community which contrasts sharply with the individualism of modern liberalism that has unfortunately infected the Western church. There are secondly, differences in ecclesiology.

---

21. For much of the analysis in this section, I am drawing on Guroian, "Evangelism and Mission in the Orthodox Tradition," 237-44. It should perhaps be noted Guroian is an Armenian Orthodox, and thus a member of the family of non-Chalcedonians who are not in communion with other Orthodox. However, I do not believe this undermines the observations made by Guroian regarding Orthodox theology generally. See also Kärkkäinen, "Proselytism," for a focus on theological issues underlying this debate; and Bria, "Evangelism, Proselytism, and Religious Freedom in Romania," for a careful analysis of this debate within the context of Romania.

22. Bria, "My Pilgrimage in Mission," 76. In an interview with *Christianity Today*, Patriarch Aleksii II of Russia initially expressed gratitude for the efforts of various American Christian agencies in helping the Orthodox Church in Russia in the 1990s. However, when it was discovered these agencies were really intent on building Protestant churches, opposition to proselytism grew. See Glanzer, *Quest for Russia's Soul,* 161, 177-81.

In Orthodox theology, the church is understood corporately and organically, and is identified with a people, a land, and a nation.[23] Evangelicals, however, have a voluntaristic conception of the church and adhere to a separation of the church and state. Thirdly, evangelicals and Orthodox have a very different understanding of what salvation means. There is a strong individualism inherent in an evangelical understanding of salvation. Orthodox theology, on the other hand combines the personal and corporate in its understanding of salvation. Finally, Orthodox theology defines mission in terms of redeeming sinful and divided humankind and reuniting humanity within the mystical body of Christ. Any mission that divides Christians further is condemned as going contrary to the Pentecostal vision of overcoming the divisions of humankind begun at the Tower of Babel.[24] Hence, the strong Orthodox objections to evangelical proselytism in their territories.

This is not the place to provide a careful critique of Orthodox theology as it relates to evangelism and proselytism. Indeed, it is important to keep in mind the focus of this chapter is on the ethics, not the theology of proselytism. But I do want to point to some emerging tensions within Orthodox theology that might have some relevance to the ethics of proselytism.

The first set of tensions has to do with the understanding of the church and who is considered a Christian. Various writers have pointed out that vast parts of national populations that are claimed to be Orthodox are at best only nominal, lapsed, or inactive Christians.[25] Of course, the very idea of "a nominal Christian" is disputed within Orthodoxy because such a person is still a baptized member of the Orthodox Church. However, even members of the Orthodox hierarchy in Russia, for example, are forced to admit there are "unchurched members of Orthodox families," or that it would be "naïve" to consider large numbers of those who claim to be Orthodox as "believers" with "true religious sentiment."[26] All this leads some Orthodox leaders to admit there is a need "to reevangelize the large numbers of unchurched

---

23. A Russian Orthodox Archbishop, for example, refers to Russia as "a monoconfessional state whose history is closely related to the Orthodox Church." Glanzer, *Quest for Russia's Soul*, 176, cf. 182–83.

24. On the unity of the one holy, catholic, and apostolic Church, see Meyendorff, *Orthodox Church*, chapter 10.

25. Guroian, "Evangelism and Mission in the Orthodox Tradition," 243. For a good summary of the issue of "nominal Christians," see Glanzer, *Quest for Russia's Soul*, 181–84. Glanzer reviews a 1999 study which found that only 2.5 to 3 percent of those who identify themselves as Orthodox are actively involved in the church and around 10 percent attend church at least once a month (181).

26. Quoted in Glanzer, *Quest for Russia's Soul*, 182, 181. Orthodox sources also talk about "the Christian who is not a Christian." Quoted in Nichols, "Mission, Evangelism, and Proselytism in Christianity," 628.

persons."[27] Another Orthodox writer talks about the "re-Christianization of Christians," as an important part of the church's evangelistic witness.[28] Of course, the need for reevangelism and re-Christianization also applies to Western churches.[29] Indeed, there are frequent biblical warnings about Christians drifting away from the faith, forsaking their first love, being led astray, or falling away.[30] Jesus himself told parables to illustrate the possibility of God's people getting lost—sheep that were once part of the sheepfold who wander away on their own and get lost, or the moving story of a son who leaves a loving household only to squander his life in wild living.[31]

I would suggest there are several tensions in Orthodox theology here that need to be faced. First, there is the tension between saying someone is a believer, but not a true believer. Second, the notion of reevangelism seems to recognize the individual person, and this raises questions about a more corporate understanding of salvation within Orthodoxy. While the ideal might be for a whole people to worship and serve God, we must be careful to acknowledge the individual dignity and freedom of the individual.[32] I have argued elsewhere that a healthy understanding of the human person must balance an emphasis on the individual and an emphasis on community.[33] There is also an important ethical question that needs to be raised. Surely it is unethical not to allow a person who has been baptized into the Orthodox church to change his or her identity and become an atheist. Not to allow such a change of identity again violates the freedom and dignity of the person (Guideline #C9).

There are also growing tensions within Orthodoxy regarding their understanding of a national church. Guroian, for example, points out this

---

27. Guroian, "Evangelism and Mission in the Orthodox Tradition," 241. See also Kishkovsky, "Orthodox-Evangelical Encounter," 114. The notion of reevangelization was also introduced by Pope John Paul II in his *Redemptoris Missio*, issued on Dec. 7, 1990. See Donders, "Mission of the Redeemer," 154.

28. Quoted in Nichols, "Mission, Evangelism, and Proselytism in Christianity," 628.

29. Walter Brueggemann reminds us of this need: "Indeed, I imagine that the evangelizing of insiders (i.e., most of the whole of the Western church) may be our primary agenda in evangelism" (Brueggemann, *Biblical Perspectives on Evangelism*, 73).

30. See, for example, Amos 2:4–5; Hosea; Gal 1:6–9; 1 Tim 6:3–10; 2 Tim 4:3–4; Heb 2:2; 3:7–11; 5:11—6:6; Rev 2:4.

31. Matt 18:12–14. Green suggests the context in Matthew 18 is pastoral in nature, in contrast to the same parable given in Luke 15:3–7. Green, *Message of Matthew*, 193.

32. It is interesting to note that the dignity, freedom, and responsibility of the human person was highlighted in a statement growing out of a recent synaxis of Orthodox primates held in Chambésy, Switzerland, Jan 21–28, 2016. See Synaxis of the Orthodox Churches' Primates, "Mission of the Orthodox Church in the Contemporary World."

33. See Thiessen, *In Defence of Religious Schools and Colleges*, 216–17.

notion doesn't fit in with the globalization of the modern human community.[34] More importantly, this corporate and organic view of the church doesn't take into account the growing secularization and even atheism within Orthodox nations.[35] There is therefore, again, a need for evangelism or reevangelism within Orthodox countries, and thus, as already noted, various Orthodox leaders have challenged the Orthodox church to take up the challenge of evangelizing its own people.

The admission there are many nominal or lapsed Christians and even unbelievers in the Orthodox Church raises the further question as to who is responsible for the evangelism or reevangelism of these people. Various statements by Orthodox leaders and the actions of various Orthodox churches clearly indicate that nominal or lapsed Christians, or unbelievers in Orthodox countries, may only be evangelized by the Orthodox Church.[36] Here the Orthodox notion of "canonical territory," comes into play according to which other Christian bodies are deemed to be trespassing by seeking to evangelize in areas falling within the jurisdiction of an Orthodox church.[37] But the notion of canonical territory is not only difficult to define, it also flies in the face of Orthodox principles of catholicity and unity, as well as the globalization of the modern human community. Indeed, some Orthodox theologians see this regional understanding of the church as only temporary.[38]

As we have seen, Orthodox opposition to proselytism is also rooted in a concern for unity. This concern is also shared by the World Council of Churches, which likes to highlight the need for "a common witness."[39] Here we need to be careful not to make too much of the ideal of unity. Plurality is a feature of a post-Babel world, and Pentecost did not erase this plurality, as is sometimes claimed. Realism demands an emphasis on both unity and plurality. There are also different kinds of unity. The unity of the body of Christ can also be understood as spiritual in nature rather than in terms

---

34. Guroian, "Evangelism and Mission in the Orthodox Tradition," 242.

35. Nicastro quotes Orthodox priest Fr. Alexander Veronis, who points out that 210,000,000 of Russia's 280,000,000 people are not members of the Orthodox Church" (Nicastro, "Mission Volga," 228).

36. Nichols, "Mission, Evangelism, and Proselytism in Christianity," 629.

37. See World Council of Churches, "Towards Common Witness," 469, #e. This principle can be seen as supported by Paul in Rom 15:20. See also my comments in chapter 5, page 91.

38. For a classic statement of this ideal, see Alexei Khomiakov, "The Church is One." Elliott identifies some examples where the Orthodox Church has itself not upheld the notion of canonical territory ("Evangelism and Proselytism in Russia," 74).

39. World Council of Churches, "Towards Common Witness."

of a denominational or territorial unity.[40] I would also suggest evangelical evangelism in Orthodox countries can be done in such a way as to foster unity between denominations.

GOLDEN RULE

There is another theological/practical principle that needs to be considered in relation to this problem. I would remind those opposed to proselytism of the Golden Rule taught by Jesus. "In everything, do to others what you would have them do to you" (Matt 7:12). In chapter 7, I introduced the Golden Rule as a foundational procedural guideline for ethical evangelism (Guideline #A5). The Golden Rule surely entails that if you want to engage in evangelism, you should allow others to do the same.[41] Indeed, it is unethical to assume or to work towards a monopoly in evangelism. Of course, all this is very much in keeping with the ideal of religious freedom.[42] As noted in chapter 2, man and woman were created in the image of God. They were also given the freedom to obey or disobey God. God does not force anyone to accept his revelation or his offer of salvation. Religious freedom is central to upholding the dignity of human beings (Guideline #A3).[43] It was considerations such as this that led the World Council of Churches to develop a definition of religious freedom as a fundamental human right. This right was subsequently incorporated in the Universal Declaration of Human Rights.

> Everyone has the right to freedom of thought, conscience and religion. This right includes the freedom to change his/her religion or belief, and freedom, either alone or in community with others, in public or in private, to manifest his/her religion or belief, in teaching, practice, worship and observance.[44]

---

40. See Meyendorff, *Orthodox Church*, chap. 10. For a classic Orthodox statement of the Church bearing "witness to the extension of her mystical territory even beyond her canonical borders," see Florovsky, "Limits of the Church."

41. Guroian makes this point in *Ethics After Christendom*, 180–81.

42. Guroian maintains the ideal of religious freedom is supported by Orthodoxy, though its meaning might be slightly different from the liberal and democratic ideal of religious freedom (Guroian, "Evangelism and Mission in the Orthodox Tradition," 243).

43. For an Orthodox defense of freedom of conscience, see Bartholomew, *Encountering the Mystery*, chapter 7.

44. Quoted in World Council of Churches, "Towards Common Witness," 467. For a review of international covenants regarding liberty of conscience, religious pluralism and equality, free exercise of religion, nondiscrimination on religious grounds, and autonomy for religious groups, see Lerner, "Proselytism, Change of Religion, and International Human Rights."

What is puzzling here is that the 1997 World Council of Churches statement on proselytism, "Towards Common Witness," acknowledges the importance of religious freedom and specifically refers to the Golden Rule as a norm.[45] I find it difficult to harmonize this with the repeated call in the document to renounce all proselytism.[46] Surely religious freedom entails that proselytism should be allowed.

Here I would also remind the reader of the story which appears at the beginning of this chapter. It is a story told by an Orthodox priest. Eric Tosi tells this personal story to illustrate his notion of "koinonic evangelism," evangelism that is deeply personal and grows out of the church community. It is a moving story, and a delightful illustration of proselytism growing out of a little accident at a softball game, but there is one little detail that should not be overlooked. The couple being proselytized by Tosi and his wife were in fact associated with another church, though one in which they were not entirely happy. What we have here is an example of Orthodox proselytism.[47] Again, I want to stress that I find nothing unethical in Tosi's beautiful story of care for someone in need.

What I find puzzling though is Tosi's strong opposition to evangelical proselytism. Indeed, Tosi even talks about "the sin of proselytism."[48] How can he use such language when he himself engages in proselytism? Tosi fails to face this inconsistency because he draws a sharp contrast between his Orthodox koinonic approach to evangelism and proselytism understood as a sin.

> Evangelism is constructive and respects the freedom and dignity of the person whereas proselytism is destructive, deceptive, and manipulative. Evangelism is a witness to the truth of Christ and allows a person the freedom to respond to the message whereas proselytism is a corruption of the Christian witness.[49]

But this contrast is quite arbitrary and rests on the confusion I have already drawn attention to—a confusion between proselytism understood as evangelistic malpractice, and proselytism understood simply as

---

45. Ibid., 467.

46. Ibid., 463, 470, 472. Of course, in condemning proselytism, the World Council of Churches statement is assuming unethical means are being used. I would suggest, however, that implicit in the World Council of Churches statement is a condemnation of all proselytism, quite apart from unethical means being used.

47. Elsewhere, Tosi cites many examples of people moving from other Christian faiths to the Orthodox Church. Tosi, "Koinonic Evangelism: Case Study," 33, 35. Active recruitment of Protestant seekers by the Orthodox Church in America is also described by Gillquist, *Becoming Orthodox*, 163, 168–74.

48. Tosi, "Koinonic Evangelism: Case Study," 35.

49. Ibid., 32.

sheep-stealing. Most evangelicals would heartily endorse Tosi's description of koinonic evangelism which respects the freedom of a person to change churches. It is simply unfair to paint Orthodox proselytism in positive terms and then to impose on evangelical proselytism all the negative characteristics that belong to evangelistic malpractice. Tosi also needs to be reminded of the Golden Rule. If he can engage in proselytism, he should not condemn others doing the same.[50]

STEALING LOST SHEEP

There is an oddity about the very notion of sheep-stealing that needs to be brought to the fore. Is it even appropriate to talk about sheep (i.e., church members) being stolen? Or owned? There is a possessiveness here that is surely problematic. Of course, this relates to a theological understanding of the church and sheep in a church. I would suggest that ultimately the sheep are not *owned* by any church. If anything, we should rather talk about sheep being owned by the Good Shepherd who laid down his life for the sheep (John 10).

Further, as was noted in chapter 3, the Good Shepherd is very concerned about sheep that get lost (Luke 15). Both Orthodox and evangelical Christians need to acknowledge that church members can get lost. There are many Christians who are only nominally Christian, as has already been noted, and in our secularized world, many leave the faith entirely. The Good Shepherd asks us as Christians, whatever our denomination, to go and look for these sheep and bring them back into the fold.[51] These sheep need to be reevangelized, to use a term I have already introduced and that is in fact used by some Orthodox and Catholic writers. But here again, does it really matter who does the reevangelism? Surely Orthodox Christians should have no objections to evangelicals helping them in the task of reevangelism.

There is another oddity to the notion of sheep-stealing that needs to be highlighted. Describing proselytism as sheep-stealing creates a distorted picture because people aren't exactly like sheep. It is much harder to steal a person than it is to steal a sheep. In fact, stealing persons is generally described as kidnapping, and one has to take very special measures to

50. Orthodox missiologist, Petros Vassiliadis, is more consistent when he suggests the Orthodox Church in the West should abandon all efforts at proselytism in America, given its general condemnation of proselytism (Vassiliadis, "Mission and Proselytism," 273). Of course, I prefer a consistent application of the Golden Rule, which allows for ethical proselytism everywhere.

51. See chap. 3, pp. 53–54. Of course, the "fold" is understood in a rather narrow sense in Orthodox theology. I am calling for a more generous understanding of the "fold" as including the universal or catholic church.

kidnap a person. Surely it is not fair to describe evangelical proselytism as kidnapping, at least in most cases. I believe proselytism can, and sometimes does, violate a person's freedom, in which case the analogy to kidnapping is appropriate.[52] But the analogy is not always appropriate. Claims about the probability of proselytism as kidnapping occurring are empirical claims that require evidence. I would suggest occurrences of kidnapping persons who are in some way related to another church are in fact rare.

Let me illustrate this point by painting a scenario of proselytism. A native Albanian evangelical Christian (Eduard) is in a coffee shop with a longstanding friend of his (Luan) who is nominally Orthodox. A pleasant conversation eventually shifts to the topic of religion, as has been happening fairly often in their recent conversations. Luan, who hasn't attended church for several years, asks Eduard why he so committed to his faith and to his church. Eduard explains his own religious commitment to Jesus Christ, which in turn expresses itself in a commitment to his own church. In the ensuing conversation, Luan expresses a desire to attend Eduard's church at some point in time. Further conversations and visits to the evangelical church eventually result in Luan becoming serious about his own religious commitment, and in the end he requests to be baptized and to become a member of Eduard's evangelical church.[53]

I want to suggest it is very difficult to find anything morally blameworthy in the above scenario. Luan was a willing participant in the conversations and he freely made a decision to be baptized and join an evangelical church. If this assessment is correct, we have to conclude that ethical proselytism is indeed possible. Here it needs to be stressed I am only talking about the ethics of proselytism. Clearly, there are some theological considerations that might give Orthodox theologians some concerns, but these are not the focus here.

Of course, a change in some of the details of the above scenario might result in a different ethical evaluation. For example, suppose we introduce another variable, involving vulnerability, to follow up on an association sometimes linked to proselytism.[54] In this revised scenario, we are still dealing

---

52. I believe the recruiting activities of some cults and new religious movements can be described in terms of kidnapping, but even here the charge is often overstated. For a review of the literature on cult recruitment and the danger of overstating the charge of kidnapping see Thiessen, *Ethics of Evangelism*, 81–83, Appendix 2, 248–49.

53. From an Orthodox perspective, there is no need for Luan to be rebaptized, because he is already baptized. However, Luan might be of the conviction that his original baptism was invalid, because it occurred while he was an infant and therefore he had no say in the matter. I also know of evangelical churches who would not require rebaptism when persons claim their original baptism was valid.

54. See World Council of Churches, "Towards Common Witness," 468, #g and #i. See also Mar Demetrios who objects to evangelicals and Pentecostals targeting

with a long-standing friendship between Eduard, an evangelical Christian, and Luan, a nominal Orthodox "Christian," but now Luan gets very sick. As a close friend, we would of course expect Eduard to visit Luan. Again, on one of these visits the conversation turns to religion, and to make a long story short, further visits and conversations eventually lead to Luan making a renewed confession of faith in Jesus Christ, and expressing a desire to join Eduard's church. Is this exploiting vulnerability? I'm not so sure. I would rather see this as a friend caring for another friend. Luan doesn't even think of inviting an Orthodox priest to come and visit him, because he hasn't attended an Orthodox church in years. Instead, he turns to a friend for help, and the ensuing conversations eventually leads to a change in Luan's church affiliation. Here again, I do not think there is anything unethical occurring.

This is not to say there is no danger of exploiting vulnerability when engaged in proselytism (or evangelism). Indeed, the problem of exploiting vulnerability can be seen as a violation of my guideline on "Freedom and Coercion" (Guideline #C9). But I suggest we need to be careful not to exaggerate this danger. The notion of exploiting vulnerability is vague, and caution is in order when making this charge.[55] It should be noted in passing that Tosi's example at the beginning of this chapter can also be described as a case of an Orthodox priest exploiting vulnerability, but again, I see this charge as entirely unwarranted. Yes, there were needs that Tosi and his wife were responding to. Indeed, they were acting as "good Samaritans," but it is quite unfair to characterize this example of proselytism as exploiting vulnerability. We need some Christian charity here on the part of those who like to make the charge of exploiting vulnerability.

It should further be noted that by introducing the issue of vulnerability we are adding a feature to proselytism that need not be viewed as an essential component. This relates to the confusion I dealt with in an earlier section of this chapter. To combine proselytism with exploiting vulnerability is to confuse matters. All Christians, including evangelical Christians, agree it is wrong to exploit vulnerability when evangelizing or proselytizing. The central issue of this chapter is on the ethics of proselytism itself, quite apart from accidental features that are sometimes associated with proselytism.

---

members of an established church "when they are in vulnerable situations emotionally, sick or distressed, or alone and isolated" ("Response 2," 145).

55. For a more detailed treatment of the problem of vulnerability, see Thiessen, *Ethics of Evangelism*, 88–91, 172–76.

STEALING SHEEP

Lest it be thought my scenarios in the previous section skirt the real issue, let me suggest another scenario, similar to the first one except for one important detail. Suppose Luan is not just nominally Orthodox as in the first scenario, but a sincere, faithful, and committed Orthodox Christian. Of course, now it is quite inappropriate to talk about Eduard trying to evangelize or reevangelize Luan. Luan (and Eduard) are both Christians, and if their friendship is a genuine one, and if they are mature Christians, they will both acknowledge the same. If Eduard did not realize this beforehand, he will in fact apologize for even attempting to evangelize Luan.[56]

Now suppose we change the scenario once again, and assume Eduard refuses to acknowledge Luan's genuine Christian commitment, and thus tries to evangelize Luan and persuade him to switch churches. Now we are dealing with what can be considered a full-fledged case of attempted sheep-stealing. But, is it unethical? Here again we need to be careful. If we are dealing with two mature adults who are friends, there are some problems in describing even this scenario as unethical. Luan is after all free to say no in this exchange. Remember also, kidnapping a mature adult is difficult! On the other hand, it can be argued that Eduard is not treating Luan with dignity and respect (Guideline #A3). So, I believe persistent evangelizing on the part of Eduard in this scenario should be considered unethical.

There is further something very unecumenical about Eduard's continuing efforts to evangelize Luan and persuade him to change churches. Surely, Luan's existing church membership should be respected by a friend. Of course, we need to keep in mind my earlier question regarding who owns the sheep. I have argued there is something inappropriate about the language used when we talk about a church "owning" its members. And yet, if Luan is a genuine believer and content with his belonging to the Orthodox Church, this should surely be respected. If, however, Luan expresses unhappiness with the Orthodox Church, then the dynamics change once again, and we are dealing with a scenario similar to the story considered at the beginning of this chapter. We have here a complex interplay between personal and institutional identities, and as mentioned before, I believe these identities need to be kept in balance.

---

56. Here I agree with Robeck that "most evangelicals would agree that those who have a demonstrably active living faith in Jesus Christ should not be treated as persons to be evangelized" (Robeck. "Mission and the Issue of Proselytism," 7).

ETHICAL EVANGELISM AND REEVANGELISM, AND COMMON WITNESS

I conclude this chapter by returning to the problem of definitions. Lawrence Uzzell describes "proselytism" as having become "the world's most overused religious term," and growing "less and less precise the more often the word is used."[57] I concur and will have more to say on this in the final chapter. In this chapter, I have tried to limit my discussion to a specific meaning of proselytism as sheep-stealing. However, even with this special meaning of the term, there is confusion. Proselytism in this special and narrow sense should simply mean trying to influence someone to change church affiliation. But as we have seen, most often proselytism is associated with using improper means to influence someone to change church affiliation. And the list of improper means is long.[58]

The problem here is that this makes proselytism (in its special and narrow sense) unethical by definition. This approach refuses to allow for the possibility of ethical means of influencing someone to change church affiliation. Further, the majority of Christians, including evangelicals, will agree that coercion and inducements to convert are unethical. As argued earlier, we need to separate proselytism, understood in the narrow sense of sheep-stealing, from these obviously unethical practices, and we must allow for the possibility of ethical proselytism, particularly with regard to individuals who are only nominal or lapsed members of another church.

There are other problems with the charge of unethical proselytism. Many of the terms used to identify unethical means are vague. At what point is psychological pressure excessive and unethical? Is offering humanitarian aid to someone in need always an inducement to join another church?[59] What does exploitation of illness or loneliness mean? I would also suggest the charge of proselytism (understood as unethical sheep-stealing) is often exaggerated. There are many Christians today who change their church affiliation entirely on their own.[60] Many members of Orthodox and Catholic

---

57. Uzzell, "Don't Call it Proselytism," 16, 14.

58. See the list from the World Council of Churches, "Common Witness," 468, and quoted in part on page 199 of this chapter.

59. See the example I give at the beginning of chapter 10. See Elliott, "Evangelism and Proselytism in Russia," for examples where this charge is both legitimate and illegitimate.

60. This point is acknowledged by the World Council of Churches' statement on proselytism, "Towards Common Witness." "Nevertheless, it must be acknowledged that some people may move from one church to another out of true and genuine conviction, without any proselytistic pressure or manipulation, as a free decision in response to their experience of the life and witness of another church" (468). Yes, indeed, and I

churches change church affiliation because they are not happy with their churches, and when evangelical churches welcome these people into their midst, this should not be labeled as proselytism.[61] Then there are the people who leave a church because they experience love and care from members of another church, as illustrated in the example given at the beginning of this chapter. In all of these cases, the charge of unethical proselytism is quite inappropriate. There is a need for more charity on the part of Christians making these charges.

This is not to say the charge of proselytism is not sometimes legitimate. When this happens, repentance is what is called for. But we must allow for the possibility of ethical proselytism. So, what does ethical proselytism look like? Here I would suggest the biblical guidelines for ethical evangelism summarized in chapter 7 can be equally well applied to proselytism and the reevangelism of lapsed, nominal, or inactive Christians. The dignity of persons needs to be respected (Guideline #A3). Great care needs to be taken not to use coercive measures in reevangelism (Guideline #C9). This includes taking care not to exploit vulnerabilities, as mentioned earlier in this chapter. Further, and as I have already argued in chapter 10, creating inducements to convert is unethical. Those engaged in evangelism or reevangelism need to display humility and a servantlike attitude (Guidelines #C10 & #C13). They must also be careful to always speak the truth with love. Making false claims about another church is unethical (Guideline #D11). Ethical reevangelism is also tolerant (Guideline #F18). It treats persons holding beliefs which differ from that of the evangelist with love and respect.

It is also important to contextualize the gospel (Guideline #I28). Here I have some sympathy with Orthodox objections to foreign missionaries who often fail to integrate the gospel with local culture, thus creating the impression that Christianity is a "foreign religion," which in turn poses a threat to local stability and harmony.[62] Preoccupation with growing one's own church is also inappropriate in reevangelism (Guideline #I30). Indeed, I would suggest when persons are reevangelized, it might be more appropriate to encourage this "new convert" to return to his/her original church. And, in cases where this doesn't happen, for whatever reason, it would be well to have in place a code of conduct, where pastors/priests of the two communities involved would inform each other of the change of affiliation

---

would add such moves can be made even in cases where there has been some reevangelism by another church or church member.

61. It has been well said that the key to solving the "problem" of proselytism is to ensure the church is healthy.

62. Mar Demetrios, "Response 2," 145.

of the "new convert."[63] Such candid communication would, I believe, go a long way towards building understanding between Orthodox and evangelical Christians when proselytism does occur.

Allowing for the possibility of ethical proselytism should not be seen as precluding the possibility of cooperation and common witness. Guroian suggests that in an increasingly global and secularized human community there are "compelling practical reasons" that we cooperate rather than compete.[64] I have already alluded to the need for reevangelism within Orthodox countries. Why not invite evangelicals, who have a passion for evangelism, to help the Orthodox church engage in reevangelism? And might not evangelicals cooperate with Orthodox Christians in evangelizing their own people? Indeed, evangelicals could be seen as helping the Orthodox church to grow. Rather than starting another denomination, why not encourage all new Christians to join the Orthodox church and reevangelized Christians to return to the Orthodox Church? New Christians and revitalized Christians in a church are an important resource for renewal.[65]

The above appeal for cooperation rather than competition in the task of reevangelism assumes the Orthodox church might be in need of help in the task of reevangelism. What if the Orthodox church is in fact actively engaged in the task of reevangelism in predominantly Orthodox countries? I would suggest here (foreign) evangelicals might have something to learn from that great evangelist, the Apostle Paul, who was concerned about not encroaching on someone else's territory. For example, in his letter to the saints in Rome, Paul says his ambition has always been "to preach the gospel where Christ was not known, so that I would not be building on someone else's foundation."[66] So perhaps there is some legitimacy to the notion of

---

63. Manastireanu, "Response 1," 139–40. For a good example of such cooperation at an interreligious level, see Sider, *Doing Evangelism Jesus' Way*, 91–93.

64. Guroian, "Evangelism and Mission in the Orthodox Tradition," 239. Nicastro describes a good example of such cooperation in Russia in the spring of 1992, where Russian Orthodox hierarches sat down with evangelical parachurch leaders and agreed on plans for a joint evangelization project along the Volga River (Nicastro, "Mission Volga"). This essay also includes a helpful analysis of problems associated with this project. I concur with the author that this project deserves further study with regard to the issue of proselytism (242).

65. Glanzer makes this point with regard to the Protestant evangelical presence in Russia, which has the possibility of energizing Russian Orthodoxy in the same way the Reformation stimulated reform within Roman Catholicism (Glanzer, *Quest for Russia's Soul*, 184).

66. Rom 15:20. See also 2 Cor 10:12–18, where Paul talks about "the field God has assigned to us," and not boasting "about work already done in another man's territory" (v. 16). These verses are not easy to interpret given the difficulties of identifying the false "super-apostles" being referred to in 2 Corinthians, but it would seem Paul is referring to

canonical territory, to which evangelicals need to be more sensitive. But where the task of reevangelism can be aided by outside help, this should not be refused.

I conclude by returning to the theological differences between Orthodox/Catholic and Evangelical/Pentecostal Christians. Ultimately, I don't think these differences can be entirely overcome. And this leaves us with the question as to what we do with irreconcilable differences. Here I would like to suggest there are some additional ethical issues that need to be faced.[67] We need to be sensitive to the needs, struggles, and aspirations of each of our churches. Evangelicals need to be sensitive to the struggles of the Orthodox Church in their sometimes difficult contexts, and the Orthodox need to be sensitive to the aspirations of evangelicals. We need to listen to each other. Evangelicals need to listen carefully to what the Orthodox say about themselves, and the Orthodox needs to listen carefully to what evangelicals say about themselves.[68] We also need to speak the truth in love (Eph 4:15). Evangelicals need to testify to the Orthodox what they believe to be the truth about God's word, and the Orthodox need to testify to evangelicals what they believe to be the truth about God's word. And both groups need to repeatedly remind themselves they do not invent or create truth. Rather the truth of the Gospel is given to us, and it is our duty to search for it together. As we are reminded by Miroslav Volf, "We are not at liberty to change what we believe to be truth in order to reach some cheap consensus."[69] Our aim instead is to try hard to find and acknowledge the truth, wherever it lies. For it is only the truth which will set us free.

I return to Eduard, an evangelical Christian, and Luan, a lapsed Orthodox who hasn't gone to an Orthodox Church in years and who in fact openly renounces the faith of his birth. I realize Orthodox Christians want to say Luan is still an Orthodox Christian, because he was baptized into the Orthodox faith, but as an evangelical Eduard disagrees. He sincerely believes Luan needs to be reevangelized and even rebaptized upon confession of faith in Jesus Christ. I want to suggest Orthodox Christians need to respect Eduard's conscience and beliefs. There are some theological disagreements that cannot be resolved, and so in the end we need more tolerance

---

a missionary concordat made a decade earlier in Jerusalem in which it was agreed James, Peter, and John should go to the Jews while Paul and Barnabas would take the gospel to the Gentiles (Gal 2:7–9). See Barnett, *Second Epistle to the Corinthians*, 20, 162.

67. I am drawing on a useful discussion of dealing with theological differences in Volf, "Fishing in the Neighbor's Pond."

68. Kishkovsky highlights this point by suggesting each side needs to help the other to see themselves as they really are ("Orthodox-Evangelical Encounter," 110).

69. Volf, "Fishing in the Neighbor's Pond," 29.

and respect on both sides of this ecclesiastical divide.[70] Only in this way will we achieve a genuinely "common witness."

---

70. Archbishop Anastasios of Albania, in his book, *Facing the World*, has highlighted this requirement of international interfaith dialogue, and he goes on to say "This truthful approach is at bottom a loving approach, one that promotes a koinonia of love." Yannoulatos, *Facing the World*, 48.

Chapter 12

Conclusion

Sheryl Haw tells this story of her work as a team leader of a medical team and nursing director of a clinic in Alula, Somalia, in 1993. The story is followed by a commentary also written by Haw.[1]

A woman entered our clinic in Somalia and sat down in front of me. She never looked up, keeping her eyes downcast towards the floor. I greeted her and asked her how we could help her and to explain what her health needs were. She did not respond. My interpreter sitting next to me muttered angrily. I felt God prompt me to speak truth to her and said "Do you know that God knows your name." She immediately looked up at me and peered intensely into my eyes, tears building up and spilling over. I rested my hand on her shoulder and affirmed the truth she so needed to hear, she was someone whom God knew and loved. With this bond of trust established, she opened up to explain that she had a prolapsed uterus. We were then able to help her medically.

Would our institutional donors consider this proselytism? Would you feel uncomfortable with this?

Here was a lady in obvious need. Her medical condition had exacerbated her feeling of isolation and worthlessness. Being present with her and out of compassion to her, prompted by God to speak truth, both her emotional and medical needs were reached, plus a spiritual truth declared, opening her heart to healing. **This was Good News to her.**

1. Sheryl Haw is currently International Director of the Micah Network. This story and commentary appeared in the introduction of the June 2016 issue of the monthly on-line Newsletter of the Micah Network, under the title, "Shalom is Good News," and is used here with her kind permission, including some minor edits.

> *At no point in this meeting was there any agenda to convert her. Nor was there a mental dialogue going on in my head to ensure I was balancing word and deed. It was a simple act of love springing out of Spirit led discernment.*
>
> **Integral Mission is action.**
>
> *Many of us feel comfortable with doing good works. We hesitate with speaking truth, fearing that this will be construed as proselytism. We also need to hear the Good News—speaking truth brings liberation, healing, reconciliation, wholeness and Shalom, not just to those whom we serve and love but to ourselves.*
>
> **Ethical Position**
>
> *The real concern is that we do not use a position of power to coerce or manipulate someone to convert. The story above demonstrates well that there was no coercion and no intention to try and convert.*
>
> *(The commentary concludes with a brief review of some ethical principles that should govern Christian aid and evangelism.)*

The above story and commentary provide a suitable introduction to the final chapter of this book in which I want to make some concluding observations and also express some final concerns about the state of evangelism and the ethics of evangelism in the Christian church today.[2] Here I will not be limiting myself to issues related to the ethics of evangelism. After several decades of research and writing on the ethics of evangelism, there are a few things I want to say about evangelism generally. This chapter may therefore have a sermonic feel to it!

I found Haw's story deeply moving when I first read it. Here we have a wonderful example of Christian love in action, combined with a sensitive proclamation of part of the good news of the Christian gospel. In her commentary, Haw shows how this combination of word and deed flowed quite naturally and spontaneously from a heart filled with Christ's love. This is what ethical evangelism looks like.

Haw specifically addresses the ethics of evangelism in the last paragraph of her commentary. She is sensitive to the danger of using her position of power as a dispenser of medical aid to coerce or manipulate someone to

---

2. My aim in this chapter is in part captured by Walter Brueggemann in his fine book on evangelism: "Part of the task concerning evangelism is to recover nerve about our modes of speech in church traditions that have debased our speech, either by conservative reductionism or by liberal embarrassment" (Brueggemann, *Biblical Perspectives on Evangelism*, 14).

convert. Evangelism that is coercive or manipulative is unethical, as we have discovered in our biblical study, and as was summarized in chapter 7, under Guideline #C9. Clearly, there was no coercion or manipulation involved when Sheryl, as a nurse, rested her hand on her patient's shoulder and told her she was known and loved by God. This was a spontaneous expression of loving witness in word and deed. It would also be quite unfair to describe this case as one of exploiting vulnerability and abuse of power.[3] Instead, what we have here is a powerful and positive example of ethical evangelism.

Some readers will no doubt question my description of the above story as a case of evangelism. Indeed, Sheryl Haw herself might not be entirely happy with my associating her story with evangelism. After all, she informs us she had no intent to convert this patient. But I would suggest there is a tension in her commentary. There are parts of her story that lend support to my describing her words and actions as involving evangelism. In the second-to-last paragraph, Haw speaks to our tendency of feeling more comfortable with just doing good works. We are hesitant about speaking gospel truth because this might be construed as proselytism. Then she adds: "We also need to hear the Good News—speaking truth brings liberation, healing, reconciliation, wholeness and Shalom." And Haw did in fact speak truth to her patient. Surely speaking truth, and sharing the good news, even though only a portion of it, is evangelism. I suggest we have here an example of healthy holistic mission, where word and deed come together. Indeed, it is hard to separate word and deed. The deed of compassionate medical care itself speaks in some way, and the words actually spoken in fact do something by way of bringing liberation and wholeness. In this story, word and deed come together to demonstrate and proclaim the good news.

Here let me raise a few minor quibbles about Haw's commentary on this story. The second-to-last paragraph is entitled, "Integral Mission is action," but, as I noted in chapter 10, the concept of integral mission, when first introduced, included both word and action. We need to acknowledge the importance of both word and deed, acknowledging at the same time that they are distinct and yet closely interrelated. So, a better heading for the paragraph would be "Integral Mission Combines Word and Action."

Haw's commentary also illustrates some problems which I have addressed in chapters 1 and 11, regarding the use of the word "proselytism." The word has multiple meanings and this leads to confusion. The first heading of Haw's commentary asks two questions: "Would our institutional donors consider this proselytism? Would you feel uncomfortable with this?" The assumption behind these questions seems to be that proselytism is

---

3. See chap. 11, pp. 208–9.

something to be avoided. Then under the heading, "Integral Mission is action," she makes the following statement: "We hesitate with speaking truth, fearing that this will be construed as proselytism." Again, proselytism is portrayed as something to be avoided. Given these negative connotations, it would seem Haw is assuming a common understanding of proselytism as "evangelistic malpractice" that involves coercion or manipulation. Indeed, she expressly refers to coercion and manipulation when dealing with ethics in the final section.

But proselytism can also be used as a synonym of evangelism. Indeed, I believe Haw's commentary is implicitly also using the word in this way. As I have already argued, Haw is really talking about evangelism, and her actions and words are a beautiful display of ethical evangelism, even though she does not use the word. I believe introducing the word proselytism (understood as evangelistic malpractice) detracts from the central thrust of the story, because as Haw herself admits, the issue of coercion is really beside the point. As I have already pointed out in previous chapters, talking about evangelism and proselytism within the same context creates confusion. It is all too easy for Christians to say they are opposed to proselytism when what they really mean is they are opposed to evangelism. I am sure Haw is not opposed to evangelism, but the ambiguity surrounding her use of the word proselytism in her story and commentary creates confusion. I believe it is better to use one word—evangelism—and then distinguish between ethical and unethical evangelism.

A final comment on intentions. Haw says there was no intention of trying to convert her patient. I would suggest Haw is here referring to conscious intent, but this doesn't preclude an unconscious intention to convert. Indeed, surely everything we as Christians do and say in our interactions with others who do not belong to Christ can and should include a desire to bring them to know the Lord Jesus Christ. In chapter 9, I described my work as a professor at a college or university. My hope and prayer has always been that my teaching and interactions with students would bring them closer to the kingdom of God. Of course, this idea is not always uppermost in my mind. I suspect this is what Haw has in mind when she suggests she didn't have an agenda to convert the patient. But absence of a conscious intention doesn't preclude having an unconscious intention to convert. Such an intention is simply part of our make-up as Christians. We long for others to know Jesus Christ, and there is nothing wrong with that. Indeed, with Paul, we as Christians say our "heart's desire and prayer to God" is that all "may be saved" (Rom 10:1).

DEFINITIONS ONCE AGAIN

I have already begun to address some of my concerns about definitions relating to evangelism in my commentary on Haw's story. But there is more to be said about proselytism, and there are other definitional problems I want to raise, as I move on to a consideration of some additional concerns I have about the place and practice of evangelism in our churches today.

As was noted in the introductory chapter, we have trouble defining evangelism. Indeed, one writer has identified seventy-nine different definitions of evangelism, and David Bosch suggests even more definitions could be added to this list.[4] My worry here is that in our confusion about definitions, we simply forget about the central meaning of evangelism found in the New Testament—verbal proclamation of the gospel. Bosch also points to the continuing controversy surrounding the relation between mission and evangelism. Whereas we used to talk a lot about evangelism, there would seem to be a marked preference for the use of missional language in contemporary churches, including the Evangelical Church.[5] A significant component of this preference is an increasing emphasis being given to building the kingdom of God, to deeds of compassion, and to advancing social justice. While I have a good deal of sympathy with the approach to mission found in emerging missional movements, I do have some concerns about their skittishness in using the word "evangelism," and at times their tendency to underemphasize evangelism.[6]

Then there are the problems of definition surrounding the term "proselytism," which I have already dealt with in the above section and in chapter 11, where I focused on the issue of proselytism as sheep-stealing. Lawrence Uzzell has highlighted the overuse of the word proselytism, suggesting this has contributed to the word becoming less and less precise.[7] Whereas once proselytism had a neutral connotation, today the term has acquired a widespread negative and even sinister connotation. Uzzell recommends we retire the term "to the linguistic museum where it belongs." I tend to agree. At the very least, we need to make sure we give the word a clear definition every time we use it. Uzzell also concurs with a point I have already made

---

4. Bosch, *Transforming Mission*, 409.

5. See Richardson, "Emerging Missional Movements," Oxbrow, "Christian Mission," 56–59, and Vassiliadis, "Mission and Proselytism."

6. While there is still an emphasis on evangelism in some of the various streams of missional movements, there is a tendency "to jettison the word 'evangelism' so as to escape its historical baggage." Richardson, "Emerging Missional Movements," 134.

7. Uzzell, "Don't Call it Proselytism." For a history of the concept, see Stalnaker, "Proselytism or Evangelism?"

in the previous section. He suggests the word proselytism is "most often invoked by those who ultimately oppose all forms of Christian evangelism."[8] I suggest we need more honesty here. "Simply let your 'Yes' be 'Yes,' and your 'No,' 'No,'" Jesus said (Matt 5:3). To hide one's opposition to evangelism by using the word proselytism is a betrayal of forthrightness that Jesus demands. This would suggest even more caution whenever we use the word. Perhaps it would be better to simply call a moratorium on the use of the word "proselytism."

I have similar concerns with regard to the concept of integral mission. I have dealt with these concerns at length in chapter 10, and so will say little here. While I endorse the original intent behind introducing this concept, I believe the notion of integral mission is misleading and often misapplied. Again, I suggest a moratorium on the use of the concept "integral mission."

WORD AND DEED

Another definitional problem has to do with the increasing tendency today to talk about proclaiming the gospel in word and deed.[9] Now there is something right about this expression, and I will get to it shortly, but I fear Christians today are in danger of replacing evangelism as verbal proclamation with proclaiming the gospel in deed. As was noted by Sheryl Haw, many of us feel more comfortable with doing good works, and we hesitate speaking the truth of the gospel. Indeed, there are some Christians today who argue there is no need for speaking the truth of the gospel. Deeds are enough. The very notion of witness seems to have changed to refer simply to being the church or being a model Christian, doing good deeds, and being involved in relief, development, and advocacy for justice.[10] Evangelism understood as verbal proclamation of the gospel is seen as outdated.

This position would seem to have a long history in my own denomination, the Mennonite Church, as is shown in an important early essay attempting to articulate a theology of service, written by veteran Mennonite

---

8. Uzzell, "Don't Call it Proselytism," 16. For a forthright statement about opposition to proselytism really being opposition to evangelism, see Vassiliadis, "Mission and Proselytism," (esp. 260–61). Vassiliadis suggests this assessment applies both to the Orthodox Church and to ecumenical circles.

9. See chap. 1, n. 51, and chap. 10, n. 35 for some examples.

10. See, for example, Bryan Stone, who argues "the most evangelistic thing the church can do today is to be the church" (Stone, *Evangelism After Christendom*, 15). For Stone, proclamation of the gospel is dismissed as "more noise" in a noisy world (254). See also Johnson, "Proselytism and Witness in Earliest Christianity."

Central Committee (MCC) worker Peter Dyck.[11] The best of Mennonite tradition is described as one in which "words and works are one"—an early version of integral mission.[12] But the article goes on to show it is all too easy to do the one and neglect the other. Dyck then goes on to describe "the swinging of the pendulum" to an extreme where "deeds are above words."[13] He also refers to a MCC filmstrip entitled, "Sermons in Overalls."[14] Willard Metzger, the executive director of Mennonite Church Canada, admits he is frequently asked, "Why don't Mennonites believe in evangelism?" Metzger maintains Mennonites do still believe in evangelism, though not in ways traditionally understood.[15] Mennonites prefer evangelism in overalls.

Of course, Mennonites aren't the only ones who have a preference for evangelism in overalls, as Dyck himself notes in the article just referred to.[16] I find a similar tendency in notions of integral or holistic mission in the church today. Since I have dealt with these notions at length in chapter 10, I will not say more about them here.

Lest I be misinterpreted, let me remind the reader once more—I believe deeds are very important. I believe in the importance of the larger mission of the church. I believe in integral mission, if properly defined. Our words need to be backed up by deeds. Verbal proclamation of the gospel needs to be accompanied by a demonstration of the gospel. Indeed, if we don't embody the good news we proclaim, our verbal witness will be hollow and lack integrity. That is why, in my summary of the ethics of evangelism as found in the New Testament, the second foundational guideline for ethical evangelism was labeled "Incarnational Witness" (Guideline #A2). The

---

11. Dyck, "Theology of Service."

12. Ibid., 265. The essay goes on to recount Paul's words, "You yourselves are our letter (of recommendation) . . . known and read by everybody" (2 Cor 3:1–3). We are also reminded of John the Baptist's question as to whether he was the Messiah. Jesus replied, "Go back and report to John what you hear and see: The blind receive sight, the lame walk, those who have leprosy are cured, the deaf hear, and the dead are raised, and the good news is preached to the poor" (Matt 11:3–6). "Our Anabaptist forefathers seem also to have been very clear on the fact that for the disciple word and deed cannot be separated." Ibid., 266.

13. Ibid., 266.

14. Ibid., 267. Dyck goes on to refer to a letter from an MCC worker who admits "he has much free time in which to do another kind of work," but he goes on to say, "As of yet, I have done no oral witnessing and don't have a definite plan to start this." This MCC worker hopes "the way I live" will be helpful to those he is working with, "but please don't say I should tell them" (268).

15. Metzger, "Sharing the Faith." See also Sawatzky, quoted in chapter 1, footnote 7.

16. Dyck, "Theology of Service," 266.

combination of word and deed is not only an ethical requirement, but also the key to effective mission.[17]

So, my aim in this section (and in this book) is not to downplay the importance of "proclamation in deed." Nor do I want to undermine the importance of Christian witness in relief, development, and advocacy. I am only objecting to the assumption, frequently made today, that we don't need words in evangelism, that deeds are sufficient. I am even willing to use the phrase "proclamation in deed," as long as it is understood that proclamation is here being used in a metaphorical sense. My concern is to make sure we do justice to the important place evangelism as verbal proclamation of the gospel has in the New Testament.[18]

GOSPEL MESSAGE

The above concerns about how we define evangelism raise some parallel concerns about the gospel message being conveyed when we evangelize. Ethical evangelism is always careful to proclaim the gospel of Jesus Christ, not "a different gospel" (Gal 1:6–9). Here I worry about two distortions of the Christian message—two extremes, if you will. There has been, and still is

---

17. Ron Sider describes the challenge in this way: "I have absolutely no doubt whatsoever that if ten percent of Christians in the world today would obey Jesus' commission in John 20:21, we would experience explosive church growth and sweeping social transformation. 'As the Father has sent me, I am sending you,' Jesus commanded. Our Lord cared about the whole person in community, and so should we. When we share the whole gospel with the whole person, God works miracles in the lives of the poor, broken, and hopeless. Individuals are remade and societies are transformed" (Sider, *Cup of Water, Bread of Life*, 12–13).

18. Vassiliadis ("Mission and Proselytism") tries to reinterpret, from an Orthodox and ecumenical perspective, New Testament passages that have been typically used to support the traditional notion of evangelism as verbal proclamation of the good news (e.g., Matt 28:18–20). But I find his interpretation rests on special pleading and frequently commits the either-or fallacy. For example, Vassiliadis suggests if we would have retained "the Trinitarian dimension" of Matthew 28 ("baptizing them in the name of the Father and of the Son and of the Holy Spirit"), we would have understood that "mission does not aim primarily at the propagation or transmission of intellectual convictions, doctrines, moral commands, etc., but at the transmission of the life of communion that exits in God" (262, quoting from Ion Bria). But why can't a Trinitarian approach to evangelism include both verbal proclamation and the transmission of a life of fellowship in the Trinity? Vassiliadis also highlights Paul's holistic and cosmic view of salvation in Col 1:19–20, with which I agree (266–67), but he fails to do justice to the fact that in this same context Paul also argues Christ's sacrifice reconciles people to God (Col 1:21–22). It is not either-or, but both-and. I would also remind Vassiliadis that Jesus and the apostles *both* proclaimed the good news *and* healed the sick. For other examples of this both-and argument, see chapter 10, page 177. See also chap. 1, n. 17.

a tendency in popular evangelical discourse to reduce the gospel to personal salvation that gets you to heaven. I believe this understanding of the good news is profoundly limiting. It fails to capture the all-encompassing nature of the gospel message I outlined in Chapter 1.[19] Jesus had much to say about the kingdom of God, and so should we.

Many Christians today have reacted (and overreacted) to such a reductionistic account of the gospel message, and have stressed instead the radical and society-transforming nature of the gospel. On this account, the gospel message is interpreted as caring for the poor and the oppressed, and seeking for justice and peace in this very broken world of ours. While this kingdom focus is certainly an important part of the gospel message, there is more to the good news than this. We cannot forget the personal dimension of salvation. Sadly, the message of peace and justice has become idolatrous in some Christian circles, a cause which has all too often lost its mooring in Jesus as Savior and Lord. A one-sided emphasis on the broader social implications of the gospel also fails to see that societal transformation might best be accomplished by personal transformation.

Another way in which the gospel message is sometimes distorted today has to do with an unwillingness to proclaim uncomfortable truth (Guideline #F17). We hesitate proclaiming Jesus as the way, the truth, and the life. We don't like to talk about sin. We underemphasize the ethical demands of Christian discipleship that must necessarily follow a commitment to Jesus Christ.[20] We don't like to identify the idols worshipped in today's culture. We like to make the gospel seem respectable and forget the gospel message will always appear scandalous when it is proclaimed faithfully and truthfully. The scandalous nature of the gospel is highlighted by Peter, drawing on Isaiah 8:14 (1 Pet 2:8). Christ is described as a stone over which some people stumble. The Greek word used here for stumbling is *skandalon*, from which our word scandalous is derived. Interestingly, Paul, in his first letter to the Corinthian church, uses the very same word when describing the reaction of Jews and Greeks to the preaching of Christ. Jews and Greeks, for very different reasons, considered the preaching of Christ crucified as scandalous or foolishness (1 Cor. 1:22). I suggest that in different times and

---

19. David Bosch too worries about a theology that has "increasingly individualized, interiorized, ecclesiasticized, and privatized salvation" (Bosch, *Believing in the Future*, 34). Concerns about starting with the individual are also expressed by Lesslie Newbigin. The gospel is first of all a story about the meaning of all of history, which of course includes our personal histories (Newbigin, *Gospel in a Pluralist Society*, esp. 124, 128).

20. See chapter 9, footnote 13 for an example of confronting society's sexual standards as part of our Christian witness. See also Willard on the need for "discipleship evangelism," evangelism that "would naturally lead to a decision to become an apprentice to Jesus in The Kingdom Among Us" (Willard, *Divine Conspiracy*, 304).

places, the gospel will be considered scandalous for different reasons. Evangelism that is faithful to the New Testament is willing to appear scandalous.

Ethical evangelism will proclaim the whole gospel of Jesus Christ. It will dare to lovingly confront the world with God's own standards of right and wrong and with the fact that all have sinned, all the while recognizing that ultimately it is God's Spirit who convicts the world of sin and righteousness and judgment (John 16:8). Truthful evangelism will include both the reconciliation of individuals to God and the reconciliation of all things in heaven and earth to God through the shed blood of Jesus Christ on the cross (Col 1:19-22). Conversion will not be understood as an end in itself, but as an experience that leads to an ongoing transformation into the likeness of Jesus Christ (2 Cor 3:18). Conversion will also be seen as including a commitment to live as a follower of Jesus Christ, building the kingdom of God and praying as Jesus taught us to pray, "Your kingdom come; Your will be done on earth as it is in heaven" (Matt 6:10).

There is a desperate need today to avoid accommodation, oversimplification, and overreaction when we think about the content of the evangelistic message.

TRUTH

The focus of the previous section on the content of the gospel message, and notions of truth, moral truth, exclusive truth, and uncomfortable truth, will no doubt have raised concerns for some of my readers. So let me hasten to add some concerns of my own. In today's postmodern climate there is of course a lot of skepticism about overarching narratives and truth. My worry here is that Christians today succumb to the postmodern worldview and the "dictatorship of relativism" that permeates Western culture. In the end, this approach undercuts evangelism itself, and hence the doubts about evangelism among many Christians today. More on this shortly.

My second concern is that Christians react and overreact to postmodern skepticism and become dogmatic dispensers of truth. This too is a betrayal of biblical norms. While we as Christians must affirm there is truth, we also need to be very careful to affirm that our understanding of the truth is finite and fallible. We only know in part, Paul reminds us in his famous chapter on love (1 Cor 13:12). I fear too many evangelical Christians today have not learned how to navigate the difficulties of proclaiming the gospel with humility. We dare not come across as pompous proclaimers of truth.

When we proclaim truth, let's not forget this needs to be done with humility (Guideline #E13). We need to be careful about claiming to *possess* truth with a capital "T."[21] Rather than being possessors of truth we are pointers to truth. Like John the Baptist, we point to Jesus, the source of all truth. Indeed, a humble mindset in evangelism is perhaps best expressed in terms of walking together with unbelievers in the search for truth.[22] Or, as is often stated, evangelism is really one beggar telling another beggar where to find food. There is no room for pride here. Just thankful and humble sharing of good news.

WHERE HAVE ALL THE EVANGELISM CONFERENCES GONE?

This is the question asked by Ed Stetzer, Senior Fellow of The Billy Graham Center for Evangelism at Wheaton College, in a January 2016 blog which appeared in a number of online magazines, including *Christianity Today*.[23] Stetzer sees the current sparsity of evangelism conferences as a symptom of a larger problem:

> [E]vangelism has fallen out of style in much of evangelicalism in America the last decade or so. Today, too many of us roll our eyes at evangelism strategies, calling them hokey and ineffective, and, instead of coming up with other evangelism strategies, we just don't evangelize. This is a problem, and we need to fix it.

The blog ends by promoting a conference on evangelism that Stetzer was organizing, the purpose of which was to help the body of Christ "share the gospel like we once did."[24]

I believe Stetzer is right in suggesting the paucity of evangelism conferences is symptomatic of a deeper problem—evangelicals have become skittish about evangelism itself. Evangelism has fallen out of style in much of evangelicalism and the broader church in North America. We don't talk much about evangelism today. We are embarrassed by evangelism, and many just don't do evangelism.

Why is this? Stetzer seems to suggest we have, in the past, been too preoccupied with tools and strategies for doing evangelism. But there is an ambiguity in Stetzer's analysis of the deeper problem underlying the evangelical neglect of evangelism. As already mentioned, he concedes evangelism

---

21. Here it is most important to distinguish between truth and the human search for truth. See Thiessen, *Ethics of Evangelism*, 67–71. See also Newbigin, *Gospel in Pluralist Society*, chapter 13, and Newbigin, *Proper Confidence*.

22. See Richardson, *Reimagining Evangelism*.

23. Stetzer, "Where have All the Evangelism Conferences Gone?"

24. The Conference, "Amplify 2016," was held June 28–30, 2016, at the Billy Graham Center for Evangelism at Wheaton College. About 500 people were in attendance.

conferences of the past might have been too focused on tools and strategies for doing evangelism. He responds by quoting a famous statement of D. L. Moody, "Well, I like my way of doing it better than your way of not doing it!" Stetzer's challenge is that if we don't like past tools and strategies, then we should come up with better ones. And presumably, we need more evangelism conferences in order to come up with better tools and strategies. We see here Stetzer hasn't given up on tools and strategies. I want to dare to suggest this continuing focus on tools and strategies might itself be a problem. Indeed, I believe such a focus contributes to unethical evangelism.

A focus on strategies has the effect of reducing people to the status of objects that can be manipulated in order to get them to convert. It violates the dignity guideline of ethical evangelism (Guideline #A3).[25] There is also a danger of relying too much on human effort and strategies, even to the point of forgetting it is ultimately God in Christ who calls people to himself (Guideline #B6). We need to pay more attention to the ethics of using tools and strategies for doing evangelism. As already noted in chapter 1, evangelicals are beginning to pay some attention to the ethics of evangelism, but much more needs to be done in this area. My hope and prayer is that this book will contribute to a much-needed ongoing discussion of the ethics of evangelism.

EMBARRASSMENT ABOUT EVANGELISM

I have already alluded to the embarrassment about evangelism felt by many evangelicals and Christians today. Some of this embarrassment is of course justified. The history of the Christian church is littered with obviously immoral approaches to evangelism, from which contemporary Christians want to distance themselves. Not only in the past, but even today, there is some justification for feeling embarrassed about some of the unethical tools and strategies used by evangelicals to do evangelism. I too feel embarrassed about past and present unethical practices in evangelism within

---

25. These points were well expressed in one of the responses to Stetzer's blog by Jennifer Cheek, posted on Jan. 9, 2016, and used here by permission, including some minor edits. "For this reason, I would say that holding another evangelism conference would have a negative result and not a positive one because conferences tend to dehumanize people into projects and categories of disbelief. People cannot be reduced to columns on a handout. All people, sinners and believers, have dignity as image-bearers of God. Tools can be effective, but evangelism conferences tend to reduce evangelism to simply learning how to use the tools.... I know this won't be a popular opinion, but I'm thankful that there are fewer evangelism conferences because without ethics, without love, our message of the beautiful gospel of grace we've been given is slandered."

the Christian church. But past failures should not lead us to a wholesale condemnation of all evangelism as unethical. Instead, these failures call for repentance, not an abandonment of evangelism.[26] What is further required is that we distance ourselves from unethical evangelism, and boldly engage in ethical forms of evangelism. Here we need to follow the example of the Apostle Paul who says this about his approach to evangelism: "*Unlike so many*, we do not peddle the word of God for profit" (2 Cor 2:17—my emphasis). Paul doesn't give up on evangelism just because there are many who have tainted motives for evangelizing. He just makes sure he does evangelism in an ethical manner. So should we.

Here we need to be careful, however, to make an important distinction. In the previous paragraph, I am calling for repentance from, and reform of, those practices in evangelism that are clearly unethical. These need to be distinguished from additional charges about supposedly unethical evangelistic practices often made against Christians that are in fact difficult to substantiate, if not entirely unwarranted. What I have in mind here are charges of coercion, exploiting vulnerability, offering humanitarian aid as an inducement to convert, missionary colonialism, abuse of power—including abuse of persuasive power—and finally the charge that evangelism creates divisions within societies. These charges are plagued with vagueness and ambiguity, as I have pointed out in some of the previous chapters of this book. Here Christians need to be bolder in defending themselves against these charges.[27] With criticisms expressed in vague generalities, Christians are perfectly justified in demanding more precise definitions and concrete evidence of wrongdoing. At the same time, Christians need to be sensitive to the legitimate concerns being expressed by these vague generalities. Indeed, Christians should join critics in condemning coercion, exploitation of vulnerabilities, etc. But critics should also recognize that most Christians want to avoid these unethical practices.[28]

---

26. Sadly, even the idea of repenting over past failures of the church has been turned into another evangelism strategy in multiple congregations in the United States. John Fletcher labels this a "Confessions of a Sinful Church" strategy, in a careful review of various contemporary strategies in evangelism. Fletcher, *Preaching to Convert*, 124–28.

27. This is what I have tried to do in my previous book. See Thiessen, *Ethics of Evangelism*, chap. 3–6.

28. I believe this is the point being made by Paul Bickley who warns about exaggerating the prevalence of evangelistic malpractice, which he calls *The Problem of Proselytism*. Indeed, Bickley goes so far as to suggest the problem of proselytism (i.e., evangelistic malpractice) is really no problem at all (62). I believe this claim is itself an exaggeration, but Bickley is certainly justified in demanding more precision and more evidence when making charges against Christian evangelism (12, 58).

There is however another reason why Christians are embarrassed about evangelism, and why many Christians today are nearly as skeptical about evangelism as are their secular critics, atheists, and agnostics. And this reason I find to be more worrisome. I believe all too often the thinking of Christians is shaped too much by the world around them, especially the chattering classes, the educated, and the journalists, who are most often steeped in the values of liberalism.[29] We are therefore worried about evangelism being intolerant. We don't want to appear fanatical about our Christian faith. We think of religion as belonging to the private domain and so hesitate talking to others about our Christian convictions. It seems arrogant to claim to have the truth. The thinking of many Christians today is shaped by these liberal values, and they cause us to be embarrassed about being engaged in evangelism. Indeed, we have absorbed these values to such an extent we rarely if ever evangelize.[30]

Let me illustrate with one of the most important of these liberal values—the desire to be "pleasingly tolerant."[31] Many Christians today are so enamored with the liberal virtue of tolerance, and have so capitulated to the popular understanding of tolerance, that they object to evangelism, as do the skeptics, because it is felt that evangelism is intolerant by its very nature. Now I think there are some problems with this objection to evangelism,[32] but that is not my concern here. Instead, my concern has to

---

29. See John Gray's *Liberalism*, for a summary of the liberal intellectual tradition. Paul Marshall describes modern liberalism as "a variable political attitude" that stresses some or all of the following: "individuality, freedom, autonomy, rights, the separation of religion and politics, reason, tolerance, the non-imposition of belief, and decent progressiveness." Marshall, "Liberalism, Pluralism and Education," 47.

30. John Fletcher comes to a similar conclusion in his recent and careful study of various forms of evangelical outreach, by suggesting "entire outreach strategies have been premised upon Christians' embarrassment at and desire not to be lumped in with the always-be-Christianizing, everyone-is-a-potential-prospect conversationalist or the homophobic street preacher haranguing mourners at a funeral. Indeed, so great is the desire to 'leave everybody else alone,' so painful the self-inflicted wounds of awkward/offensive/presumptive evangelism, that most self-identified evangelicals rarely evangelize at all, at least not with any frequency" (Fletcher, *Preaching to Convert*, 305). Fletcher goes on to express some sympathy with those sounding the alarm about the gap between profession and action with regard to evangelism among evangelicals and Christians. This gap is an indication of "a malaise in the US Church more generally, an ailment brought on in part by evangelical maladaptation to twentieth-and twenty-first-century culture" (Ibid., 305.).

31. Fletcher introduces this term as a way of summarizing a recent major study of religion in the United States which concludes that at the heart of "American Grace," there is a desire to be "pleasingly tolerant, faithful-but-non-fanatic" (Ibid., 309). See also, Putnam and Campbell, *American Grace*.

32. For a detailed analysis of these problems, see Thiessen, *Ethics of Evangelism*,

do with Christians uncritically absorbing liberal values like tolerance, and for that reason having suspicions about the possibility of ethical evangelism. What is needed instead is to think critically about tolerance, and to reshape this virtue so it is in keeping with biblical teaching.[33] Jesus and the apostles called Christians to be separate from the world, and that includes separation from worldly thinking (John 15:19; Rom 12:2). So, the challenge for us as Christians is to think biblically about these liberal values and about the ethics of evangelism.[34]

A FINAL PLEA TO EVANGELIZE, BUT . . .

Jesus looked on the crowds and "had compassion on them, because they were harassed and helpless, like sheep without a shepherd" (Matt 9:36). This is an accurate portrayal of people even today. There are many living in a wasteland. Meaninglessness, despair, and emptiness are rampant. Many people today are nomads, desperately looking for a home—willing to follow mirages that promise great things but deliver only more of the same—barrenness and death. We have good news, and we have nothing to be ashamed of. The Apostle Paul puts it this way: "I am not ashamed of the gospel, because it is the power of God for the salvation of everyone who believes" (Rom 1:16). As we have seen, Paul extends this salvation to the entire cosmos in a later epistle. What an "evangel"! And what a privilege to be an evangelist! "How beautiful are the feet of those who bring good news," Paul says later in his masterful summary of the gospel in his epistle to the saints in Rome (Rom 10:15).

Those of us who are laypersons might find these references to Paul a bit intimidating. After all, we are not the Apostle Paul, and we are not called to be a missionary like he was. So, does this even apply to us? Studies of Paul's missionary journeys were part of my early Sunday school education, as I am sure they were and still are for many children in church today. As I reflect on my Sunday school experience now, I must confess I wish I had been told that Paul was given a special call to be an evangelist, that God gives some people in the church a special call to be evangelists, just as he calls some to be apostles, and pastors, and teachers (Eph 4:11). We need

---

105–14.

33. I have begun to do this with regard to tolerance in chapter 7, pages 125–27.

34. Brueggemann too worries about "culture-accommodating Christians" who have succumbed to "liberal embarrassment" about evangelism. Indeed, he goes so far as to suggest the church in the United States is facing "a crisis of accommodation and compromise that is near to final evaporation" (Brueggemann, *Biblical Perspectives on Evangelism*, 14, 15, 18).

to distinguish this special gifting and calling to be an evangelist from the more general challenge to all Christians to be salt and light in the world.[35] This distinction is important, because without it we create unnecessary guilt by treating all Christians as having the gifting and calling to be full-time evangelists. And yet, all of us as lay Christians are called to be witnesses to the truth of the gospel in word and deed.

So what does it mean for ordinary people in the workforce, in our professions, in our neighborhoods, to be witnesses for Jesus Christ? The practices of the early church can help us to answer this question. In chapter 6 we looked at Peter's description of what evangelism means for the layperson. "Always be prepared to give an answer to everyone who asks you to give the reason for the hope that you have" (1 Pet 3:15). What should be noted here is that this kind of evangelism occurs in response to people asking questions. Our lifestyle, our character, the way we do our work, the way we interact with people, should be such that it prompts people to ask us why we live the way we do, and how we have hope in the midst of so much despair. This is natural evangelism that grows out of who we are and what we do in the workplace and in our neighborhoods.[36] Michael Green, in his study of evangelism in the early church, devotes a chapter to answering the question: Who were the early evangelists? Clearly, the apostles played a significant role in spreading the gospel. They were the professional evangelists. But Green goes on to argue "the prime agent in mission" in the early church was "the little man, the unknown ordinary man," or the "informal missionaries."[37] And in the subsequent centuries of the early church, it was the exemplary behavior and witness of ordinary Christians that led to the phenomenal growth of the early church, as various studies have shown.[38]

Here I want to recommend an inspiring recent book by the late Alan Kreider, *The Patient Ferment of the Early Church: The Improbable Rise of Christianity in the Roman Empire*.[39] Kreider's careful research shows much

---

35. This distinction is reflected in a recent book by Teasdale, *Evangelism for Non-Evangelists*.

36. Natural evangelism is in part the thrust of an excellent book on evangelism written by John Bowen, *Evangelism for "Normal" People*.

37. Green, *Evangelism in the Early Church*, 242–43. Oxbrow reminds us that even today most people come to faith with the simple words and actions of friends and neighbors (Oxbrow, "Christian Mission," 52).

38. Rodney Stark has estimated that in the first three centuries after the death and resurrection of Jesus, the churches grew at an average of 40% per decade, and that this growth can be attributed to person-to-person sharing of the gospel, combined with demonstrating the gospel by living transformed lives and caring for people in often desperate circumstances. Stark, *Rise of Christianity*, especially chap. 4 and 7, and pp. 161, 208.

39. Kreider, *Patient Ferment of the Early Church*.

of the evangelism of the early church was "casual and unsystematic."[40] There were no missionary societies, few full-time evangelists, and there was little by way of exhorting believers to evangelize or giving them techniques to evangelize. Instead, careful attention was paid to catechesis which focused largely on helping new Christians to live the Christian life, to exemplify Christian virtues, and to care for the poor and the needy. These new believers emerged from their catechesis "as wise doves, helpers of God who by intriguing behavior and appropriate words contributed to the church's primary mode of growth—attraction."[41] The growth of the church of the first three centuries was accomplished by patient "witness in word and deed" of ordinary men and women, and very much in keeping with the advice given by Peter to the churches of the diaspora.

So, here is another reason for the "but" in the heading of this section. I believe we have something to learn from the "casual and unsystematic" way in which the early church did evangelism. Perhaps what we need is not more evangelism conferences, but discipleship conferences. And just perhaps this might result in our being more effective in evangelism today.

A FINAL PLEA FOR ETHICAL EVANGELISM

Being effective in evangelism is of course different from being ethical in the way we do evangelism. The central thrust of this book has been on the ethics of evangelism. I conclude with some of Jesus' own reflections on evangelism and the ethics of evangelism towards the end of his time here on earth. In the Gospel of John, a succinct version of the Great Commission is stated once before and once after Jesus' resurrection. "As the Father has sent me, I am sending you" (John 17:18; 20:21). Clearly there is an underscoring of the continuity of Jesus' own mission and the mission of the disciples and the church, both an expression of the missionary heart of God. But there is also an ethical component to this commission which is easily missed. We are called to imitate God's way of doing mission and evangelism—love, incarnation, servanthood, and the cross. May God help the Christian church today to proclaim the gospel of Jesus Christ in Christ's way.

---

40. Ibid., 231.

41. Ibid., 241. This statement sums up the approach to catechesis found in the *Didascalia*, a church order that comes from a cluster of communities in Syria in the third century (chap. 8).

Bibliography

Abraham, William J. *The Logic of Evangelism*. London: Hodder & Stoughton, 1989.
———. "A Theology of Evangelism: The Heart of the Matter." In *The Study of Evangelism: Exploring a Missional Practice of the Church*, edited by Paul W. Chilcote and Laceye C. Warner, 18–32. Grand Rapids: Eerdmans, 2008.
Astley, Jeff. "Evangelism in Education: Impossibility, Travesty or Necessity?" *International Journal of Education and Religion* 3.2 (2002) 179–94.
Attfield, D. G. "Child-evangelism and Religious Education." *British Journal of Religious Education* 16.1 (1993) 39–46.
Augustine. *The Confessions*. Translated by Maria Boulding. New York: Vintage, 1997.
Bailey, Kenneth E. *The Good Shepherd*. Downers Grove, IL: IVP Academic, 2014.
Bakke, O. M. *When Children Became People: The Birth of Childhood in Early Christianity*. Minneapolis: Augsburg Fortress, 2005.
Barclay, William. *Gospel of Matthew*, Vol. 1. Edinburgh: Saint Andrew, 1956.
Barnett, Paul. *The Second Epistle to the Corinthians*. Grand Rapids: Eerdmans, 1997.
Bartholomew, Craig G., and Michael W. Goheen. *The Drama of Scripture: Finding Our Place in the Biblical Story*. Grand Rapids: Baker, 2004.
Bartholomew, Patriarch. *Encountering the Mystery: Understanding Orthodox Christianity Today*. New York: Doubleday, 2008.
Bauer, Walter, et al. *A Greek-English Lexicon of the New Testament and Other Early Christian Literature*. 3rd ed. Chicago: University of Chicago Press, 2000.
Bayle, Pierre. *A Philosophical Commentary on These Words of the Gospel, Luke 14:23, "Compel Them to Come in, that My House may be Full."* Edited by John Kilcullen. Indianapolis: Liberty Fund, 2005.
Berner, Ashley. "Persuasion in Education." *Comment* 31.1 (2013) 28–33.
Bickley, Paul. *The Problem of Proselytism*. London: Theos, 2015.
Boesveld, Sarah. "Suspended Nova Scotia Student Defiantly Wears T-shirt with Pro-Jesus Message." *National Post*, May 3, 2012. http://nationalpost.com/holy-post/suspended-nova-scotia-student-defiantly-wears-t-shirt-with-pro-jesus-message.
Boffetti, Jason. "How Richard Rorty Found Religion." *First Things* (2004) 24–30.
Bonk, Jonathan. "The Gospel and Ethics." *Evangelical Review of Theology* 33.1 (2009) 47–61.

Bosch, David J. *Believing in the Future: Toward a Missiology of Western Culture*. Valley Forge, PA: Trinity International, 1995.

———. "Evangelism: Theological Currents and Cross-Currents Today." In *The Study of Evangelism: Exploring a Missional Practice of the Church*, edited by Paul W. Chilcote and Laceye C. Warner, 4–17. Grand Rapids: Eerdmans, 2008.

———. "Toward a Hermeneutic for 'Biblical Studies and Mission.'" *Mission Studies* 3.2 (1986) 65–79.

———. *Transforming Mission: Paradigm Shifts in Theology of Mission*. Maryknoll, NY: Orbis, 1991.

Bowen, John P. *Evangelism for "Normal" People*. Minneapolis: Augsburg Fortress, 2002.

Bradbury, Steve. "The Micah Mandate: An Evangelical View." In *Mission and Development: God's Work or Good Works*, edited by Matthew Clarke, 103–22. London: Continuum, 2012.

———. "Mission, Missionaries and Development." In *Handbook of Research in Development and Religion*, edited by Matthew Clarke, 413–29. Cheltenham, UK: Edward Elgar, 2013.

Bradley, Raymond D. "From Fundamentalist to Freethinker (It All Began with Santa)." In *Religious Upbringing and the Costs of Freedom: Personal and Philosophical Essays*, edited by Peter Caws and Stefani Jones, 50–72. University Park, PA: Pennsylvania State University Press, 2010.

Brennan, Patrick McKinley, ed. *The Vocation of the Child*. Grand Rapids: Eerdmans, 2008.

Brewster, Dan. *Child, Church and Mission, Revised*. Colorado Springs, CO: Compassion International, 2011.

Bria, Ion. "Evangelism, Proselytism, and Religious Freedom in Romania: An Orthodox Point of View." *Journal of Ecumenical Studies* 36.1–2 (1999) 163–83.

———. "My Pilgrimage in Mission." *International Bulletin of Missionary Research* 26.2 (2002) 74–77.

Brueggemann, Walter. *Biblical Perspectives on Evangelism: Living in a Three-Storied Universe*. Nashville: Abingdon, 1993.

———. *Theology of the Old Testament: Testimony, Dispute, Advocacy*. Minneapolis: Fortress, 1997.

Buckley, William F. "Onward, Christian Missionaries." *National Review* 55.12 (2003), 58.

Bunge, Marcia J. "The Vocation of the Child: Theological Perspectives on the Particular and Paradoxical Roles and Responsibilities of Children." In *The Vocation of the Child*, edited by Patrick McKinley Brennan, 31–52. Grand Rapids: Eerdmans, 2008.

Caws, Peter, and Stefani Jones, eds. *Religious Upbringing and the Costs of Freedom: Personal and Philosophical Essays*. University Park, PA: Pennsylvania State University Press, 2010.

Chan, Simon. "The Evangelical Understanding of Conversion." In *The Mission of God: Studies in Orthodox and Evangelical Mission*, edited by Mark Oxbrow and Tim Grass, 175–82. Oxford: Regnum, 2015.

Chester, Tim, ed. *Justice, Mercy and Humility: Integral Mission and the Poor*. Carlisle, UK: Paternoster, 2002.

Citizenship Foundation. "Teaching About Controversial Issues: Guidance for Schools." http://www.citizenshipfoundation.org.uk/lib_res_pdf/0118.pdf, 2003.

Clarke, Matthew. "Understanding the Nexus Between Religion and Development." In *Handbook of Research on Development and Religion*, edited by Matthew Clarke, 1–13. Cheltenham, UK: Edward Elgar, 2014.

Clowny, Edmund. *The Message of 1 Peter*. Leicester, UK: InterVarsity, 1988.

Collier, John, ed. *Toddling to the Kingdom*. London: Child Theology Movement, 2009.

Cooling, Trevor. *A Christian Vision for State Education*. London: SPCK. 1994.

———. *Doing God in Education*. London: Theos, 2010.

———. "Evangelism in the Classroom: A Response to Elmer Thiessen." *Journal of Education and Christian Belief* 17.2 (2013) 259–69.

Das, Rupen. *Compassion and the Mission of God: Revealing the Invisible Kingdom*. Leicester, UK: Langham Global Library, 2015.

———. "God and Refugees: Foundations for Hope." https://dasworld.files.wordpress.com/2015/12/god-and-refugees-final.pdf.

Dau, Isaiah Majok. *Suffering and God: A Theological Reflection on the War in Sudan*. Nairobi: Paulines, 2002.

Davis, James Calvin. *Forbearance: A Theological Ethic for a Disagreeable Church*. Grand Rapids: Eerdmans, 2017.

Davis, Stephen T. "How Christians Should Teach Philosophy at Secular Institutions." http://epsociety.org/userfiles/Davis-HowChristiansShouldTeachPhil%20[final].pdf.

Dawson, Lorne. *Comprehending Cults: The Sociology of New Religious Movements*. Oxford: Oxford University Press, 1998.

DiSilvestro, R. "What's Wrong with Deliberately Proselytizing Patients?" *The American Journal of Bioethics* 7.7 (2007) 22–24.

Dodd, C. H. *The Apostolic Preaching and its Developments*. New York: Harper and Row, 1936.

Donders, Joseph G., ed. "The Mission of the Redeemer." In *John Paul II: The Encyclicals in Everyday Language*, 143–72. Maryknoll, NY: Orbis, 1996.

Dyck, Peter. "A Theology of Service." *The Mennonite Quarterly Review* 44 (1970) 262–80.

Dykstra, Craig, and Sharon Parks, eds. *Faith Development and Fowler*. Birmingham, AL: Religious Education, 1986.

Elliott, Mark. "Evangelism and Proselytism in Russia: Synonyms or Antonyms?" *International Bulletin of Missionary Research* 25.2 (2001) 72–75.

Etherington, Matthew, ed. *Foundations of Education: A Christian Vision*. Eugene, OR: Wipf & Stock, 2014.

Evangelical Philosophical Society. "Christian Philosophers in the 'Secular Academy.'" http://www.epsociety.org/library/articles.asp?pid=212.

Evans, Craig A. *Matthew*. New York: Cambridge University Press, 2012.

Ewert, David. "Evangelism by Lifestyle." *Direction: A Mennonite Brethren Forum* 28.1 (1999) 18–27.

Fee, Gordon D. *Paul's Letter to the Philippians*. Grand Rapids: Eerdmans, 1995.

Fish, Stanley. *Save the World on Your Own Time*. Oxford: Oxford University Press, 2008.

Fletcher, John. *Preaching to Convert: Evangelical Outreach and Performance Activism in a Secular Age*. Ann Arbor, MI: University of Michigan Press, 2013.

Florovsky, Georges. "The Limits of the Church." *Orthodoxy and Heterodoxy* (blog). Ancient Faith Ministries, June 28, 2012. https://blogs.ancientfaith.com/

orthodoxyandheterodoxy/2012/06/28/the-limits-of-the-church-by-fr-georges-florovsky.

Fountain, Philip. "Proselytizing Development." In *The Routledge Handbook of Religions and Global Development*, edited by Emma Tomalin, 80–97. New York: Routledge, 2015.

French, Edgar. Review of *The Ethics of Evangelism*, by Elmer John Thiessen. *Direction: A Mennonite Brethren Forum* 42.1 (2013) 110–11.

Friesen, Abraham. *Erasmus, the Anabaptists, and the Great Commission*. Grand Rapids: Eerdmans, 1998.

Gillquist, Peter. *Becoming Orthodox: A Journey to the Ancient Christian Faith*, 3rd ed. Ben Lomond, CA: Conciliar, 2009.

Glanzer, Perry. *The Quest for Russia's Soul: Evangelicals and Moral Education in Post-Communist Russia*. Waco, TX: Baylor University Press, 2002.

———. "Teaching Christian Ethics in Russian Public Schools: The Testing of Russia's Church-State Boundaries." *Journal of Church and State* 41.2 (1999) 285–306.

Goheen, Michael. "A Critical Examination of David Bosch's Missional Reading of Luke." In *Reading Luke: Interpretation, Reflection, Formation*, edited by Craig G. Bartholomew, 229–64. Milton Keynes, UK: Paternoster, 2005.

———. *A Light to the Nations: The Missional Church and the Biblical Story*. Grand Rapids: Baker, 2011.

Goheen, Michael W., and Craig G. Bartholomew. *Living at the Crossroads: An Introduction to Christian Worldview*. Grand Rapids: Baker, 2008.

Gooch, Paul W. *Partial Knowledge: Philosophical Studies in Paul*. Notre Dame, IN: University of Notre Dame Press, 1987.

Gould, Paul. M. *The Outrageous Idea of the Missional Professor*. Eugene, OR: Wipf & Stock, 2014.

Gray, John. *Liberalism*. 2nd. ed. Minneapolis: University of Minnesota Press, 1995.

Green, Joel B. *1 Peter*. Grand Rapids: Eerdmans, 2007.

Green, Michael. *Evangelism in the Early Church*. Rev. ed. Grand Rapids: Eerdmans, 2003.

———. *The Message of Matthew*. Downers Grove, IL: InterVarsity, 2000.

Greener, Susan Hayes. "Children-at-Risk and the Whole Gospel: Integral Mission 'To, For, and With' Vulnerable Agents of God." *Transformation* 33.3 (2016) 159–70.

Guinness, Os. *The Call: Finding and Fulfilling the Central Purpose of Your Life*. Nashville: W Group, 2003.

Guroian, Vigen. *Ethics After Christendom: Toward and Ecclesial Christian Ethic*. Grand Rapids: Eerdmans, 1994.

———. "Evangelism and Mission in the Orthodox Tradition." In *Sharing the Book: Religious Perspectives on the Rights and Wrongs of Proselytism*, edited by John Witte and Richard C. Martin, 231–44. Maryknoll, NY: Orbis, 1999.

Harvey, Robert, and Philip H. Towner. *2 Peter & Jude*. Downers Grove, IL: InterVarsity, 2009.

Hauerwas, Stanley. *Vision and Virtue: Essays in Christian Ethical Reflection*. Notre Dame, IN: University of Notre Dame Press, 1983.

Haughey, John C. "The Complex Accusation of Sheep-stealing: Proselytism and Ethics." *Journal of Ecumenical Studies* 35.2 (1998) 257–68.

Haw, Sheryl. "Shalom is Good News." http://createsend.com/t/r-4CA521D291EF1B1A2540EF23F30FEDED.

Hays, Richard B. *The Moral Vision of the New Testament: Community, Cross, New Creation—A Contemporary Introduction to New Testament Ethics.* San Francisco: HarperSanFrancisco, 1996.

Hiebert, Paul G. *Anthropological Reflections on Missiological Issues.* Grand Rapids: Baker, 1994.

Hill, Brian V. "Proselytizing in the State School." *Journal of Christian Education* 55.1 (May 2012/2013) 21–27.

Hillion, Daniel. "Does Integral Mission Include Everything that God Requires of Us and Does God Require of Us Everything Included in Integral Mission?" http://www.micahnetwork.org/sites/default/files/doc/page/does_im_include_everything_that_god_requires_of_us_daniel_hillion.pdf.

Hirst, Paul H. *Moral Education in a Secular Society.* London: University of London Press, 1974.

Hunter, James Davison. *To Change the World: The Irony, Tragedy, & Possibility of Christianity in the Late Modern World.* Oxford: Oxford University Press, 2010.

International Federation of Red Cross and Red Crescent Societies and the ICRC. "The Code of Conduct for the International Red Cross and Red Crescent Movement and NonGovernmental Organisations (NGOs) in Disaster Relief." http://www.ifrc.org/Global/Publications/disasters/code-of-conduct/code-english.pdf.

Jayasinghe, Saroj. "Faith-based NGOs and Health Care in Poor Countries: a Preliminary Exploration of Ethical Issues." *Journal of Medical Ethics* 33.11 (2007) 623–26.

Johnson, Luke Timothy. "Proselytism and Witness in Earliest Christianity." In *Sharing the Book: Religious Perspectives on the Rights and Wrongs of Proselytism*, edited by John Witte & Richard C. Martin, 145–57. Maryknoll, NY: Orbis, 1999.

Johnstone, Henry, Jr. "Towards an Ethics of Rhetoric." *Communication* 6 (1981) 305–14.

Joint Working Group between the World Council of Churches and the Roman Catholic Church. "The Challenge of Proselytism and the Calling to Common Witness." *The Ecumenical Review* 48.2 (1996) 212–21.

Jones, Stefani. "Finding My Voice." In *Religious Upbringing and the Costs of Freedom: Personal and Philosophical Essays*, edited by Peter Caws and Stefani Jones, 192–213. University Park, PA: Pennsylvania State University Press, 2010.

Kaiser, Walter C., Jr. *Mission in the Old Testament: Israel as a Light to the Nations.* Grand Rapids: Baker, 2000.

Kandiah, Krish. "Lesslie Newbigin's Contribution to a Theology of Evangelism." *Transformation* 24.1 (2007) 51–60.

Kärkkäinen, Veli-Matti. "Proselytism and Church Relations: Theological Issues Facing Older and Younger Churches." *The Ecumenical Review* 52.3 (2000) 379–90.

Keller, Timothy. *Every Good Endeavor: Connecting Your Work to God's Work.* New York: Riverhead, 2012.

Kerr, David A. "Christian Understandings of Proselytism." *International Bulletin of Missionary Research* 23.1 (1999) 8–14.

Kerr, Hugh T., and John M. Mulder. *Famous Conversions: The Christian Experience.* Grand Rapids: Eerdmans, 1994.

Khomiakov, Alexei. "The Church is One." http://orthodoxinfo.com/general/khomiakov_church.aspx.

Kishkovsky, Leonid. "The Orthodox-Evangelical Encounter: To See Yourself as You Really are." In *The Mission of God: Studies in Orthodox and Evangelical Mission*, edited by Mark Oxbrow and Tim Grass, 110–16. Oxford: Regnum, 2015.

Kreider, Alan. *The Change of Conversion and the Origin of Christendom.* Harrisburg, PA: Trinity International, 1999. Reprint. Eugene, OR: Wipf & Stock, 2007.

———. *The Patient Ferment of the Early Church: The Improbable Rise of Christianity in the Roman Empire.* Grand Rapids: Baker Academic, 2016.

Kreider, Alan, and Eleanor Kreider. *Worship and Mission After Christendom.* Scottdale, PA: Herald, 2012.

Lausanne Covenant. 1974. https://www.lausanne.org/content/covenant/lausanne-covenant.

Lausanne Occasional Paper #21, "Evangelism and Social Responsibility: An Evangelical Commitment." June 26, 1982. www.lausanne.org/content/lop/lop-21.

Lerner, Natan. "Proselytism, Change of Religion, and International Human Rights." *Emory International Law Review* 12.1 (1998) 477–563.

Lewis, C.S. *Surprised by Joy.* New York: Harcourt Brace Jovanovich, 1955.

Loewen, Jacob A. *Educating Tiger: My Spiritual and Intellectual Journey.* Hillboro, KS: Centre for Mennonite Brethren Studies, Tabor College, 2000.

Lynch, Cecelia, and Tanya B. Schwartz. "Humanitarianism's Proselytism Problem." *International Studies Quarterly* 60 (2016) 636–46.

Malik, Charles. "The Other Side of Evangelism." *Christianity Today* (Nov. 7, 1980) 38–40.

Manastireanu, Danut. "Response 1: Ethical Witness, Absolutely! Proselytizing, Hopefully Not!" In *The Mission of God: Studies in Orthodox and Evangelical Mission*, edited by Mark Oxbrow and Tim Grass, 135–42. Oxford: Regnum, 2015.

Mar Demetrios, Yuhanon. "Response 2: The Challenges of Proselytism in the Context of Christianity in Asia." In *The Mission of God: Studies in Orthodox and Evangelical Mission*, edited by Mark Oxbrow and Tim Grass, 143–47. Oxford: Regnum, 2015.

Marshall, Paul. "Liberalism, Pluralism and Education." In *Agenda for Educational Change*, edited by John Shortt and Trevor Cooling, 45–56. Leicester, UK: Apollos, 1997.

McCarthy, Rockne, et al. *Society, State and Schools: A Case for Structural and Confessional Pluralism.* Grand Rapids: Eerdmans, 1981.

McKnight, Scot. *Turning to Jesus: The Sociology of Conversion in the Gospels.* Louisville: Westminster John Knox, 2002.

McLaughlin, Terry. "Parental Rights and the Religious Upbringing of Children." *Journal of Philosophy of Education* 18.1 (1984) 75–83.

Mennonite Central Committee. "Principles and Practices." https://mcc.org/sites/mcc.org/files/media/common/documents/mccprinciplesandpracticesweb2.pdf.

Metzger, Willard. "Sharing the Faith." *Canadian Mennonite* 18.19 (2014) 7.

Meyendorff, John. *The Orthodox Church: Its Past and its Role in the World Today.* 4th ed. Crestwood, NY: St. Vladimir's Seminary, 1996.

Micah Network. "Micah Network Declaration on Integral Mission." September 27, 2001. 1–4. http://www.micahnetwork.org/sites/default/files/doc/page/mn_integral_mission_declaration_en.pdf.

———. "Proselytism" (2007) 1–3. http://www.micahnetwork.org/sites/default/files/doc/library/proselytism_policy_statement.pdf.

Michaels, J. Ramsey. *1 Peter.* Waco, TX: Word, 1988.

Middleton, Richard J. *The Liberating Image: The Imago Dei in Genesis 1.* Ada, MI: Brazos, 2005.

Minnerath, Roland. "An Ethical/Catholic Perspective of Proselytism," *FIDES ET LIBERTAS* (2000) 42–51.

Motyer, J. A. *The Message of Philippians*. Leicester, UK: InterVarsity, 1984.

Naugle, David. "Traits of Christian Philosophers." http://www.epsociety.org/userfiles/art-Naugle%20(TraitsOfChristianPhilosophers).pdf.

Neuhaus, Richard John. "While We're at it." *First Things* 178 (2007) 74.

Newbigin, Lesslie. *The Gospel in a Pluralist Society*. Grand Rapids: Eerdmans, 1989.

———. *Proper Confidence: Faith, Doubt & Certainty in Christian Discipleship*. Grand Rapids: Eerdmans, 1995.

Nicastro, R. Vito, Jr. "Mission Volga: A Case Study in the Tensions between Evangelizing and Proselytizing." *Journal of Ecumenical Studies* 31.3–4 (1994) 223–43.

Nichols, Alan. "Ethical Issues in Evangelism and Justice Among the Poor." *Evangelical Review of Theology* 18 (1994) 137–51.

Nichols, Joel A. "Mission, Evangelism, and Proselytism in Christianity: Mainline Conceptions as Reflected in Church Documents." *Emory International Law Review* 12.1 (1998) 563–656.

Novak, David. "Proselytism in Judaism." In *Sharing the Book: Religious Perspectives on the Rights and Wrongs of Proselytism*, edited by John Witte, Jr. and Richard C. Martin, 17–44. New York: Orbis, 1999.

Oakeshott, Michael. "Education: The Engagement and its Frustration." In *Education and the Development of Reason*, edited by R. F. Dearden et al., 19–49. London: Routledge & Kegan Paul, 1972.

Ordway, Holly. *Apologetics and the Christian Imagination: An Integrated Approach to Defending the Faith*. Steubenville, OH: Emmaus Road.

Ostling, Richard N. "The New Missionary" *Time* (Dec. 27, 1982) 42–48.

Oxbrow, Mark. "Christian Mission: Contemporary Theology and Practice with Reference to Children." In *Theology, Mission and Child: Global Perspectives*, edited by Bill Prevette et al., 47–63. Eugene, OR: Wipf & Stock, 2014.

Oxbrow, Mark, and Tim Grass, eds. *The Mission of God: Studies in Orthodox and Evangelical Mission*. Oxford: Regnum, 2015.

Packer, J. I. *Evangelism and the Sovereignty of God*. Downers Grove, IL: InterVarsity, 1961.

Peace, Richard V. *Conversion in the New Testament: Paul and the Twelve*. Grand Rapids: Eerdmans, 1999.

Peters, Frank C. "Brother, Your Work is not Your Calling." *The Mennonite Brethren Herald* (August 27, 1971) 2–3.

Peters, R. S. *Authority, Responsibility and Education*. 3rd ed. London: George Allen and Unwin, 1973.

———. *Ethics and Education*. London: George Allen and Unwin, 1966.

Peterson, Eugene H. *Five Smooth Stones for Pastoral Work*. Grand Rapids: Eerdmans 1980.

———. *Growing Up with Your Teenager*. Grand Rapids: Fleming H. Revell, 1987.

———. *Reversed Thunder: The Revelation of John & the Praying Imagination*. San Francisco: HarperSanFrancisco, 1988.

Pilavachi, Mike. *When Necessary Use Words: Changing Lives Through Worship, Justice and Evangelism*. Ventura, CA: Regal, 2006.

Prevette, Bill. "The Disturbance of God, Holistic Mission and Children in Crisis: Lessons from a Study of Partnership in Romania." In *Theology, Mission and Child:*

Global Perspectives, edited by Bill Prevette et al., 90–108. Eugene, OR: Wipf & Stock, 2014.

Prevette, Bill, et al., eds. *Theology, Mission and Child: Global Perspectives.* Eugene, OR: Wipf & Stock, 2014.

Prior, David. *The Message of 1 Corinthians.* Leicester, UK: InterVarsity, 1985.

Pritchard, G. A. *Willow Creek Seeker Services: Evaluating a New Way of Doing Church.* Grand Rapids: Baker, 1996.

Putnam, Robert D., and David E. Campbell. *American Grace: How Religion Divides and Unites Us.* New York: Simon and Schuster, 2010.

Ramachandra, Vinoth. "What is Integral Mission?" http://www.micahnetwork.org/library/integral-mission/what-integral-mission-vinoth-ramachandra.

Rawls, John. *Political Liberalism.* New York: Columbia University Press, 1993.

Reno, R. R. "American Satyricon." *First Things* 116 (2001) 35–41.

Richardson, Rick. "Emerging Missional Movements: An Overview and Assessment of some Implications for Mission(s)." *International Bulletin of Missionary Research* 37.3 (2013) 131–36.

———. *Evangelism Outside the Box.* Downers Grove, IL: InterVarsity, 2000.

———. *Reimagining Evangelism: Inviting Friends on a Spiritual Journey.* Downers Grove, IL: InterVarsity, 2006.

Ridderbos, Herman. *The Coming of the Kingdom.* Philadelphia: Presbyterian and Reformed, 1962.

Riley-Smith, Louise, and Jonathan Riley-Smith. *The Crusades: Idea and Reality, 1095–1274.* London: Edward Arnold, 1981.

Robeck, Cecil M. "Mission and the Issue of Proselytism." *International Bulletin of Missionary Research* 20.1 (1996) 2–9.

Rorty, Richard. *Consequences of Pragmatism.* Minneapolis: University of Minnesota Press, 1982.

Salladay, Susan Anthony. "Christian Ethics: Proselytizing or Spiritual Care." *Journal of Christian Nursing* 23.3 (2006) 37.

Samuel, Vinay K., and Albrecht Hauser, eds. *Proclaiming Christ in Christ's Way: Studies in Integral Evangelism.* Oxford: Regnum, 1989.

Sandsmark, Signe. *Is World View Neutral Education Possible and Desirable?* Carlisle, UK: Paternoster and the Stapleford Centre, 2000.

Sawatzky, Katie D. "Ready to Listen and Learn." *Canadian Mennonite* 19.22 (2015) 9.

Schirrmacher, Thomas. "The Code: 'Christian Witness in a Multi-Religious World'—Its Significance and Reception." *Evangelical Review of Theology* 40.1 (2016) 82–89.

Schirrmacher, Thomas, and Thomas K. Johnson. "Why Evangelicals Need a Code of Ethics for Mission." *International Journal of Religious Freedom* 3.1 (2010) 23–37.

Schuurman, Douglas. *Vocation: Discerning Our Callings in Life.* Grand Rapids: Eerdmans, 2004.

Sherman, Amy L. *Kingdom Calling: Vocational Stewardship for the Common Good.* Downers Grove, IL: IVP, 2011.

Sider, Ronald J. *Cup of Water, Bread of Life: Inspiring Stories about Overcoming Lopsided Christianity.* Eugene, OR: Wipf & Stock, 2010.

———. *Doing Evangelism Jesus' Way: How Christians Demonstrate the Good News.* Nappanee, IN: Evangel, 2003.

———. "Evangelism, Salvation, and Social Justice: Definitions and Interrelationships." In *The Study of Evangelism: Exploring a Missional Practice of the Church*, edited by Paul W. Chilcote and Laceye C. Warner, 185–204. Grand Rapids: Eerdmans, 2008.

———. *One-Sided Christianity?: Uniting the Church to Heal a Lost and Broken World*. Grand Rapids: Zondervan, 1993.

Smedes, Lewis B. *Caring and Commitment: Learning to Live the Love We Promise*. San Francisco: Harper & Row, 1988.

Smith, Gordon. *Transforming Conversion: Rethinking the Language and Contours of Christian Initiation*. Grand Rapids: Baker, 2010.

Smith, James K. A. "The Lost Art of Persuasion." *Comment* 31.1 (2013) 2–3.

———. *Who's Afraid of Postmodernism?* Grand Rapids: Baker, 2006.

Stackhouse, John G., Jr. *Humble Apologetics: Defending the Faith Today*. Oxford: Oxford University Press, 2002.

Stalnaker, Cecil. "Proselytism or Evangelism?" *Evangelical Review of Theology* 26.4 (2002) 337–53.

Stark, Rodney. *The Rise of Christianity: A Sociologist Reconsiders History*. Princeton, NJ: Princeton University Press, 1996.

———. *The Triumph of Christianity: How the Jesus Movement Became the World's Largest Religion*. San Francisco: HarperOne, 2011.

Stetzer, Ed. "Where have All the Evangelism Conferences Gone?" *The Exchange (blog)*, January 6, 2016, http://www.christianitytoday.com/edstetzer/2016/january/where-have-all-evangelism-conferences-gone.html.

Stone, Bryan P. *Evangelism After Christendom: The Theology and Practice of Christian Witness*. Grand Rapids: Brazos, 2007.

Stott, John R. W. *The Message of Acts*. Leicester, UK: InterVarsity, 1990.

———. *The Message of Ephesians*. Downers Grove, IL: InterVarsity, 1979.

———. *The Message of Thessalonians*. Leicester, UK: InterVarsity, 1991.

Strachan, Wendy, and Simon Hood, eds. "Evangelization of Children." https://www.lausanne.org/wp-content/uploads/2007/06/LOP47_IG18.pdf

Synaxis of the Orthodox Churches' Primates. "The Mission of the Orthodox Church in the Contemporary World." http://pemptousia.com/2016/01/synaxis-of-the-orthodox-churches-primates/.

Taylor, John V. *The Go-between God: The Holy Spirit and the Christian Mission*. London: SCM, 1972.

Taylor, Richard. *Metaphysics*. 4th. ed. Engelwood Cliffs, NJ: Prentice Hall, 1992.

Teasdale, Mark R. *Evangelism for Non-Evangelists: Sharing the Gospel Authentically*. Downers Grove, IL: InterVarsity, 2016.

Teitel, Emma. "A Tiring Tempest in a T-shirt." *Maclean's Magazine* 21 (2012) 12.

Thacker, Justin. "Holistic Gospel in a Developing Society: Some Biblical, Historical and Ethical Considerations." *Evangelical Review of Theology* 33.3 (2009) 213–20.

Thangaraj, M. Thomas. "Evangelism Sans Proselytism: A Possibility?" In *Sharing the Book: Religious Perspectives on the Rights and Wrongs of Proselytism*, edited by John Witte, Jr. and Richard C. Martin, 335–52. Maryknoll, NY: Orbis, 1999.

Thiessen, Elmer John. "Christians and Jews and Proselytizing: A Response to David Novak." *Religious Studies and Theology* 22.2 (2003) 55–63.

———. "Ethical Evangelism and Proselytizing." In *The Mission of God: Studies in Orthodox and Evangelical Mission*, edited by Mark Oxbrow and Tim Grass, 117–34. Oxford: Regnum, 2015.

———. *The Ethics of Evangelism: A Philosophical Defense of Proselytizing and Persuasion.* Downers Grove, IL: IVP, 2011.

———. "Evangelism in the Classroom." *Journal of Education & Christian Belief* 17.2 (Fall, 2013) 221–41. Reprinted in *Journal of Christian Education* 55.1 (May 2012/2013) 7–20.

———. *In Defence of Religious Schools and Colleges.* Montreal and Kingston: McGill-Queen's University Press, 2001.

———. "The Offensiveness of Evangelism." June 8, 2012. https://www.firstthings.com/web-exclusives/2012/06/the-offensiveness-of-evangelism.

———. "A Philosopher's Journey with Christ: An Intellectual and Spiritual Autobiography." https://elmerjohnthiessen.wordpress.com/2013/06.

———. "Reply to Responses." In *The Mission of God: Studies in Orthodox and Evangelical Mission*, edited by Mark Oxbrow and Tim Grass, 148–54. Oxford: Regnum: 2015.

———. *Teaching for Commitment: Liberal Education, Indoctrination, and Christian Nurture.* Montreal and Kingston: McGill-Queen's University Press; Leominster, U.K: Gracewing, 1993.

———. "The Vocation of the Child as a Learner." In *The Vocation of the Child*, edited by Patrick McKinley Brennan, 381–407. Grand Rapids: Eerdmans, 2008.

Thiessen, Jacob. "We are Pilgrims." Unpublished manuscript, 1974.

Toews, John B. "The Calm Before the Storm: Mennonite Brethren in Russia (1900–1914)." *Direction: A Mennonite Brethren Forum* 31.1 (2002) 74–95.

Tomko, Jozef. "Missionary Challenges to the Theology of Salvation: A Roman Catholic Perspective." In *Sharing the Book: Religious Perspectives on the Rights and Wrongs of Proselytism*, edited by John Witte, Jr. and Richard C. Martin, 174–200. Maryknoll, NY: Orbis, 1999.

Tosi, Eric George. "Koinonic Evangelism: A Case Study of the Theology and Practice of Evangelism as Practiced in Three Parishes of the Orthodox Church in America." DMin diss., University of Trinity College and Toronto School of Theology, 2015.

———. "Koinonic Evangelism: The Community as the Evangelist." In *The Mission of God: Studies in Orthodox and Evangelical Mission*, edited by Mark Oxbrow and Tim Grass, 155–72. Oxford: Regnum, 2015.

Uzzell, Lawrence A. "Don't Call it Proselytism." *First Things* 146 (2004) 14–16.

Vassiliadis, Petros. "Mission and Proselytism: An Orthodox Understanding." *International Review of Mission* 85.337 (1996) 257–75.

Vischer, Robert K. "The Best Interests of the Child: Modern Lessons from the Christian Traditions." In *The Vocation of the Child*, edited by Patrick McKinley Brennan, 408–31. Grand Rapids: Eerdmans, 2008.

Volf, Miroslav. "Fishing in the Neighbor's Pond: Mission and Proselytism in Eastern Europe." *International Bulletin of Missionary Research* 20.1 (1996) 26–31.

———. *Work in the Spirit: Towards a Theology of Work.* Eugene, OR: Wipf & Stock, 2001.

Waltner, Erland. *1 Peter.* Scottdale, PA: Herald, 1999.

Webb, Barry G. *The Message of Isaiah.* Downers Grove, IL: InterVarsity, 1996.

Wells, David F. *God the Evangelist: How the Holy Spirit Works to Bring Men and Women to Faith.* Grand Rapids: Eerdmans, 1987.

Wells, Samuel. *Improvisation: The Drama of Christian Ethics.* Grand Rapids: Baker, 2008.

Willard, Dallas. *The Divine Conspiracy: Rediscovering Our Hidden Life in God*. San Francisco: HarperSanFrancisco, 1998.

Willmer, Haddon, and Keith J. White. *Entry Point: Towards Child Theology with Matthew 18*. London: WTL, 2013.

Wood, Donald K. "The Ethics of Evangelism in the Doctor-Patients Relationship. *Today's Christian Doctor* 30.1 (1999) 14–16.

World Council of Churches. "Towards Common Witness: A Call to Adopt Responsible Relationships in Mission and to Renounce Proselytism." *International Review of Mission*, LXXXVI.343 (1997) 463–73.

World Council of Churches, Pontifical Council for Interreligious Dialogue, and World Evangelical Alliance. "Christian Witness in a Multi-Religious World: Recommendations for Conduct." http://www.worldevangelicals.org/pdf/1106 Christian_Witness_in_a_Multi-Religious_World.pdf.

Wright, Christopher J. H. *The Mission of God: Unlocking the Bible's Grand Narrative*. Downers Grove, IL: IVP, 2006.

———. *The Mission of God's People*. Grand Rapids: Zondervan, 2010.

Wright, N. T. *The New Testament and the People of God*. London: SPCK, 1992.

Yancey, Philip. *The Jesus I Never Knew*. Grand Rapids: Zondervan, 1995.

Yannoulatos, Anastasios. *Facing the World: Orthodox Christian Essays on Global Concerns*. Translated by Pavlos Gottfried. Crestwood, NY: St. Vladmir's Seminary, 2003.

Subject Index

(**Note**: A list of guidelines for ethical evangelism which are discussed in chapter 7 is found under the index entry, "Guidelines for ethical evangelism." This list will refer readers to the relevant key concepts in the index where, for each guideline, they will find three subheadings in bold: **Guideline**, **Biblical basis**, and **Application**. After the subheading, **Guideline**, readers will find the identifying number of the guideline and the page number of the relevant guideline. After the subheading, **Biblical basis**, readers will find page numbers that provide the biblical basis for this guideline as found in Chapters 2–6. The page numbers after the subheading **Application** identify any pages where this particular guideline is applied to historical and contemporary situations.)

abuse of power. *See* power; abuse of
acceptance of rejection of evangelistic appeals. *See* gracious acceptance of rejection of evangelistic appeals
Anabaptists, 9n22, 15n41
    self-identification of author, 6–7
apologetics, 65, 66–68, 82, 83, 96, 106n34, 116, 122, 123n19, 161, 169. *See also* persuasion and apologetics
arrogance. *See* pride and boasting; humility
autonomy, 147–50, 148n38

baptism, 149–50, 152n49
biblical guidelines for ethical evangelism, chap. 7. *See concepts related to each guideline;* guidelines for ethical evangelism

Calvin, John, 146
child evangelism, chap. 8
    parental, 143–50
    beyond the family, 150–54
children
    vulnerability of, 147, 167
    becoming adults, 146–50
    Jesus' love for, 146–47
    at risk, 152–54
Christian nurture, 143–50
civil disobedience, 72
codes of conduct in evangelism, 6, 6n12, 6n13, 189n55, 193–94, 212–3
coercion
    Guideline #C9, 120. *See also* Guidelines #G19 & 20, 128; 123, 131
    Biblical basis, 3, 7, 32, 33, 34, 42, 50–51, 54–55, 67, 68–70, 71, 98, 109, 117–8, 118n12

SUBJECT INDEX

coercion *(continued)*
   Application, 28, 67, 98, 118, 119, 131, 148–50, 151–52, 153, 168, 187–88, 189, 191, 199, 203, 207–9, 212, 218
   degrees of, 118, 187
   in humanitarian aid (*See* humanitarian aid: coercion; humanitarian aid and enticement to convert*)*
CoMission, 200
common witness. *See* competition vs. cooperation
communication of the gospel. *See* contextualization
competition vs. cooperation, 132, 211–215
confrontation in evangelism. *See* uncomfortable truth in evangelism
conscience, 84, 96, 100, 113, 121, 158n10, 160, 205
contextualization
   Guideline #I28, 131
   Biblical basis, 40, 66, 66n28, 87–89, 108
   Application, 34, 212
conversion, 12–14, 13n36, 50, 56n48, 63, 70, 70n37. *See also* Holy Spirit and conversion
   as change of belief, behavior and belonging, 13, 39
   in the early church, 14n38
   of Levi, 39
   of Philippian jailor, 68–9
   of Saul, 12, 69–70
   of Zacchaeus, 177
   slow or sudden, 12–13, 68–70
creation mandate, 28
creation story, 27–28, 29, 112–13, 143n22
criticizing other religions, 2, 99, 121, 126–7, 169, 199. *See also* tolerance
cults, 115, 115n9, 208n52

Dalai Lama, 173n3
determinism, 187

development and religion, 173n2
dignity of persons, 203n32
   Guideline #A3, 114
   Biblical basis, 28, 31, 50, 98, 101, 107, 117
   Application, 28, 114, 126, 131, 147, 154, 167–68, 189, 191, 203, 205, 210, 212, 227
disciple-making, 15, 16, 50, 63, 75–78, 81n16, 105, 114–15, 232
dogmatism, 123, 169, 188, 225–6. *See also* humility in evangelism
dualism of evangelism and social action, 176, 176n14, 178. *See also* integral mission
   justification of, 175–80, 178n22

early church. *See* evangelism in particular contexts: early church
education and evangelism. *See* evangelism and related concepts: education. *See also* liberal education
effectiveness in evangelism. *See* evangelism, effectiveness of
emotional appeals and rhetoric, 118, 123n20
   Guideline #E15, 124
   Biblical basis, 33–34, 65, 68–70, 81–83, 86n29
   Application, 123, 123n22, 151-2
end justifying the means. *See* means and ends in evangelism
enemies of the gospel. *See* loving enemies of the gospel
Enlightenment, 25n10, 147, 162, 162n15
ethical relativism, 30n30, 160, 160n13, 225
ethics
   approach taken in the book. *See* ethics: modes of ethical discourse in Scripture
   biblical, 22–27
   common ground between Christians and non-christians, 5, 21
   etiquette, vs. 119n14
   foundations of, 5, 5n8, 5n9, 112–13

SUBJECT INDEX   247

guidelines for ethical evangelism, chap. 7 (See Guidelines for ethical evangelism)
modes of ethical discourse in Scripture, 24–26, 58–59, 78–79, 111–12, 132
nature of, 4
need for discernment, 112
rules, 23, 24. *See also* laws, biblical; ten commandments
sexual, 160n13
teaching of, 160
universal or transcultural norms, 25

evangel (*to euaggelion*, good news), 8n18, 10, 40, 43, 230. *See also* gospel message and *kerygma*.

evangelical
neglect of ethics of evangelism, 6
relationship with Orthodox, 6, 138, chap. 10
self-definition, 6
self-identification of author, 6
suspicions about evangelism, 4, 174
understanding of conversion, 12, 13n36
understanding of ecclesiology, 202
understanding of evangelism, 7, 11, 47, 64, 114, 123, 126, 131, 152, 174, 175–76, 180, 186, 202, 224, 225, 226–30
understanding of social action, 11–12, 34, 175–76, 180, 186, 194n72, 223–24

evangelism. *See also* codes of conduct in evangelism; natural evangelism; pre-evangelism; re-evangelism

evangelism conferences, 226–27, 227n25, 232

evangelism, criteria to distinguish ethical from unethical evangelism, chap. 7. *See concepts related to each guideline;* Guidelines for ethical evangelism

evangelism, definitions of, 7–10, 14–16, 175, 220
author's definition, 15–16
objections to author's definition, 16–18

evangelism, effectiveness of, 19, 34, 62, 68, 100, 113, 119, 131,168, 179, 223, 226, 227n25, 232

evangelism, embarrassment about, 226, 227–30, 229n30, 230n34. See also evangelism: objections against

evangelism, expectations. *See* expectations in evangelism; success and results

evangelism, goal of, 12, 15, 16, 63. *See also* results and success in evangelism

evangelism, guidelines for ethical evangelism, chap. 7. *See concepts related to each guideline;* Guidelines for ethical evangelism

evangelism and humanitarian aid. *See* humanitarian aid

evangelism, objections against, 1–3, 140–42, 161–64, 169–71, 228, 228n27
as intolerant, 125–27, 229–30, 229n31
responses to objections, 3–4, 140–42, 161–64.
Christians making these objections, 4, 174–5, 229–30

evangelism, opposition to, 50, 51–53, 55, 70–73, 76, 137–38, 140–42, 217n2, 221n8. *See also* persecution

evangelism in particular contexts
academy, chap. 9
children (See child evangelism)
early church, chap. 4, 97, 97n11, 177n21, 231–32, 231n38
medical profession, 156, 163n26, 216–17
professional life, chap. 9, 156, 157, 163n26, 164
Russia, 198, 200

evangelism and related concepts
"attraction," 17, 32, 61n10, 97–98, 98n14, 98n15

evangelism and related concepts (*continued*)
- "education," 162–63, 165.
- "fishing for men," 47–48 (*See also* seeking and welcoming sinners)
- "friendship evangelism," 114
- "incarnational evangelism" (*See* incarnational witness)
- "initiation," 16, 143n21, 148
- "koinonic," 13n34, 206–7
- "lifestyle evangelism," 93n42, 97, 98n14, 98n15, 113, 182, 182n37, 182, 182n37, 231
- "mission," 17–19, 175–80, 220 (*See also* humanitarian aid; distinct yet related; as equal)
- "natural evangelism," 231, 231n36
- "presence," 17, 33, 56
- "word and deed," 17–18, 17n51, 17n52, 97, 102, 104n74, 113, 181–85, 183n42, 218, 221–23, 222n12, 232 (*See also* incarnational witness)

evangelism, scandal of, 2, 82, 82n21, 224–25
evangelism vs. social action, 17–18, 44n10, 49, 63, 64, 104n74, 154, 175–80, 181–85, 181n35
evangelism strategies, 48, 56, 226–27, 227n25, 228n26
evangelistic intentions, 219
evangelistic sermons and speeches, 64–66
evangelists vs. lay evangelism, 230–1
exclusive truth. *See* truth: exclusive truth
expectations in evangelism
- **Guideline** #G19, 128
- **Biblical basis**, 48, 50, 51–53, 56, 67–68
- **Application**, 51, 67–68, 117, 128

exploiting vulnerability, 143, 147, 151, 154, 156, 167, 188n52, 189, 190–93, 194n74, 199, 208–9, 209n55, 211
- how to avoid, 192–93

faith-based organizations (FBOs), 173n2, 180n33, 183, 184, 193
false apostles or false evangelists, 80–81, 80n14, 85, 104, 105
Francis of Assisi, 181
free will and choice, 28, 117, 148, 176, 187, 190. *See also* coercion; determinism
Four Spiritual Laws, 69, 121
freedom. *See* coercion
friendship evangelism. *See* evangelism and related concepts: friendship evangelism

gentleness in evangelism, 96, 99, 102, 117, 123 128. *See also* humility
gifts of the Spirit, 157, 179
God. *See also* reverence for God and Christ; Great Commandment
- as evangelist, 41–42
- as foundation of ethics, 113
God and human effort
- **Guideline** #B6, 116–17
- **Biblical basis**, 48, 54, 56, 60–63, 81–83, 86
- **Application**, 124, 131, 131n34, 227
good deeds. *See* humanitarian aid
gospel message, 10–12, 40, 43, 65, 66, 81. *See also* evangel; *kerygma*
- complete gospel, 44, 64, 120–21, 225
- distortions of, 85, 223–25
- foolishness of, 81–83, 224–5
- hiddenness of, 83n22
- as including cosmic redemption, 11–12, 43, 44n10, 64, 121, 177, 223n17, 223n18, 224–25
- as including individual salvation, 11, 12–14, 43, 44n10, 50, 54, 63, 121, 177, 202, 223n17, 223–25, 224n19, 225
- universal in scope, 108
Golden Rule
- **Guideline** #A5, 115
- **Biblical basis**, 30, 92
- **Application**, 115n9, 150, 151, 205–7
government prohibitions against evangelism, 103, 129, 183–4.

See also prohibitions against evangelism
gracious acceptance of rejection of evangelistic appeals
    Guideline #G20, 128
    Biblical basis, 50, 51–53, 68, 70–74, 75–78, 98
    Application, 149, 168
Great Commandment, 177–8
    Guideline #A4, 115
    Biblical basis, 30, 36, 49–50, 64, 66, 75–78, 92, 144
    Application, 31, 115, 126, 146, 150, 153, 168, 180, 186, 192, 195, 217
Great Commission, 8, 9, 14, 49, 49n28, 50n29, 60, 150, 177–78. *See also* Holy Spirit and the Great Commission
Guidelines for ethical evangelism, chap. 7
    #A1. God and Christ as Lord, 113 (*See* reverence for God and Christ as Lord)
    #A2. Incarnational Witness, 113 (*See* incarnational witness)
    #A3. Dignity, 114 (*See* dignity)
    #A4. Great Commandment, 115 (*See* Great Commandment)
    #A5. Golden Rule, 116 (*See* Golden Rule)
    #B6. God and Human Effort, 116–17 (*See* God and human effort)
    #B7. Holy Spirit and Conversion, 117 (*See* Holy Spirit and conversion)
    #B8. Prayer, 117 (*See* prayer)
    #C9. Freedom and Coercion, 120 (*See* coercion)
    #C10. Power in Weakness, 120 (*See* power in weakness; servanthood in evangelism)
    #D11. Truthfulness, 121 (*See* truth, truthfulness)
    #D12. Integrity, 121 (*See* integrity)
    #E13. Humility, 123 (*See* humility)
    #E14. Persuasion and Apologetics, 124 (*See* persuasion and apologetics)
    #E15. Rhetoric and Emotions, 124 (*See* emotional appeals and rhetoric)
    #F16. Seeking and Welcoming Sinners, 125 (*See* seeking and welcoming sinners)
    #F17. Uncomfortable Truth, 125 (*See* uncomfortable truth)
    #F18. Tolerance, 127 (*See* tolerance)
    #G19. Expectations, 128 (*See* expectations)
    #G20. Gracious Acceptance of Rejection, 128 (*See* gracious acceptance of rejection)
    #G21. Loving Enemies, 128 (*See* loving enemies)
    #G22, 128. Persecution (*See* persecution: responding to)
    #G23, 129. Prohibitions against Evangelism (*See* prohibitions against evangelism)
    #H24–27, 130. Motivation (*See* motivation)
    #I28. Communication and Contextualization, 131 (*See* contextualization)
    #I29. Means and Ends, 132 (*See* means and ends)
    #I30. Results and Success, 132 (*See* success and results)

hate speech, 1–2, 52–53
hermeneutics, 22–27, 25n10
hidden agendas and identities. *See* integrity in evangelism
Holy Spirit, 52, 57, 58, 64, 64n22, 72, 73, 86, 150n55
Holy Spirit and conversion
    Guideline #B7, 117 (*See also* #E14, 124; 122)
    Biblical basis, 13, 14, 36, 48, 48n22, 56n48, 59–62, 66–68, 69, 83n22, 86, 116
    Application,116n11, 225
Holy Spirit and the Great Commission, 8, 9, 49–50, 61, 116n11, 223n18

250   SUBJECT INDEX

human effort and divine initiative. *See* God and human effort
humanitarian aid, chap. 10. *See also* secular humanitarian organizations
   Code of Conduct, 189n55, 193–94
   and coercion, 187–88, 190–93
   danger of becoming secularized, 183, 183n40
   imbalance of power in, 190–3, 191n61
   motivation for, 184, 185–86
   transparency about identity, in, 184, 184n43
humanitarian aid and enticement to convert
   charge of, 173, 173n3, 173n4, 190–3, 199
   examples of, 172, 188–89
   responding to charge, 173–75, 187–88, 190–93
humanitarian aid and evangelism, conceptual relationship, 17–18, 104n74
   distinct yet related, 175–80
   equated, 181–85, 181n35
humanitarian aid and evangelism, practical relationship
   continuum, from complete separation to concurrence, 191–92
   examples of healthy relation, 113, 180n32, 191n60
   examples of unhealthy relation, 180, 180n33, 192n65, 222, 222n14
   exploiting vulnerability (*See* exploiting vulnerability)
   government demands to separate, 184
   imbalances in relation, 180, 180n33, 180n34
   priorities, 179–80
   leading to conversions, 177, 177n21, 182, 182n38
   made conditional on conversion, 189, 189n54
   made conditional on listening to evangelistic appeals, 188–9
   opportunism 185–6

humility in evangelism. *See also* pride and boasting
   Guideline #E13, 123–24 (See also #B8, 117; #C10, 120)
   Biblical basis, 34, 41–43, 47, 55–56, 82–83, 86, 96, 99, 102, 104, 120, 122, 128
   Application, 124, 128, 146, 168–69, 212, 225–26

incarnational witness
   Guideline #A2, 113
   Biblical basis, 30, 31, 32, 34, 41–42, 93, 96–8
   Application, 101–2, 156–8, 168, 185, 222
incomplete gospel. See gospel message: complete
indoctrination, 140–2, 163
initiation. See evangelism and related concepts: "initiation"
integral mission, holistic mission, 17–18, 17n57, 17n59, 172n1, 175–76, 218, 222
   and children, 153, 153n53
   critique of, 176–77, 183n40, 221
   definition of, 176, 176n13
integrity in evangelism. *See also* motivation
   Guideline #D12, 121
   Biblical basis, 44, 52, 75–78, 83–85, 90, 93, 96, 98, 100
   Application, 121, 151, 168, 184, 185, 194, 200
International Federation of Red Cross, 189n55, 193

Jesus as a model for ethical evangelism, 41–46
Jonah, 20–21, 35–36
judgment and judgmentalism in evangelism, 20–21, 35–36, 43, 44, 48n22, 110, 124–25, 124n24, 225

kerygma, 11
kingdom of God, 11, 11n27, 12, 16, 43, 43n9, 50, 56, 59–62, 63–64, 64, 64n18, 64n20, 89, 121, 157

laws, biblical, 29–31. *See also* ethics: ten commandments; rules
liberalism, 166, 201, 229, 229n29. *See also* public/private distinction of liberalism
love, 30–1, 30n30, 34, 51n31, 94, 128, 142, 152, 176, 196
   and communication, 66, 198, 232
   and disciple-making, 50
   for enemies (*See* loving enemies of the gospel)
   God's, 30, 35, 36, 146, 149, 177, 186, 216–7
   and hate speech (*See* hate speech)
   Jesus', 34, 39, 44, 46, 46n16, 147
   of God (*See* Great Commandment)
   and motivation (*See* motivation)
   of neighbor (*See* Great Commandment)
   for sinners, 44, 45, 124 (See also seeking and welcoming sinners)
   speaking truth with, 47, 126, 212, 214
   and tolerance (See tolerance)
loving enemies of the gospel
   Guideline #G21, 128
   Biblical basis, 30–31, 35–36, 51–53, 57–58, 99, 101, 126
   Application, 128, 168

martyr, martyrdom, 55, 57–58, 73, 73n42, 74, 106, 107, 128
means and ends in evangelism
   Guideline #I29, 132
   Biblical basis, 87–89
Mennonite Central Committee, 183, 183n41, 221-2, 222n14
Mennonites and evangelism, 4n7, 221-2
Micah Network, 18n57, 18n59, 172n1, 175-6, 176n13, 178, 180n33, 183n40, 184n44, 194n72, 216n1
mission, missional, *missio Dei*, 17, 17n55, 17n56, 175, 179, 185, 220, 232. *See also* humanitarian aid
   of Israel, 31–34
   professors, 158, 158n6, 158n10, 171
   relation to evangelism, 18–19, 175–80, 220, 220n6
motivation for ethical evangelism, 4
   Guidelines #H24, #H25, #H26, #H27, 130 (*See also* #D12, 122)
   Biblical basis, 30–31, 33, 42–43, 53, 62, 75–78, 84, 89–92
   Application, 132, 182, 184, 184n43, 185–86, 200
   difficulty in assessing, 174, 186

narrative of the bible, 24, 24n8, 30, 31
neutrality in teaching, 162, 162n19, 163–4, 170n40
new religious movements. *See* cults
nominal Christians, 54, 202, 202n26, 203, 204, 207

objectives of book, 6
Orthodoxy, Orthodox churches, chap. 11, 196, 196n1, 198, 200, 201–5
   ecclesiology, 13n34, 202, 202n23
   notion of canonical territory, 204, 213–14
   relationship with evangelicals, 6, 138, 197, 198, 201–5, 214
   religious freedom, 205, 205n42
   understanding of evangelism, 181n35, 197n5, 197n6, 203, 221n8, 223n18
   understanding of mission, 197n6, 202
   understanding of persons, 201
   understanding of salvation, 202
   understanding of who is a "Christian," 202–3
   and unity, 202, 204–5

Padilla, René, 176
parables of Jesus, 53–56
persecution, responding to
   Guideline #G22, 128–9
   Biblical basis, 51–53, 55, 57–58, 70–74, 86, 96, 100–101, 106–7
   Application, 71–74, 86, 97, 100–101, 107, 128

SUBJECT INDEX

persuasion and apologetics
    Guideline #E14, 124 (See also #B7, 117)
    Biblical basis, 11, 26, 57–58, 66–68, 67n29, 81–83, 96, 116, 122
    Application, 67, 160, 161, 169
    as inherent in human nature, 162, 162n20
philosophy, 4, 5, 118, 138, 140, 157–61, 161n14, 165–66, 168n37, 169–70
pluralism, 125, 143n22, 160–1, 166–70, 169, 205n44
postmodernism, 3, 160n13, 162, 225
power, 3, 11, 151, 154, 167
    abuse of power, 118, 122, 131, 151, 168, 189, 190–3, 212, 217–18, 228
    of the gospel, 9, 55, 56, 71, 81, 230
    of the Holy Spirit, 8, 53, 60–2, 117, 122, 130
power in weakness. See also servanthood in evangelism
    Guideline #C10, 120. See also 122, 131
    Biblical basis, 34, 42, 56, 74, 81–83, 85–87, 86n29, 118
    Application, 122, 128, 168, 212
prayer, 43, 77
    Guideline #B8, 117 (See also 122)
    Biblical basis, 49n26, 60, 62, 72, 85n27
    Application, 116, 149, 201, 219
pre-evangelism, 159, 159n12
pride and boasting, 82, 82n20, 90, 104, 169
prohibitions against evangelism. See also government prohibitions against evangelism
    Guideline #G23, 129
    Biblical basis, 70–74, 102, 103
    Application, 103, 129, 183–4
proselytism, chap. 11
    confusion over definition, 55n46, 189, 197, 198–200, 209, 211, 218–19, 220–1
proselytism as sheep-stealing, chap. 11
    definition, 6, 197, 199
    examples, 196, 206, 208–9, 210
    opposition to, 197–98, 208n54
    practiced by the Orthodox church, 196, 206, 207n50, 209
    problems with the notion of stealing sheep, 207–10
public/private distinction of liberalism, 2, 36, 162, 162n18, 229

Red Crescent Societies, 189n55, 193
redemption, personal and cosmic. See gospel message: as including cosmic redemption; as including individual salvation
re-evangelism, 54, 202, 203, 203n27, 207, 213
rejection of evangelistic appeals. See gracious acceptance of rejection of evangelistic appeals
relativism, 99, 126, 160n13, 225. See also ethical relativism
religious freedom, 1–2, 115, 205, 205n42, 205n44
repentance, 13, 43, 44, 62, 64
resistance to evangelism. See gracious acceptance of rejection of evangelistic appeals; persecution
respecting persons. See tolerance
results and success in evangelism
    Guideline #I30, 132
    Biblical basis, 48, 50, 53, 56, 62, 75–78, 83, 131
    Application, 131, 132, 212
reverence for God and Christ as Lord, 100, 102, 113
    Guideline #A1, 113 (See also Guideline #A4, 115)
    Biblical basis, 29, 44–46, 76, 92, 99–100, 102, 107–9
    Application, 186, 195, 195n75
rhetoric. See emotional appeals and rhetoric
Roman Catholic, 138, 181n35, 197, 197n7, 198, 199n12

sacred/secular dualism, 156–57
salvation. See redemption
secular, secularization, 166, 160, 204

SUBJECT INDEX   253

secular humanitarian organizations, 174, 174n7
   hidden agendas of, 174, 174n7, 193
   influence on Christians, 174–75
seeking and welcoming sinners
   Guideline #F16, 125
   Biblical basis, 39, 44, 54, 124, 125n25
   Application, 124, 150-1, 158, 159, 207
self-righteousness
   in evangelism, 44
   of Pharisees, 45–46, 46n16
servanthood in evangelism
   Guideline #C10, 120 (See also Guidelines #H25, 130; #H28, 131; 122)
   Biblical basis, 14, 31, 33–34, 42–43, 52, 88–89, 107, 118, 130
   Application, 35, 94, 118, 131, 168, 191, 212, 232
sin, sinners, 39, 44–45, 44n10, 54 123n22, 124, 227n25. See also seeking and welcoming sinners
social action and church growth, 177, 177n21. See also evangelism vs. social action; humanitarian aid and evangelism, practical relationship
social sanctions against evangelism. See prohibitions against evangelism
Stephen, 57–58, 73–74
strategies in evangelism. See evangelism strategies
structural pluralism, 143n22
success. See results and success in evangelism

teaching for autonomy, 146–50
teaching for commitment, 143–50, 149, 156, 159, 160
ten commandments, 23, 24, 29, 30, 120
tolerance. See also criticizing other religions
   Guideline #F18, 127
   Biblical basis, 1–2, 30, 31, 50, 52–53, 66, 96, 101, 125–27

   Application, 30–31, 127n31, 126–27, 169, 212, 214–15
   definition, 31, 53n37, 126–27, 168, 169, 212, 229–30
truth, truthfulness. See also uncomfortable truth in evangelism
   Guideline #D11, 121
   Biblical basis, 23, 29, 30–31, 40, 42, 44, 46–47, 64, 75–78, 83–85, 103, 104, 105, 126
   Application, 43, 64, 85, 125, 152, 169, 200, 212, 225–26
   confrontational truth-telling, 45, 46n16
   exclusive truth, 26, 47, 47n18, 125
   vs. the search for truth, 226n21

uncomfortable truth in evangelism
   Guideline #F17, 125
   Biblical basis, 26, 30–31, 34, 36, 45, 47
   Application, 34, 37, 224
Universal Declaration of Human Rights, 205

vocation, 156–57, 171

Wesleyan Quadrilateral, 26n16
witness, meaning of, 8, 31, 33
word vs. deed. See evangelism and related concepts: "word and deed." See also incarnational evangelism; integral mission
words, as weapons, 2–3, 52, 67
work, 156–57, 171
World Council of Churches, 6, 6n13, 181n35, 197n5, 198, 199n12, 204, 205–6, 206n46, 211n60
   and religious freedom, 205–6, 205n44
World Evangelical Alliance, 6, 6n13
worldview, biblical, 24, 24n8, 28, 65, 65n22, 66, 166
World Vision, 189
worship. See reverence for God and Christ as Lord

Author Index

Abraham, William J., 7n15, 9n20, 11n27, 15n42, 16, 16n49, 18n60, 143n21
Astley, Jeff., 165
Attfield, D.G., 143n21, 149n40
Augustine, 51n31, 69n34, 94, 101

Bailey, Kenneth E., 30n30, 53n38, 54n40
Bakke, O.M.. 130n9
Barclay, William, 46n9
Barnett, Paul, 80n10, 80n14, 85n28
Bartholomew, Craig G., 26n18, 28n23
Bartholomew, Patriarch, 205n43
Bauer, Walter, 51n32
Bayle, Pierre, 51n33
Berner, Ashley, 162n21
Bickley, Paul, 188n52, 191n60, 195n74, 228n28
Boffetti, Jason, 168n38
Bosch, David J., 7, 17, 18n58, 25n10, 121n15, 175, 220, 224n14
Bowen, John P., 231n19
Bradbury, Steve, 176n13, 180n33, 184n43, 184n46, 190, 192, 193n69, 194n72, 194n73
Bradley, Raymond D., 142n16
Brennan, Patrick McKinley, 140n9, 154n57
Brewster, Dan, 140n9, 152n49, 153n53,
Bria, Ion, 201, 201n21, 223n18
British Citizenship Foundation, 162n16

Brueggemann, Walter, 9n21, 11n29, 16n44, 31n34, 144n25, 203n29, 217n2n 230n34
Buckley, William F., 127n31
Bunge, Marcia J., 147n33

Campbell, David E., 229n
Chan, Simon, 13n36
Chester, Tim, 18n57, 180n33
Clarke, Matthew, 173n2
Clowny, Edmund, 100n20, 100n21
Collier, John, 139n9
Cooling, Trevor, 162n19, 164n28, 164n29

Das, Rupen, 182n38, 185n47
Dau, Isaiah Majok, 185
Davis, James Calvin, 126n30
Davis, Stephen T., 161n14, 164
Dawson, Lorne, 115n9, 198n9
DiSilvestro, R., 163n26
Dodd, C.H., 11n25, 15n42
Dyck, Peter, 222, 222n14, 179n29, 183n42
Dykstra, Craig, 149n40

Elliott, Mark, 204n38, 211n59
Evangelical Philosophers Society, 158n7
Evans, Craig A., 48n24, 52n34
Ewert, David, 182n37, 97n9, 98n14

255

AUTHOR INDEX

Fee, Gordon D., 89n31
Fish, Stanley, 162n15
Fletcher, John, 123n23, 228n26, 229n30
Florovsky, Fr. Georges, 205n40
Fountain, Philip, 173n5
French, Edgar, 5n8
Friesen, Abraham, 9n22, 15n41, 50n29

Gillquist, Peter, 206n47
Glanzer, Perry, 200, 202n23, 202n25, 213n65
Goheen, Michael, 25n11, 26n18, 32n38
Gooch, Paul W., 82
Gould, Paul. M., 158n9
Gray, John, 229n29
Green, Joel, B., 95n3, 101n23, 102n26
Green, Michael, 8, 8n18, 10, 11n25, 15n42, 46n16, 64n20, 67n29, 203n31, 231
Greener, Susan Hayes, 140n9, 153n50, 153n53,
Guinness, Os, 157n4
Guroian, Vigen, 201n21, 197n6, 202n25, 203n27, 204n34, 205n41, 205n42

Harvey, Robert, 104n29, 104n30
Hauerwas, Stanley, 30n30
Haughey, John C., 162n20
Hauser, Albrecht, 176n13
Haw, Sheryl, 216n1, 216–9, 220, 221
Hays, Richard B., 22–5, 79n7, 111, 138, 138n5, 139, 139n7
Hiebert, Paul G., 14n40
Hill, Brian V., 164n28, 164n29
Hillion, Daniel, 154n54, 178n22
Hirst, Paul H., 162n15
Hood, Simon, 150n42
Hunter, James Davison, 34n45, 62n12

International Federation of Red Cross, 189n55, 193

Jayasinghe, Saroj, 189n54
Johnson, Luke Timothy, 8n17, 221n10
Johnstone, Henry Jr., 162n20
Joint Working Group between the World Council of Churches and the Roman Catholic Church, 181n35, 199n12
Jones, Stefani, 137–8, 141, 141n13, 142

Kaiser, Walter C. Jr., 31n33, 32n39, 35n46
Kandiah, Krish, 7n15, 18n58
Kärkkäinen, Veli-Matti, 201n21
Keller, Timothy, 157n4
Kerr, David A., 197n7
Kerr H.T., 70n37
Khomiakov, Alexei, 204n38
Kishkovsky, Leonid, 214n68
Kreider, Alan, 12, 13, 13n32, 13n38, 32n39, 96n6, 98n15, 118n12, 177n21, 181n35, 195n75, 231–2
Kreider, Eleanor, 18n58, 96n6, 181n35, 195n75

Lausanne Covenant, 178n22
Lerner, Natan, 197n7, 205n44
Lewis, C.S., 14
Loewen, Jacob A., 114, 188–9
Lynch, Cecelia, 174, 174n7, 190n58, 191n60

Malik, Charles, 158n7
Manastireanu, Danut, 196n1, 213n63
Mar Demetrios, Metropolitan Yuhanon, 196n1, 208n54
Marshall, Paul, 229n29
McCarthy, Rockne, 143n22
McKnight, Scott, 12n30, 70n37
McLaughlin, Terry, 148n38, 149n40
Mennonite Central Committee, 183, 183n41
Metzger, Willard, 222
Meyendorff, John, 202n24
Micah Network, 18n57, 18n59, 172n1, 175–6, 178, 180n33, 183n40, 194n72, 216n1
Michaels, J. Ramsey, 100n19
Middleton, Richard J., 28
Minnerath, Roland, 198n8
Motyer, J.A., 90n35, 91n36
Mulder, J.M., 70n37, 197n7

Naugle, David, 171n42

AUTHOR INDEX 257

Neuhaus, Richard John, 132
Newbigin, Lesslie, 7n15, 18n58, 67n31, 182, 224n19, 226n21
Nicastro, R. Vito, Jr., 199, 204n35, 213n64
Nichols, Alan, 192n65, 197n5
Nichols, Joel A., 202n26, 203n28
Novak, David, 32n37

Oakeshott, Michael, 143n20
Ordway, Holly, 106n34
Ostling, Richard N., 182n38
Oxbrow, Mark, 175n11, 197n3, 220n5, 231n37

Packer, J.I., 116n10,
Parks, Sharon, 149n40
Peace, Richard V., 13n38
Peters, Frank C., 156n2
Peters, R.S., 143n20, 167
Peterson, Eugene H., 105–6, 106n34, 149n40, 168n37
Pilavachi, Mike, 195n75
Prevette, Bill, 139n8, 139n9, 153n51, 154n54, 180n33, 180n34
Pontifical Council for Interreligious Dialogue, 6
Prior, David, 85n28,
Pritchard, G.A., 123n21, 131n33, 131n34, 131n35

Ramachandra, Vinoth, 176, 176n15, 176n17, 177n18, 178n23
Rawls, John, 166n33, 166n34
Red Crescent Societies, 189n55, 193
Reno, R.R., 160n13
Richardson, Rick, 13n37, 17n55, 176n14, 220n6
Ridderbos, Herman, 11n27
Riley-Smith, Louise and Jonathan, 51n31
Robeck, Cecil M., 197n7, 210n56
Roman Catholic Church, 138, 181n35, 197, 197n5, 198, 213n65
Rorty, Richard, 166n33, 168n38

Salladay, S.A., 163n26
Samuel, Vinay K., 176n13

Sandsmark, Signe, 162n19
Sawatzky, Katie Doke, 4n7
Schirrmacher, Thomas, 6n13
Schuurman, Douglas, 157n4
Schwartz, Tanya B., 174, 174n7, 190n58, 191n60,
Sherman, Amy L., 157
Sider, Ronald J., 17n51, 17n52, 177, 179–80, 180n32, 180n33, 182n38, 213n63, 223n17
Smedes, Lewis B., 149n39
Smith, Gordon, 13n36
Smith, James K.A., 3n4, 68n33
Stackhouse, John G. Jr., 169n39
Stalnaker, Cecil, 220n7
Stark, Rodney, 97n11, 97n12, 177n21, 231n38
Stetzer, Ed, 226–7, 227n25
Stott, John R.W., 57n1, 61n10, 64n21, 65, 66n27, 69n35, 76n2, 77n5, 146n30
Strachan, Wendy, 150n42
Stone, Bryan P., 221n10
Synaxis of the Orthodox Churches' Primates, 203n32

Taylor, John V., 116n11
Taylor, Richard, 187n51
Teasdale, Mark R., 231n35
Teitel, Emma, 2–3
Thacker, Justin, 177n18
Thangaraj, M. Thomas, 55n46, 115n8
Thiessen, Elmer John, 1n1, 5n8, 6n12, 16n44, 47n18, 53n37, 114n5, 118n132, 121n17, 123n20, 126n27, 127n31, 140n10, 141n15, 144n23, 147n35, 152n48, 155, 160, 162n17, 163n23, 164n28, 165n30, 166n34, 167n36, 170, 173n3, 187n51, 208n52, 209n55, 226n21, 228n27, 229n32
Thiessen, Jacob, 198
Tosi, Eric George, 13n34, 181n35, 196, 199, 206, 206n47, 206n48, 207, 209
Towner, Philip H., 104n30, 104n29

Uzzell, Lawrence A., 211, 220, 221n8

Vassiliadis, Petros, 207n50, 221n8, 223n18
Vischer, Robert K., 149n41
Volf, Miroslav, 197, 214, 214n67

Waltner, Erland, 102n27
Webb, Barry G., 33n41, 33n43
Wells, David F., 41n6
Wells, Samuel, 25n12
Willard, Dallas, 15, 15n41, 43n9, 44n10, 158n8, 224n20

Willmer, Haddon, 139, 139n9
White, Keith J., 139, 139n9
Wood, Donald K., 163n26
World Council of Churches (WCC), 6, 181n35, 197n5, 198–9, 199n13, 204, 205, 206, 206n46, 211n60
World Evangelical Alliance, 6
Wright, Christopher J. H., 17n56
Wright, N.T., 26–7

Yannoulatos, Anastasios, 215n70

Scripture Index

OLD TESTAMENT

Genesis

1:26	28
1:28	28n23
2:15	28n23
2:17	29
2:24	29n25
3:1	52n34
12:1–3	31
18:19	144n26

Exodus

19:5–6	31
20:2	29
20:16	29n26
22:21	126n28
22:22	185n47

Leviticus

19:11	23, 29n26
19:18	30n28, 114n7, 126n28
19:33	126n28
19:34	126n28

Deuteronomy

5:1–21	29
6:1–3	30
6:4–9	144
6:4–5	30, 114n7
6:20–21	144
10:18	30, 185n47
10:19	30n27, 126n28
11:18–21	144n24
11:26–32	29n24
16:11	185n47
16:14	185n47
21:23	82n21
30:15–20	29n24
30:19	148n36
31:12–13	144n24

Joshua

24:15	148n36

Judges

21:25	29n25

I Samuel

2:26	147

Job

4:8	29n24
19:16	185n47

Psalms

1	29n24
2	29n24
7:9	90n33
8:5–6	28
19:12	91n38
23	53
25:9	122n18
41:1	185n47
67:1–2	32n35
68:5	185n47
72:13	185n47
75:1	92n41
78:1–8	144n26
127:3	144
147:15–18	29

Proverbs

3:34	122n18
4	144n26
16:18–19	122n18
17:3	90n33
22:6	144n26

Isaiah

2:2–3	32n35, 61n10, 97n10
2:5	32
5:18–23	46n16
8:12	100n18
8:14	224
10:2	185n47
28:23–29	29n25
32:15–18	60n7
40:14	33n42
41:8–9	31
42:1–7	33, 33–34
42:6	31n33
49:6	31n33, 32n39
56:3	30n27
60:3	31n33
62:1–2	32n32, 122n18
62:12	32n32

Jeremiah

23:1–8	54n42

Ezekiel

3	148n36
11:18–20	60n7
34	48n23, 54n42
36:24–32	60n7
39:29	60n7

Daniel

7:13–14	108n37

Hosea

1–14	203n30

8:7	29n24

Amos

2:4–5	203n30

Jonah

1–4	20–21, 35–36
4:2	35
4:11	36

Micah

4:1–5	32n35
6:8	122n18

Nahum

3:1–7	20

Zechariah

8:20–23	32n35

NEW TESTAMENT

Matthew

3:2	42
4:18–22	47n19
4:19	47n20
4:23	11
5:3	122n16
5:9–12	31n31, 52n36
5:11–12	73, 171n42
5:13–16	32, 181n36, 183
5:16	97n10
5:18	46n17
5:26	46n17
5:37	46–47
5:43–48	31n31, 52n36
6:2	46n17
6:5	46n17
6:16	46n17
6:10	43, 225
6:26	28
7:12	30n29, 115, 205
7:13–14	29n24, 131n32, 148n36
7:24–27	29n24
8:4	34n44
8:10	46n17
8:14–15	49n27
8:18–22	125n26
9:9–13	44n11, 125n25
9:30	34n44
9:35–11:1	38n24
9:35–37	11, 48, 48n23, 230
10:1	49n26
10:7–8	49n26, 183
10:12–15	50
10:14	71n38
10:15	46n17
10:16–20	52, 52n34
10:19	122
10:21–25	46n17, 52, 125n26
11:2–6	178n24, 181n36, 222n12
12:19	34
12:15–21	33
12:22–37	125n25

SCRIPTURE INDEX

13	55	5:43	33n44	14:15–23	51, 51n32
14:22	51n32	6:34	48n23	15	207
16:21–23	59	6:45	51n32	15:1–7	53n39, 54, 54n40, 54n41, 203n31
16:24–28	125n26, 148n36	8:12	46n17		
		9:1	46n17		
18:2–4	12, 122n16	9:41	46n17		
18:6	147	10:13–16	146, 146n31	15:8–10	54n40
18:12–14	53n39, 54n41, 203n31	10:43–45	88	15:11–32	54n40
		12:29–31	114n7	18:9–14	125n25
		16:15–16	49n28	18:15–17	146
19:13–15	146n31			19:1–10	44n12, 177
20:24–28	118, 191			21:3	46n17
21:15–16	147	Luke		21:12–14	96n7
22:1–14	51			23:34	73
22:16	46	1:1–4	40n3	23:46	73
22:20	124	2:11	10	24:44–47	11
22:34–38	30	2:41–50	147	24:48	8, 10
22:37–40	112n3	2:51–52	147		
22:39–40	30n28	3:1–18	10		
23	45n13	3:10–14	42	John	
23:15	45	3:16,	42		
23:37	46n16	3:18,	42	1:7	33n40
25:31–46	178, 185n47	4:18–21	8, 10, 33n40, 43, 177n19	1:8	33n40, 43
28	223n18			1:14	41, 46
28:17	68n32			1:35–51	47n19
28:18–20	9, 9n22, 14, 49n27, 50, 223n18	5:1–11	47n19	1:51	46n17
		5:5	47	3	45n14
		5:10	48n21	3:1–15	56n48
28:38–39	150n45	5:27–32	39, 44n11, 45	3:3	12, 46n17
		6:31	30n29	3:5	46n17
		7:22	63n17	3:11	46n17
Mark		8:40–48	49n27, 63n16	4	176n17, 178n25
1:4	42	8:49–60	63n16	4:1–42	44n12, 49n27
1:14–20	47n19	9	177		
1:14–15	11, 43	9:1–6	48n24	4:39	131n32
1:1	10	9:5	148n36	4:41	131n32
1:17	47n20	9:27	46n17	5:17–26	63n16
1:29–31	49n27	9:51–55	50, 72n40, 148n36	5:33	47
1:39	178n24			8:40	46
2:2	131n32	10	177	10:1–18	54n41, 55
2:13–17	44n11	10:1–24	48n24, 49n26, 53	13:1–17	122n16
2:15	131n32			14:6	46
3:7–19	48n24	10:21	146	14:15–16	46
3:14–15	48, 49n26, 178n24	11:37–54	45n15	15:18–16:16	60n6
3:28	46n17	12:11–12	96n7	15:19	230
4:26–29	56n47	12:44	46n17	16:8–11	36, 48n22, 225
5:21–43	49n27	14:1–14	45n13		

SCRIPTURE INDEX

John (continued)

17:18	49n26, 232
18:37	46
20:21	49n26, 232
20:30–31	40n2
21:1–14	48n21

Acts

1:1	58
1:3	59
1:4–5	60
1:7–8	60, 8, 33n40, 49n28
1:11	61
2:1	67n31
2:13	68
2:14–41	9
2:17–21	60n7
2:22	63
2:38–39	13, 62, 150n45
2:38	13, 62
2:40	67n29
2:41	13, 68, 131n32
2:42	62
2:45	64
2:47	131n32
3	63, 64n22, 71
3:19	14n40
3:26	14n40
4:1–21	71–72, 64n19
4:2	67n29
4:4	131n32
4:7	67n31
4:23–31	63, 72
4:29–30	177
4:33	72
4:34–35	64
5:1–11	59n3
5:12–41	72, 73
5:12	63n17
5:21	15
5:25	15
5:28	15
5:29	103n28
6:7	73
6:8–7:60	57–58, 73–74
7:1	67n31
8:4	11n26, 64n18
8:6	64n18
8:12	11, 13, 64n18
8:14	11n26
8:25	67n29
8:26–40	65n25
8:31	67n31
9:1–22	12, 69–70
9:2	63n15
9:15	78, 92n39
9:18,	13
9:32–35	63n16
9:36–43	63n16
9:42	131n32
10:1–11:30	64n19, 65n22
10	207
10:24	151n46
10:33	67n31
10:42	67n29
10:44–48	13n33, 151n46
13	65
13:5	67n29
13:15	67n31
13:38	67n29
13:44–51	70–71
13:47	32n39
14:1–7	68
14:3	63
14:8–20	59n3, 65n26
14:15	14n40
14:21–22	15
15:19–20	14n40
15:36	67n29
15:40	75n1
16:1–3	75n1
16:3	88n30
16:11	75n1
16:15	13
16:16–40	68–69, 151n46
17	75n1, 76n1
17:1–4	66
17:2–3	67n29, 76n2
17:4–5	68n32
17:5–10	76
17:10–12	66
17:12–13	68n32
17:12	131n32
17:16–34	65n26, 66, 88n30, 127
17:17	67n29
17:23	126n29
17:32–34	68
18	79
18:4	67n29
18:5	67n29, 76n3
18:8	13, 68n32
18:12	68n32
18:13	88n30
18:19	67n29
18:24–28	67n29, 80n11
18:25	63n15
18:28	67n29
19:1–41	64n19
19:8	11n28, 64n18, 67n29
19:9	63n15, 67n29, 68n32
19:19	68n32
19:23	63n15
19:37	127
20:25	11n28, 64n18
21:23–26	88n30
22	12, 70
22:1	96n7
22:20	73n42, 74
22:4	63n15
23:1	121n16
23:9	121n16
23:11	33n40, 67n29

SCRIPTURE INDEX

24:14	63n15	**1 Corinthians**		**2 Corinthians**	
24:16	121n16	1:2–3	85n29	1:5–11	85n28
24:22	63n15	1:12	80n11	1:12	82n20,
24:25	67n29	1:16	151n46		84n24,
25	67n30	1:18–2:16	81		121n16
25:16	96n7	1:20	82n18	1:15–23	80
26	12, 67n30	1:22	224	1:19	81n16
26:11	51n32	1:25	26	2:1–5	80n10,
26:14	69n35	1:29	82n20		80n11,
26:18	14n40	1:31	82n20		80n12
28:19	51n32	2:1–5	81	2:7	84
28:23	11n28,	2:1	123	2:12	81n16, 84
	64n18	2:4	123	2:14–17	85n28, 86,
28:24	68n32	2:6–16	83		92n41
28:30–31	89	2:8–10	83n22	2:17	80n14,
28:31	11n28,	2:12	82n19		84n24, 228
	64n18	2:14	83n22	3:1–3	93n42,
		2:16	82n19, 90		181n36,
Romans		3:1	78		222n12
		3:3–4	79, 80n9	3:1	80n14
1:1–3	40n1	3:5–6	14, 81n16,	3:5	86
1:13	90n34		159n12	3:12–18	84
1:14–16	9, 92n40	3:19	83n22	3:18	225
1:16	230	3:21	82n20	4:1–6	23n6
1:18–21	83n22	4:5	88n30,	4:1–2	83–4, 84
2:2–4	126n30		90n33	4:2	82n20,
9:1	121n16	4:7	82n20		84n25, 90,
10:1	219	5:1	80n9		121
10:15	230	5:9–13	80n9	4:4	83n22
12:1–2	59n4,	6:1	80n9	4:5	43, 84
	112n2, 230	7:10–12	59n5	4:7–12	85
12:7	179n27	7:12–16	101n24	5:11	84n25,
12:8	179n27	7:14	150n44		92n40
12:14–21	52n36	7:25	139n7	5:12	82n20
12:16	31n31	9:15–18	80n13,	5:14	31, 92
12:18	31n31		82n20, 92	5:20	92
12:17–21	31n32	9:19	88, 92	6:3–10	85n28
13:1–7	29n25,	9:20–22	87	6:7	85n27
	72n41	11:17–18	80n9	6:8	80n13
13:8–10	30, 92,	12:15	13	7:2	80n13
	112n2	13:12	225	7:8–12	80n12
15:1–2	126n30,	14:26–36	80n9	8:1–2	92n41
	185n47	15:1	11, 81n16	8:8–11	92n41
15:20	91n37,	15:7–10	78	9:7	92n41
	213n66	15:12	80n9	9:12	92n41
16:19	52n34	15:58	106	9:15	92n41
				10–13	82n20

2 Corinthians (continued)

10:1	80n11, 83
10:4–5	83n23, 116, 169–70
10:10	80n11
10:12–12:3	81n14
10:12–18	213n66
11:3–4	85
11:1–13	80n14
11:5	86n29
11:6	80n11
11:7–12	80n13
11:7	11
11:16–33	85n28
11:18	80n14
11:22–23	80n14
11:29–30	86n29
12:1–10	85n28
12:8	86n29
12:11	51n32, 80n14
12:13–18	80n13
12:19	81n15

Galatians

1:6–9	203n30, 223
1:8	11n26, 40n1
1:11	11n26
1:23	11n26
2:3	51n32, 88n30
2:7–9	214n66
2:14	51n32
3:13–14	82n21
5:14	114n7
6:7–8	29n24
6:12	51n32

Ephesians

1:13	85n27
3:14–15	146
4:11	179n27, 230
4:15	126, 214
5:8–10	112

5:21–6:9	145n27
5:22–6:4	29n25
6:1–9	101n22
6:1–4	145
6:5–9	29n25, 90n33
6:7	157n3
6:10–20	83n23

Philippians

1:7	96n7
1:9–11	59n4, 112n2, 148n37
1:12–14	89
1:15–18	89
1:19	89n32
1:23–24	89n32
2:2–3	90
2:3–11	122n16
2:12–13	116
2:14–16	92n42

Colossians

1:5	85n27
1:10	148n37
1:19–20	11, 177, 223n18, 225
1:21–2	223n18
1:22	177
2:3	158
2:15	11
3:12–14	126n30
3:12	122n18
3:18–4:1	101n22
3:23	157n3
4:4	84n25, 85n27
4:6	97n13

1 Thessalonians

1:5	76n4
1:8–9	78
1:9	76n2

2:1–6	75–78, 76n4, 90, 90n33, 92n39, 92n40
2:7–8	78, 92
2:9	76n4
2:10	76n4
2:11–12	78
2:16–3:13	77
3:6–8	76
3:8–9	78
3:12–13	78
4:7	77
5:14	185n47
5:21	147n37

1 Timothy

1:4	104n29
1:13	65n24
2:7	85n27
4:7	104n29
6:3–10	203n30
6:4	82n18

2 Timothy

1:3	121n16
1:13	11n25
2:15	85n27
2:23	82n18
3:7	82n18
4:3–4	104n29, 203n30
4:16	96n7

Titus

1:14	104n29
3:1	72n41

Hebrews

1:1–3	41n7
2:2	203n30
3:7–11	203n30
5:11–6:6	203n30

5:14	59n4	3:1	101, 113, 182	1:13	103
		3:4	102	1:15	103
James		3:5	96n6	1:16	103
1:27	185n47	3:6	95n5, 102	1:17–18	103
4:6	122n16	3:9	95n3, 101	1:19–21	103, 104
		3:11	95n5	2:1–3	103, 104n30
1 Peter		3:13–17	96	3:1	103
		3:13	95n5	3:18	148n37
1:1	95n4	3:14	95n3, 100n18		
1:2	32			**1 John**	
1:3	96n6	3:15–16	8n17, 23n6, 33, 95n5, 99, 100, 121n6, 192, 231	1:1–3	105
1:6	95n3			1:2	33n40
1:13	96n6			2:24–27	105
1:17	95n4			4:1–6	105
1:21	96n6			4:1	148n37
2:1	101	3:16–18	99n3		
2:4	32	3:17	95n5	**Revelation**	
2:8	101n23, 224	3:19	100		
2:9	32	3:20	101n23	1:9	106
2:11	95n4	3:21	100	1:12–16	108
2:12	32, 95n3, 95n5, 97, 181	4:1	95n3	1:17	108
		4:3	96	2:4	203n30
		4:4	96	2:13	73n42, 106
2:13–3:7	145n27	4:11	179n27	2:23	90n33
2:13–17	72n41, 103	4:12–19	95n3	3:14–22	109
2:15	95n5	4:17	101n23	3:20	109
2:17	95n5, 101, 126	5:5–6	99n17	5	106
		5:10	95n3	6	106
2:18–20	95n5, 101, 102	5:13	95n3	6:9–11	106–107
				7:9–17	107
2:21–25	52n35, 52n36, 101, 102	**2 Peter**		7:9	61
				14:6–7	107
2:21	171n42	1:12	103	19:16	108

www.ingramcontent.com/pod-product-compliance
Lightning Source LLC
Chambersburg PA
CBHW030615230426
43661CB00053B/1994